1

"THE NEARLY MAN" HAD LONG SINCE DEPARTED THE MONASTERY BUT FOUND THAT ADAPTING TO LIFE OUTSIDE OF THE CLOISTERS WAS NO EASY TRANSITION.

Publishing Information

"From Monk to Elvis"

This autobiography by author J S Nearey is published by Create Space

The Title number:

It can be ordered online via Amazon Books at:
        http://www.amazon.com

Go onto: www.amazon.com, search into the "Book" section and look for:
"From Monk to Elvis" ref:

Contents

About the Author.

Surprisingly, I became a first-time author in 2010. I say surprisingly, because I did not even read books, let alone write one. I used to be a fairly keen reader until I was in my early twenties, but much of that was related to my education. I loved English literature and so I used to read classic novels and such works. However, once I finished education and belatedly began work, when I was 22 years old, I just stopped reading books and would only read newspapers, magazines and such like. It is not something I am proud of, but given this situation, it seemed most unlikely that I would ever become an author. I heard it said recently that in order to become a good writer, one would need to be an avid reader of books in order to understand and learn the methods of writing. I really cannot argue against that statement, but I can certainly see the logic of it. The fact that my writing was an autobiography, rather than a novel, possibly made it easier for me to write, as it involved a different style of writing.

The catalyst for my becoming a first time author in my 65th year, was being encouraged by a friend to write a book about my life and experiences. It was an objective that I had considered over the years, but had never had sufficient courage or drive to undertake it. Eventually, and well into my sixties, I decided that I would write my autobiography, as several people told me that I had experienced an interesting and unusual life and that I had a story that I should tell. Even so, at that time I did not possess any of the necessary drive and enthusiasm to begin such a large undertaking. I had been suffering from severe bouts of insomnia and I was unable to sleep during long periods the night. Most times, I would arise and for something useful to do, I would go into my study in the early hours. That was the start of my writing. In fact, my first book "The Nearly Man", was only ever written during the night, due to my bouts of insomnia. Without this problem, my books may never have seen the light of day.

In 2013 I completed and published my first book "The Nearly Man", an autobiography of my young life. Most autobiographies are single volumes, as they cover an entire lifetime. In this instance, it seemed to me that my story had reached its natural conclusion, as my life had changed dramatically by the age of just twenty-two years. Even so, I truly believed my story to be complete.

Many reviewers of my book, surprised me considerably by stating that they were disappointed that the story finished when it did. The majority of my readers wanted to know much more about my later life and how it progressed. They wanted to understand how "The Nearly

Man" adapted to life after the monastery and what happened to me in my life thereafter.

On reviewing their comments and their thirst for a continuation of my true story, I have belatedly acknowledged their request for more information and have concluded that there is indeed a further section of the story to be told. As such, this new work is being prepared as a sequel to "The Nearly Man", a natural conclusion to my original story. I am however delighted to say that the majority of the writing has been during daylight hours as my insomnia has improved somewhat, if not entirely.

I wish to dedicate this sequel particularly to my wife Anne, who has been my constant mentor and has given her full support to this lengthy project. I also wish to thank my younger brother Mike who has given me continual encouragement and assistance in the production of the sequel. He has assisted me, due to various lapses in my memory, by bringing back to mind, various episodes of my young life, which had slipped into my unconscious memory. Without these, the book would not have been complete and accurate in all of its detail.

My desire to tell the remainder of my story was borne out of a wish to explain to family, friends and anybody who reads it, about my life, and the reasons why I followed this extraordinary lifestyle. It will perhaps explain to those who know me, just what makes me the person I am today and the affect that it has had on me as an adult. It lays bare my soul and exposes not just my personality traits, but also my strengths, faults and weaknesses. It describes personal details of my life that, without this book, I would have treated as personal and private and I would not have divulged. As such, it has not been easy for me to write and publish this second book and I pondered and agonized, both long and hard, before deciding that I would write this sequel and thus complete my life story.

After this 2nd volume of my autobiography, I wish to continue writing as it gives me fulfillment and pleasure. Quite what genre I will write in the future, time alone will tell.

J.S.Nearey - Author

Introduction

"From Monk to Elvis," is the second part and the sequel to the autobiography of J.S. Nearey, author of **"The Nearly Man"**.

It is the sequel to the original story. It tells of his life and work after living for ten years at Erdington Abbey, a Monastery in Perth and finally at Hawkstone, a Monastery in Shropshire. It was there that his life endured a myriad of emotions and dramas. The finale to this was the starting point for this new volume, **"from Monk to Elvis"**

The story recounts his highs, lows and how his time there reached a dramatic and emotional climax. It was to influence the remainder of his life and his varied lifestyle. The sequel story re-visits the iconic institutions from his past. He re-lives many of the dramas and experiences he had to endure. These had taken place some forty-five years earlier, and yet there was still a need for him to exorcise these ghosts from his past. The story deals with his new life, where he experiences some twenty five jobs in less than forty five years. Many of the jobs are just bizarre, or patently unsuitable to his character and background. It concludes with a phrase which gives meaning to the book title;

"from Monk to Elvis" - via twenty-five jobs

Chapter 1

Return of the prodigal son.

Fast forward from 1970 to 2012. The world has changed beyond recognition in such a short space of time. It has experienced more dramatic change in the past hundred years, than during any century since the modern world began. In global terms, the twentieth Century has seen two World Wars, the invention of electricity, oil for power and the fantastic innovation of the World Wide Web. These innovations have changed the entire globe at such a rapid pace, that it is highly unlikely that such dramatic development will ever be seen and experienced again, in such a relatively short space of time. Little wonder then, that such a rapid rate of change has also been evident in most walks of life, even those establishments and institutions that are normally the slowest to embrace such change.

With these comments in mind, on 1st September 2012, I returned to one of my former "homes," the Redemptorist Monastery in Perth, Scotland. It was the first time I had returned there, since I had departed and gone to live at Hawkstone Hall, Shropshire in 1967. I was unsure what I would find there, even though I had kept in touch, with passing interest, through the use of the internet and various websites. I was aware that life had moved on, and that monastic life was not the same as it was when I had left it in 1971. My life in Perth had helped to mould me into the person that I have become today. It has left an indelible mark on my life and it has shaped my future as a person, whether that is for good, bad or otherwise.

I had looked forward to re-visiting the monastery once more. It still had a strange attraction and fascination for me, even after all these years. Yet my expectations had not been high. I had returned to so many establishments from my younger years, only to be hugely disappointed and find that the building had now gone, been demolished, built into a housing development or had changed to such an extent, that it was no longer recognizable as the place I had once known. As I approached the high road to Perth via the lavish Scottish scenery, it was impossible not to be hugely impressed. The day was clear and crisp and the views were magnificent. The rolling countryside, the splendid mountains and lakes, surely, they would never change, and neither indeed had they. It was with great excitement, tempered by a degree of trepidation, that I spied the road signs to Perth and the local towns and lanes that I had once known so well. Certainly, the places seemed larger than I had remembered, but the views, hills, rivers and lochs, and those magnificent mountains, were just the same and equally as dramatic as they had always been. I somehow felt instantly reassured.

As I drove towards Kinnoull Hill, I recognized the Isle of Skye Hotel at the foot of the hill, where my parents had stayed overnight, when they visited Perth, to witness me take my vows. The car began its steep climb towards the Monastery. Our vehicle seemed to labour somewhat, but given the steep incline, it was barely surprising. Kinnoull Hill is a monumental mound of earth at its summit, gazing imperiously over the meandering River Tay and its surrounding fertile valley. I felt a huge surge of excitement as we climbed the hill, seemingly stuck in second gear. Then, peering out from between the monumental trees on the right hand side, there it stood, proudly, in all its dramatic and scenic beauty, the Redemptorist Monastery at Perth. I felt a sudden tinge of anticipation, even excitement, inside me, as I waited to enter its foreboding doors one more time

1. Monastery at Perth, Scotland.]

2. Rear of Monastery at Perth.

The turrets and twin steeples of the monastery protruded pompously from amongst the tall pine trees. It felt to me as if I was being welcomed back home, despite the extraordinary and medieval experiences I had lived through, decades ago. Yet driving slowly towards it, I felt only good feelings at that time. I stopped outside and gazed in admiration, not speaking. I stood there in awe and trepidation of the place I had once called home, if only for a year, back in the summer of 1966.

I parked my vehicle on the steep road outside and walked down the cinder path towards the Church. As I did so, my wife Anne, walking alongside me, I felt that I was the young eighteen-year-old Stephen Nearey, not the sixty-three-year-old man, that I was then, walking somewhat tentatively down the slippery path, just as I had done so, some forty-five years to the day, on 1st.September 1966.

The time was precisely 9.59 am. The Church Service was just about to begin at 10am. I hated being late. I had been brought up to be always on time. In the monastery we did not have watches, just the occasional ticking clock, in public areas and we had been instructed to respond to the bell, that regulated our daily schedule, indeed our entire lives, whilst living at the monastery at Perth.

We had scraped in, only just in the nick of time. As I pushed open the large wooden double doors, they creaked and groaned, so that as we entered, it seemed that the entire congregation had turned around to see who had just come in. The Church was almost full, with in excess of one hundred worshippers present. In today's terms this was a big congregation. It seemed as if they were all locals and it was evident that I was a stranger in town. In truth I did feel rather like a complete stranger. I was a man from a foreign country, even if I was only a neighbor from England. If only they knew the truth. Even though it was forty-two years since my last visit, I knew this church and this monastery, far better than any of the congregation on that day. In my time spent in Perth, I knew every inch of that Church, and every nook and cranny, having been to Mass there each day for a complete year. I knew every square inch of that monastery and grounds in fine detail. Perhaps I was not really such a stranger after all.

Immediately, I sat down in my pew and three priests entered the Church from the vestry. I did not expect to know any of them. My memory for faces and names has always been poor, so I was not expecting to remember anyone. The service was in English, with a modern liturgy, and yet from time to time, parts of it, both in speech and in song, were chanted in Latin. It took me back to the days when the entire service was played out in Latin. Despite the length of time since then, I remembered and knew every word of the liturgy which was in Latin. Of course, that language had been an integral part of my earlier education. I had studied it for six years in the Juvenate, and had passed my GCE "O" level. Since that time, I had used the Latin language, even though it has never been spoken in everyday life. It is after all, the basis of so many modern-day languages, including English, French and Spanish, all of which I had studied at Erdington Abbey in Birmingham.

At the end of the service, and just before the final hymn, the priests invited members of the congregation to join them in the monastery for coffee or tea. Apparently, this was a regular routine. Until then, I had not known quite how I was going to re-introduce myself and make myself

known to the Redemptorists monks. In fact, I did
not know if there was anyone still at Perth, who
would have even heard of Stephen Nearey. My
wife had just spoken to a lady in the congregation
to ask if she knew the names of the priests. She
most certainly did, as she was a regular
worshipper, who lived just a few yards from the
monastery and knew just about everything about it
and the priests and monks who dwelled there.
Although I did not know why, my wife had
informed the lady that I had been a Novice there
in the 1960's and within moments, the news had
spread through the congregation, like a forest fire,
and I was invited with my wife, to join the others
for coffee in the refectory.

We walked from inside the Church and through
the door that is the entrance to the monastery. The
last time I had done that in 1966, it was a door that
had been barred to women, even to nuns, as the
monastery in those days, was a place of worship
for men, and men alone.

We walked quietly along the cloister. It did look
and feel somehow different. It was less sparse than
I remembered it, all those years ago, not quite as
formal and foreboding as it had been in the sixties.
Along each of the walls of the cloister and on
either side, were photographs of the Redemptorists
from bygone eras, stretching back as far as 1885.
Judging from the photographs, it seemed that the

monastery and its inhabitants had not changed, merely the faces and names of those from different generations. As we moved along the corridor, glancing at the old photographs, one in particular caught my attention. It must have been the date that I spotted. There was a large photograph at the end of the corridor dated 1966-67. I stopped to look. There it was! A very young picture of me, fresh faced and just eighteen years old. I was among the full complement of twenty five novices and postulants from that era. Immediately, it flashed me straight back to 1966. I stood there gazing at the photograph, trying desperately to remember the names of those that I had known and lived with. As I did so, one of the Monks approached me and said: *"That's me! Second from the right, top row!"* I turned around to look at who he was, but I did not recognize him.

3. Novices at Perth 1966. Steve 3rd. left front row.

16

"That's me!", "Brother Kevin!" he said. *"I'm Father Tom McCarthy now."* He went on: *"I was fifteen years old in that picture, just after I arrived at Perth. In fact, [he continued], I remember that it was you that served me my first lunch here, just the day after I arrived at the Monastery."*

Brother Kevin had joined the Order at the tender young age of fifteen years. He had decided to join as a Brother, a Monk who would not become a priest or a missionary. Instead he would spend his life supporting the work of the Monastery as a chef, a gardener, or any other tasks involved with the running and upkeep of the building. It turned out though, that Brother Kevin had changed his mind after just a few years, and he had decided that his calling was, after all, to be a priest. All these years later, he is now a Missionary, preaching the word to people all over the United Kingdom.

As I was trying to assimilate all the news that he was giving to me, some forty-five years later, Father Kevin was dragged away by a rather too zealous lady member of the parish, who really had to speak with him rather urgently, no doubt about the Church flower arranging.

As I stood there, still gazing with a fixed stare at the picture of the novices from 1966-7, a nun approached from behind and blurted out in a powerful manner and with a strong accent: *"You'll*

17

stay for lunch Stephen?" It was a question, but it sounded more like a command. I recognized that her accent was Irish [What else?], and the name I caught, was Margaret-Mary. Word had spread like wild fire around the Monastery, that an ex-Novice had returned, and they were laying out the welcome mat. *"Stephen, You'll stay for some lunch? You will?* – She repeated. I gazed towards my wife for approval. I felt somewhat awkward. My mind told me that I still belonged there, and yet, I knew that I did not. It was all such a long time ago and my life had taken on myriad twists and turns since those emotional days. I stuttered and stammered over the answer and eventually, regaining my cool I said: *"Yes, Sister Margaret Mary, thank you, it would be lovely to join you for lunch."* Immediately it flashed across my sub-conscious mind that "The Prodigal Son" had returned and just as in the parable, in the Gospel of St. Luke 15:12:32], I was to be made to feel as if they had rolled out the red carpet and welcomed me back home. In the Gospel story, the wayward son was received back into the fold with open arms by his family. They had killed the fatted calf, roasted it and had a family feast to welcome his homecoming. The similarities ended there. I was not about to re-join the monastery, but I was made to feel as if one of their own had returned to the fold, if only for a short period of time, and we were made very welcome.

Sister Margaret-Mary informed me that lunch
would be served in about one hour and asked me
if I wanted to have a look around the monastery to
see what had changed. Strange as it may seem, the
exterior of the monastery looked practically the
same as it did back in 1966 and the grounds were
almost identical. The biggest difference was the
shortage of Monks and that it was far more open
to the public, than when I was a Novice. In it's
heyday in the 1950's and 1960's and when I first
arrived, there were some twenty five Novices and
Postulants in that year, alongside the resident
Priests Brothers and Monks. By stark comparison,
on my return visit, the entire Monastery was run as
a house of Retreats and Renewals, by just a
handful of Priests and Nuns totaling around half a
dozen and there were no Brothers living there at
all. Since the 1970's the intake of new blood had
dried up to just a slow trickle, as in the western
world, Religion has been largely ignored and
marginalized, by much of the present, unbelieving
UK population.

As I wandered up and down the monastic cloisters,
maintaining a respectful quiet, they were even
more silent than I had remembered. The rooms, or
cells, as we used to call them, were still plain and
simple, but were rather more modern than the
medieval cell that I used to call home. Yet they
retained the same simplicity, albeit they now had
the modern pre-requisites of a sink with hot and

cold water. Even so, they had not progressed as far as having en-suite facilities for the guests who were staying at the monastery. They were there in order to take part in a religious renewal or retreat. Perhaps that was for the best, so as not to detract attention from the purpose of their visit.

I walked into the common room, a place where we had spent time every day, perhaps for an hour or so, socializing and making rosary beads in order to earn our keep! These were then sold to parishioners or to the congregation on the Missions, in order to make money to help keep the Monastery financially afloat. My wife had dallied there for some minutes and so, I went alone up-to the top floor of the Monastery. Along the creaking old cloister, were the attic bedrooms that I had known so well. This was where my cell had been some forty two years earlier. The attic floor was no longer in use as letting rooms, but the cells were still just as they were in the nineteen sixties. As I entered the very cell that had been mine, a chill came all over me and down into my spine, a shiver that went through my very being. It was as if I had been transported backwards throughout time. For some moments, I just stood and gazed around that cell, just as I had done on my first day there in 1966. The walls were now bare, and without any furniture, the room took on an even more spartan appearance. I gazed for some moments through the tiny attic window. It was still a beautiful and dramatic view, looking out over the hills and down towards the City of Perth. It was summer, and yet there was a chill in the air inside the attic cell. It felt damp and unloved and oh so different to the time in September 1966, when this attic floor was inhabited by some twelve or so new Postulants and Novices. Despite the quiet life that had been the order of day for the Monks, it had then felt alive and vibrant and yet now, it felt dead, just a distant and faint memory, a shadow of the former life it had taken on. Time had indeed taken its toll on the Redemptorist Monastery at Perth.

As I meandered down the wooden spiral stairs, the only noise was from the creaky old floorboards. I felt a sort of relief, when I was back on the middle cloister and then I heard Anne, my wife, who was still in the common room talking. It shook me out of a kind of stupor. I had taken myself backwards to bygone days and it was a relief to return to 2013. As I entered the common room, my wife asked me if I was alright. She told me that I had looked withdrawn and distant, since I had returned to the monastery. While I was with her, I felt quite alone, not only with my thoughts, but I felt as if I had returned to being the solitary person that I had become in 1966. I had become calmed and withdrawn. I had retreated into myself, perhaps trying to take in the memories of the twelve long months that I had lived in the Monastery and the life changing effects, that it had on me.

It was with some degree of relief that my wife suggested: *"Shall we go outside and explore the grounds?"* I was beginning to feel confined and claustrophobic inside the Monastery. Ever since those early days of 1966, I had developed a loathing for being indoors for too long. I longed for and sought out the wide-open spaces, where I could breathe deeply into the fresh air and feel liberated once more. Without hesitation, I led Anne to the exit at the rear of the Monastery. Once outside the familiar, large wooden doors, to the rear entrance, I began to feel a little more like the person that had arrived and in good spirits, an hour or two earlier. We walked around what was left of the old farm. The remaining buildings had fallen into a dilapidated state and I felt a tinge of sadness. It seemed much smaller than I had remembered it. I found out later on, that much of the farmland had been sold off to meet the high cost of running the Monastery and it was not needed anymore. The numbers of Monks and Priests had dwindled and there were no Brothers left at all. The few that had lived there had died and there have been no new vocations to become Brothers since many years past. As I dallied by the farm buildings, I could not help but raise a secret smile and remember Brother Michael who was my "Boss" when I worked with him on the farm in 1966. I can never forget the time I slid down an embankment with a barrow-load of pig manure that I had "lovingly" shoveled up. It cost me two weeks of "solitary" in the

Monastery Infirmary, as I had damaged my back trying to rescue the runaway wheelbarrow! Could I ever forget that it was Brother Michael who provided me with my weekly contraband sports paper, which had put me in seriously bad-books with the Novice Master.

As we wandered around the gardens, they were still delightful, but slightly unkempt and unloved. The pathways were green but overgrown and the many religious statues on every corner, whilst still clearly evident, were showing the signs of neglect and wear and tear from the elements. What struck me was the quietness of it all. In 1966, it was impossible to walk through the farm or the gardens without coming across a Brother, busily working the fields or the farm, or the Novices and Priests taking the fresh air and silently walking the grounds, deep in contemplation or just quietly mulling over the meaning of life, or wondering what was going to be for breakfast! Nothing was ever said, as we quietly glided past one another in those days. There was just a slight, reverential nod of the head and a respectful glance, as we passed each other by. Now, we were alone in those gardens and with not a solitary person in sight.

As we headed back in the direction of the Monastery, I asked Anne, my wife, to go indoors and wait for me. It was a pleasant, if cool summer's day and I wanted to walk around the

Monastery Cemetery alone. She had already commented that I had become withdrawn, quiet and detached while I was at Perth. It was true, it was causing a strange and morose effect on me. I was without doubt a different person, once I was back inside the Monastery enclosure. Returning to Perth had made a profound influence on me, just as it had made a life changing influence on me when I originally became a Novice and Monk there, back in 1966.

Many of the inhabitants of the graveyard had been known to me. I was not being morbid or morose, but the reality of life, was that it had been forty two years since I had lived there, and many of the older Monks, Priests and Brothers would have died and would now be laid to rest there. Strangely, I did not feel particularly sad or morbid. These were all very good men, who had lived the life they had chosen, and were interred in the grounds of the place that they had called home, for very many years. Once their life's work was completed and had come to an end, they were anticipating, nay expecting to move onto better and greater things in their next life. This was what their life's work had been all about and they then wanted to reap the benefits of their labors, in the next world.

I walked slowly and respectfully along the long rows of Redemptorists, now buried side by side with their colleagues. Each burial plot had a simple white cross, with just their name, title, date

of birth, death and their profession. It was a
sobering journey for me and it brought home to me
my own mortality, as several of the names that I
stopped in front of, were men that I had once
known and lived alongside, for some time. In
several cases their ages were not so different to my
own. It was somewhat un-nerving though, to read
some of the names on those headstones. Some had
not lived their expected life span and it was a
shock to see their names in front of me. I had
known several of them well, as we had lived in
such close proximity. I walked along all three rows
of graves, possibly numbering sixty and while my
mind was recounting tales from many years gone
by, I quickly controlled myself, took a deep intake
of breath, breathed out slowly and then thought to
myself, that life was for the living and must be
lived to the full. I strolled rather more quickly and
with some greater purpose back into the
Monastery and met up with Anne. She was
speaking in the cloister with one of Nuns. It must
have been difficult for my wife. Here she was,
confronted with my past life, possibly like meeting
an old flame of mine and not sure how to cope with
it. It was a great deal for her to take in, but she was
trying very hard to be supportive.

Here she was, in my world, and confronted by a
lifestyle and a group of people, that had practically
owned my very existence. It was little wonder, that
she told me later, that I was a different person

when I was inside the Monastery at Perth. She barely recognized me. She told me that it was as if I belonged to someone or something else, and that during that short period of time in Perth, I was a stranger to her, an outsider that she did not really know. It was so very close to being the truth.

As she was speaking to Sister Margaret-Mary, the bell tolled. It was calling everybody from all corners of the Monastery and grounds to come and join in the luncheon. That particular sound meant something very familiar to me. For years at Erdington, Perth and again at Hawkstone, my entire life, from morning until night, had been run and controlled by the sound of a large, clanging bell. To hear it at this stage though, merely filled me with reminiscences and took me immediately back into another time zone. I had become accustomed to responding immediately to a bell. The moment it tolled, Sister Margaret-Mary ushered us into the Refectory for luncheon. To return there after so many years was again a nerve racking experience. I had so many memories: the plain but wholesome food: a refectory full of Monks, eating in silence, except for the clinking of cutlery on their plates. Most of the time, during a meal, we had listened to one of the monks reading from the pulpit throughout the repast: The only other sounds were the clink and clank of cutlery and glass, while the diners listened intently, or otherwise, to the reader. Mostly, the reading would be from a religious book, perhaps a biography of a saint, or a manuscript written by a Saint or Pope. Occasionally, the refectory could be lightened, by the reading of a novel or something a little more gripping. Yet, back to 2013, my wife and I were sat in the same place. It had scarcely changed, yet it was somewhat less austere, with tables of four replacing the heavy oak rectangular tables from yesteryear which seated ten. The refectory could have been from back then, in the nineteen sixties or somewhat earlier. Times move slowly but predictably in the monastic life.

Certainly different, was the food. It was not now provided for a Monastery full of Monks, it was now served mainly to visitors and people staying at the Monastery on retreats. The chef had provided a first class carvery, and whereas it was nothing much like a restaurant, it was more than acceptable. After lunch and a tasty dessert, Father Kevin came and sat with us at our table. It was beyond belief to me, that this was the same person who had been practically "dropped off" at the Monastery gates by his family, and left to get on with it. He was just a fifteen year old boy when he arrived at Perth, all alone, timid and extremely quiet. He joined us as a Novice with the ambition of becoming a Redemptorist Brother. In the year he spent with us, he showed no indication that he had ambitions to be anything other than that, and why should he? He had decided that he wanted to be a Monk, without the limelight, and without the serious training and responsibilities required to be a Priest. He seemed more than content to be a Religious Brother and to play a supporting role by assisting in the running of the Monastery and the Farm, and by helping the Redemptorist's Missionary effort, in whatever way he could usefully contribute. That shy young man had long since flown! The mature man now sat before us was confident, loud, perhaps even brash, with a wicked sense of humour, that I had never known from him, way back in 1966. The duckling had long since flown the nest and in its place, had returned a beautiful Swan.

After spending just a few short years as a Brother, Father Kevin believed that his vocation had changed and he had trained to be a fully-fledged Redemptorist Priest and modern day Missionary. I would not have recognized him from the picture in the cloister and yet, after not seeing me for more than forty five years, he recognized who I was instantly. He joined us at the dining table, devoid of his monastic garb and dressed as a layman. He appeared anything but a traditional monastic. He was free in his use of "industrial language", [swearing to you and I], and he called a spade, very much a spade!! We spoke about the photograph in the cloister. I was eager to learn what had happened to the twenty six faces that had sat alongside me in that line up. It was fascinating to learn which of the Novices from that group had gone all the way and were still with the Redemptorists, but there were painfully few of them, amounting to just a handful. A few had died and others had left to pursue a life in the secular world, myself included. I had secretly hoped that the Order would still be large and thriving, but, and in keeping with the real world, Religious beliefs in our part of the globe have changed dramatically and the Religious Orders such as the Redemptorists are clinging onto their Monasteries and their people, but with much smaller numbers, such has been the seismic change in religious belief during the past fifty years or so.

To make matters worse, the Catholic Church and Religious Orders such as the Redemptorists, were living in a time capsule, several hundred years behind the times. The Redemptorists are now trying desperately to meet the needs of our modern society and to appeal more to the younger generation that has largely rejected religion. The appeal of such communities has declined to such an extent, that perhaps it has changed forever and will perhaps never be quite the same again.

When lunch was over, we said our farewells to the small group of Redemptorists and nuns who are now stationed at Perth. They had all made me and my wife very welcome, and had put out the red carpet, to welcome back their prodigal son. I wished them all the best, but departed with some degree of sadness and resignation, that life had changed for the Redemptorist Community at Perth, but not for the better. I hated seeing it, in what I could only describe as terminal decline. It made me wonder what I would find if I returned in another ten or twenty years.

We walked to the front doors and I could not stop myself from glancing all around me, to take in the images of the cloisters for one final time. Perhaps, one day I would return once more, yet I would be nervous as to what I would find on such a return visit to the Monastery at Perth, a place I had once called my Home.

Before bidding our fond farewells, I lingered on the steps of the ancient building, flashing fleeting glances all-around of me, as if to take in every image of the Monastery and its grounds. I was drawn to it once more and did not want to let it go, despite many times being desperate to leave it, in the year of 1966 when I had been a Novice. It was as if the building had a giant hold over me and that it would never completely let me go.

My overwhelming feeling, as we drove away and out of sight of the Monastery, was one of sadness, that an institution that had made such an indelible impression on my young life, was slowly but surely fading away and taking me with it.

After several centuries spent as a thriving centre of the local community, practically without change, it had now altered and declined to such an extent, that it was in imminent danger of becoming untenable as a monastic community in the modern era, and possibly an irrelevance, in the not too distant future. Time alone will tell.

31

Chapter 2

A brand new dawn

After driving away from Perth that day, we eventually came to rest and I sat and relaxed, thinking of the events that had taken place that afternoon. I began to reflect on a truly memorable return visit after forty five years. In reality, it was no more than a person returning to a place where they had once lived and finding that it had changed beyond recognition. There are always going to be feelings of nostalgia in such journeys. Yet, for me, it was something entirely different and more meaningful. The Monastery at Perth had made a defining effect on my entire existence. In that short twelve month period between 1966 and 1967, I had changed my demeanor from being a happy go lucky teenager into a rather serious monastic, having become a Monk, by taking vows of poverty, chastity and obedience. That twelve-month period had transformed my life and my entire outlook. From that moment onwards, I was on a journey to becoming a Missionary and a Priest at Hawkstone. The following three years were to be a time of study and learning, interspersed by periods of anxiety, worry and stress, as I wrestled with the calling inside of me. Subconsciously, I believed that I was searching for a way out, but I could not admit it, especially to myself. Inside of me, I was searching for a genuine reason to leave, to go back to a civilian way of life, but it was my conscience and the relationship with my family and associates, that would stop me from making the decision to do so.

More and more I was unable to cope with the solitary life style, a life without a partner, without love and without a birth family to lean on. In the final analysis, it was serious illness that was the catalyst for my decision to leave the Monastic life.

Whilst I was ill in Hospital and perhaps at the lowest ebb of my young life, I had developed an emotional attachment to Margaret, my care Nurse. It was this relationship that led me to return home in order to convalesce and it made my decision to eventually return to the monastery, even more difficult. While I was agonizing as to which direction I would finally take, I returned to the Monastery for several months, before finally making the decision that I wanted to leave and return to the secular life style, with my family.

In the final analysis, I was comfortable in the knowledge that the reason I did not stay with the Redemptorists, was that the monastic life style was not suitable for me and I was not the right person for them. If I had left because of my growing attachment to my Nurse, Margaret, I would never have felt comfortable that I had gone for the right reasons. Indeed, it was even more crucial to her, that my decision to either stay or to go, was not because of the close relationship between us. Although it had been a deciding factor, it was not the defining reason for us eventually going our separate ways.

Margaret could never have lived in the knowledge that I would leave the Monastery in order to be with her. She was unable to accept that she would be responsible for me leaving Hawkstone and giving up the Monastic life. That guilt, would have been too much for her to bear and she may well have carried her guilt for a lifetime. To do so, would have wrecked our relationship. In the end, she may have made the correct decision for herself, and sadly, but ultimately, for me as well.

A few short weeks after I had arrived back at my family home, I received the shocking news that Margaret's fiancée had been killed whilst driving alongside her in a road traffic accident. She had only just become engaged and got back together with him again. I was devastated for Margaret. She deserved to be happy, as she was a wonderful and beautiful person. She had broken up with him before she met me in the hospital at Shrewsbury General, only to return to him, in the knowledge that our romantic relationship had too many problems and issues for it to ever succeed.

35

Our ill-fated liaison was bound to fail at that moment in time. The stark reality, was that I was already spoken for, albeit not with another woman. Competing with another woman would have been one challenge, but competing with the might of the Roman Catholic Church, was altogether another matter and one battle that she could never win. She had to deal, not only with the heartache of our broken romance, but only a few short weeks later, she was devastated and distraught by the unexpected loss of Dave, her husband to be, and in such tragic circumstances.

On my return back home to Marple, I had perhaps, subconsciously harbored secret thoughts that one day, I may be reunited with Margaret, that another day, we would meet up again and pick up our relationship where we had left off. Fate though has a different way of dealing with matters of the heart. For my part, it would have been insensitive, to say the least, to pursue such romantic ambitions so soon after she had suffered such a loss. For me, it seemed far too soon after leaving Hawkstone, to be making a life changing decision yet again.

Margaret had seen her relationship with me disintegrate, knowing that she could not compete with the call of the Catholic Church, and then within a matter of weeks, to lose the man she then loved. The fates just seemed to conspire against us. They came between us and although we spoke again about getting back together over the following months, it just seemed that ours was a relationship that was destined never to succeed. Too many barriers had come between us. We both had major issues that had to be dealt with, and the physical distance between us, some sixty miles, made it even more difficult. Margaret and I both had major re-building jobs to be undertaken in our lives, before either of us could deal with our emotional relationships. Gradually, we just drifted along on our chosen paths, seemingly accepting the inevitable, and eventually going our separate ways. It has been written that it is *"Better to have loved and lost, than never to have loved at all"*. That statement may be true for some, yet for me, it was the most difficult decision of my young life.

I had spent six long years at the junior seminary at Birmingham, followed by the total isolation of my year in Perth. This was followed by three long years of intense studies and education at Hawkstone. There had been precious little opportunity to ponder on such matters as emotional relationships.

For much of my time at Perth and Hawkstone, I was unaware of what was happening in the outside world. I was cocooned in my monastic bubble, where emotional attachments were trivial matters that rarely featured in our secluded lives.

37

Chapter 3

Rebuilding a life

My life in the Monasteries was always one of unwavering structure. I knew what we were going to be doing, by the day and by the hour. It was all laid out, and organized, practically written in stone and there was a routine that rarely if ever altered. It may not have been exciting, but it was there. We knew what to expect, when and how. It was always at the peal of a bell, that we knew the exact time to do the next task. It was a truism to say that there was always something to be done, a task to be carried out and very few times when there was nothing to be done. Boredom was rarely an issue.

My new life, back at home was entirely the opposite. My connections to everybody I knew at Hawkstone, Perth, and Erdington had been severed, and I would not be in contact with any of them again in the near future. The structure in my life was now a thing of the past. Back in civilian life, I had nothing to do, nowhere to go and no immediate plans to do anything. Structure and order, no longer featured in my life.

A huge gaping hole had been left in my life! Everything that I had known before and done, now had no relevance in my life. What use was Latin in the new civilian world? What benefit would Philosophy and Church History be to me now? I once had a future, but that had now ended, and here I now was, aged twenty two, with no skills, no meaningful qualifications and no contacts. Outside of the Monastery, I knew nobody except for my immediate family and I rarely saw them either. To state that I was hopelessly lost in those first few weeks back at home, was a massive understatement. I had not developed any social skills, as I had been largely silent for many years. Neither had I had any significant interaction with the civilian world or any people outside of my immediate circle in the monastery.

I felt very alone, a completely lost soul, in those first few weeks after returning from the Monastery. I really did not know quite who I was anymore. I did not know how to behave and what I was supposed to be doing. Initially, I thought I should be doing all the things I used to do in the Monastery. I would awake sharply at 6am every morning and my first inclination would be to leap out of bed and say prayers before going to meditation. It took me several weeks before it began to sink in, that I should get out of bed at a time to suit me and gradually and leisurely, go down for breakfast. At first, I was driven by the clock. I was expecting a bell to sound whenever it was nearly time for meals. I needed to remind myself to look at the clock to check the time of day. At lunchtime, I would expect a bell to ring, but when it did't I would be forever clock watching, to see what time would be right for meals. For many weeks to come, in my mind, I was still at Hawkstone and driven by all the things that used to happen. In my subconscious, I was still re-living the daily routines alongside the new daily agenda, that was my new life back at home.

Perhaps one of the most difficult habits to come to terms with, was the fact that I was allowed to speak all of the time. I still found myself keeping silent, especially in the mornings. I would do things, as I had done at Hawkstone, but I would remain quiet and do them silently, without speaking. My younger brother Mike would sometimes remind me: *"Hey, Our Kid,"* he would call me: *"You can speak, you know!"* Yet, old habits die hard and I often needed to be reminded that it was no longer a requirement to remain silent until after lunchtime. Mike would try and cajole me into adapting to my new life by asking me to join him at the Pub, for a pint or four, or a "kick around" on the football field nearby. He was only eighteen at the time, still in the throes of youth and doing impulsive things. I had become prematurely old for my twenty two years and was very reserved and rather too serious minded. I suppose that given the gravity of the life I had been leading for the past ten years, I could be forgiven for being rather too quiet and unable to let myself go. I had not been used to anything other than the grown up and conservative life style I had experienced in the Monastery. I was finding it hard to make a change.

When I first arrived back at home, it had to be remembered that I had been living at Hawkstone under a vow of poverty, not to mention chastity and obedience. My clothes, possessions and wardrobe amounted to two pairs of black trousers, two pairs of black shoes, a few "T" shirts, a couple of dark sweaters and three shirts. Added to this, a small selection of underwear, and that was that! I did not possess a coat, as I left my black raincoat along with my religious habit at Hawkstone. I did not want to be dependent upon Mum and Dad, as they were still not well off and only just had enough to get bye. I was reluctant then, when they offered me a small sum of money to go out and buy some clothes. I was used to living with just the basics of life, both in terms of clothes and possessions. I had been used to having to ask my superior for even the most basic of needs. I felt uneasy taking money from Mum and Dad. I just wanted to stay at home, as I felt somewhat conspicuous in my all black attire, especially as I was no longer a member of the clergy.

When I did finally give in and decided to go and buy some clothes with some money from my parents, it was something of a culture shock. This was 1970. The men's shops were awash with flared trousers, flowered shirts with wide wafty collars with matching ties. In 1970 the clothing was garish, in keeping with the flower power era that was typical of the nineteen seventies. To say that I was out of my comfort zone was a massive understatement and in the end, I settled for a pretty basic set of clothes, that were completely yesterday's fashion, dark colours, traditional, and more in keeping with a middle aged man than a twenty two year old. At this stage of my life, suddenly coming out into the modern world, I could not bring myself to wear 22-inch-wide flares and a brightly coloured, flowered shirt. It just was not me at that moment in time. My brother Mike taunted me about my new clothes, but after years of being on the outside of the real world, I was not quite ready to come out and join the seventies flower power brigade!

Adapting to life outside of the Monastery was proving to be no easy task. Although in my heart I knew that I had done the right thing, I was still racked with guilt over taking the decision to leave. Inside of me, I felt that I had taken the selfish, easy decision and that I had let a lot of people down. It was as if I had been the flag bearer for my family, friends and for my parish. I had been the one to make them proud, by becoming a Priest and somebody special. Now, I had left and I was just plain old me, nobody special. At that time, I was just a person who had failed to achieve his

43

ambition and I had nothing to fall back upon and nothing to look forward to. Only recently, I had been Stephen Nearey, Monk, Redemptorist and Priest in waiting. Then, in an instant, I became plain old Stephen Nearey, who does nothing in particular, and with nothing on the horizon.

In company, I imagined I could practically feel people speaking about me. There were low whispers and they could be saying: *"That's the man that's just come out of the Monastery"*, but nobody ever talked to me about it. It seemed to be a subject that people would not speak openly about, particularly to me. In truth, there was an element of wallowing in self-pity at that stage, because I was truly lost and did not know in which direction to go. Mum and Dad had been amazing. They had encouraged and supported me throughout all the ten years with the Redemptorists. I know very well, that they found my decision hard to take, yet they tried hard not to let it show. During those early weeks after returning home, I could feel their disappointment; It felt so real, that I could almost touch it. I had let them down and I was racked with guilt about it. Mum and Dad would ask me about my plans for the future, about what I would do. For weeks, all I could tell them was that I did not know what to do, as I did not know what I was capable of doing. I felt extremely limited in my options. Before I could move on, I really wanted to speak with my parents about how I felt, about the real reasons for leaving the Monastery and to try to explain to them why I had not been able to continue. In the end, I never did. I was not used to opening up to anybody and discussing my inner feelings, therefore, just as I had done at the Monastery, I kept my own council, battened down the hatches and kept everything well and truly bottled up inside of me.

As the weeks slowly passed, I gradually pulled myself together and started to think about the rest of my life. At long last, I was beginning to think about what the future held for me, instead of fretting about the past. What had happened had indeed happened and there was no point in looking back, and there was definitely no going back. I found myself lying in bed at night and thinking about yet another plan of action. My first one truly had been a master plan, but it had not reached fruition. However, I was now starting to think of the positives from those ten years and a few of them I could carry over into the next decade. At last, I was starting to emerge from my state of depression, I was beginning to look forward more and think positively about my future. The green shoots of revival had been planted and were about to spring forward. It had taken months, and it was going to be a long and arduous road, but the recovery process was at last beginning to roll.

I needed to think about what I could do for a living.

It was the first time in my young life, that I had to think about earning my own living. In the monastery, all my needs had been catered for. I had not needed a mortgage, or to pay rates or taxes. Food, clothing and all the essentials of life, had been provided for me by the Redemptorists.

However, I was realistic enough to know that my CV [well, I didn't actually have one!] would not make for good reading to any potential employer: It would have read something like:

"Aged 22 Years: Work experience: Nil. Special skills: Nil. Specialist subjects: Latin, Philosophy and Church History. Despite my seven GCE "O" levels, all I could offer an employer was a good general education, but in no useful subjects as far as the jobs markets were concerned."

I realized that before I could start building a career, I would have to get a job, any job at all, in order to earn some money and contribute to my family's financial coffers. In the slightly longer term, I thought I had already decided the overall direction which my career should take. Up to that point, my entire life had been geared to helping other people, by being involved in society through my connections to the Church. I could think of no other way of life that would be best suited to me at that time. The type of careers I was thinking of, included, social work, teaching, nursing, the police and such like. However, I knew that it would take some time to build a career in one of those sectors and so I applied my mind to finding a basic job, quickly, so that I could earn some income to fund my belated start in the real world.

As I had never been involved in employment before, I had to think about how I would find a job. In those days, the government method for finding work was via "The Labour Exchange". The words give it away somewhat: "Labour," meaning physical hard work. It was not that I was shy of physical work, but I was that not good at it. I was still pretty skinny in those days and most of the jobs in the Labour Exchange, were for hard physical work or factory jobs. It was just not for me, unless I was really desperate. I began scouring the Manchester Evening News jobs section. There were still plenty of jobs on offer, but none that suited my qualifications, or that I would be able to obtain. Either I had no experience in those job sectors, or any qualifications or my CV, would not impress. It seemed that no employer had a vacancy for a twenty-two-year-old ex-Monk, with only classical subjects in his educational portfolio. It was going to be a long, hard, and winding road in order to build my life back in civvy street.

47

Chapter 4.

Jobs, but not a career.

At long last, after scouring the employment section of the Manchester Evening News for days, I spotted a job that took my eye and did not ask for experience or qualifications. Was it just too good to be true? Probably! But I would go for it anyway. Job No.1: *"Salesman for Encyclopaedia of the World"* it read: *"No experience necessary, as full training will be given. Must be bright, hardworking and good with people"* or similar words: *"Payment will be by way of commission only. Immediate start for the right candidate."*

Eagerly I telephoned the company. To my surprise I was asked to go for an interview the very next day. It was with some misgivings that I showed the interviewer my CV. When he did not recoil in horror and seemed not to care what he had just read about my history, I felt that I must have a chance of landing the job. That evening, I had a telephone call from the Encyclopedia Company offering me the position for my local area and asking me to start on the following Monday. It all seemed too easy, too good to be true, but I knew I wanted to take it. So, there we were, Job No.1, my first ever job. I accepted it of course, albeit I was under no illusions that I would have to earn the money, as the income was on a commission basis only. Naturally, I would have preferred a salary, but it was not on offer. As I had absolutely no experience of selling, I knew that I would have to be trained, but I hoped that I had enough intelligence and drive, to make my first job a resounding success.

On the Monday morning, I called into the local office and was introduced to Derek one of the company's brightest salespeople. He did not tell me anything, or teach me anything about the company. He just told me that we were going straight out to have an appointment with a married couple in Stockport and that I was just to; *"watch, listen and learn"!* I was to have a non-speaking role! It seemed that the couple had replied to a leaflet advertisement, expressing a general interest in World Encyclopedia, in return for a free gift. The couple was late middle aged and welcoming, offering us a cup of tea on arrival. After spending about half an hour *"being friendly"* and generally gaining the confidence of the couple, Derek began his sales pitch in earnest. It was obvious to me that his sales spiel was straight out of a text book as it seemed to be word for word, in parrot fashion. He must have uttered those persuasive words hundreds of times before, so slick was his sales patter. I must confess that I just sat and listened, lost in admiration, at the way he described the

Encyclopedia products. If I had the money, I would have bought a set from him for myself, there and then; he was that good. His glowing descriptions were so convincing that it seemed as though the books were an absolute essential of life and that the couple could not possibly live without them. The pair also seemed really impressed and all was going exceptionally well until they asked Derek about the price. Yes, they had the temerity to ask what they would have to pay in order to become the proud owners of these colorful masterpieces of knowledge and literature! Derek seemed almost offended when questioned about the cost! He asked the couple if they were convinced about their need to have them. Every time he asked a question of them, he posed it in such a positive fashion that there could only be one answer, and that answer had to be "YES"! It was just like sending lambs to the slaughter!

The couple seemed almost apologetic about discussing the price, but were clearly concerned about it. Derek told them not to worry about the cost and assured the couple that he would help to make it possible for them to become the proud owners. Without mentioning the total price for the entire set of Encyclopedias, he asked them how much per week they would be willing to pay for them. He reassured them that he could spread the cost on a weekly basis. He boldly questioned how much they spent on cigarettes and drinks and then

suggested that they would be far better off
investing in their books. He described them as an
essential investment in their future and the future
of their children and grand-children. After a severe
brow-beating lasting well in excess of one hour,
the poor couple agreed that they would be far
better off spending their money on the books
rather than on their other pleasures. Derek then
convinced them to withdraw a large deposit out of
their savings and to pay the remainder over a
period of years. At this point I could feel that the
couple were becoming uncomfortable and were
searching for a reason to say "No", but they did
not dare come right out and say so. There then
followed periods of uneasy silence, as the couple
was asked to sign an agreement to buy the set of
volumes. The tension was building and Derek had
the prey in his sights and was not going to let it get
away. He asked them what was causing them not
to sign the agreement, but they were too timid to
tell him their reasons. Clearly the books were too
expensive for them, but they were backed into a
corner and did not know how to find a way out.

Every time the couple posed a tricky question,
Derek would have a slick and instant answer that
would overcome it. By this time, we had been in
the couple's home for almost four hours and I
could sense that they were weary and just wanted
it all to end. Eventually, after they had finally run
out of excuses not to buy, and Derek had given

them all the reasons why they must buy, the couple relented and wearily signed the contract to buy the set of books, paying him a substantial deposit and committing themselves to a lengthy higher purchase agreement. At the end, they did not seem delighted by their purchase of the encyclopedia.

By this time, my glowing admiration for Derek's sales skill had begun to wane and already I was beginning to question his sales technique in my mind. I wondered about his sense of morality in brow beating customers into parting with their hard earned cash. We left the couple's house, and as we got into Derek's car, he smugly smirked to me and said: *"Piece of cake! It's like taking sweets from children!"* On the journey back to the office he boastfully told me that he would be teaching me these methods and sales techniques over the next few days. When he told me that he did not accept the word *"No!,"* under any circumstances, I began to be concerned about what I had let myself in for and what type of organization I had become involved with.

That night, as I lay in bed, my mind was still awash with thoughts about my past life, not to mention what my future life may have in store for me. Already I was beginning to regret becoming involved with that type of work and with this type of company. On that first day at work, I had witnessed my colleague browbeat a couple into utter submission, buying books, and parting with a substantial amount of money, in order to buy a set of Encyclopedias. The pleasant people really did not want the books, at least, not at that price and perhaps not at all. They were too timid to refuse Derek's slick sales technique. I lay in bed thinking: *"I don't like you Derek and I don't like your company's sales methods."* I was not relishing returning to the office the following day.

The next morning, I arose very early and got dressed into my black business suit, pretending to be ready for my new job. Dad had set off for work and Mum was also about to leave. I waited until Mum had gone and picked up the telephone. Nervously I called the World Encyclopedia Company and spoke to the Manager who had interviewed me and offered me the job. *"I have decided not to continue in the job"* I said to him: *"The job is not for me,* "I continued: *"I cannot sell encyclopaedias to people who do not want them"*. There was a taut silence at the other end of the phone, so I carried on speaking: *"I can only sell to people if they really want to buy them, and I think the people we saw yesterday were forced to buy the books. If I have to sell in the way that Derek sold yesterday, then I don't want to be a part of it!"* My Manager responded: *"Stephen, this way of selling is very successful and ethical and if you don't like it, then you are better off leaving.* At that, I just replied "OK!" and I put the phone down

54

and went off to consider what I had just done.

It was with a huge sigh of relief that I had ended the conversation. I had not been looking forward to it, but I was glad I had done it. At that time I was not confident, but I knew in my heart that I could not continue working for that company. What I had seen was immoral and there was no way that I could browbeat a customer, in order to achieve a sale. I knew that if I had stayed, I would have had to do things their way and I could not live with that type of pressurized selling.

Job No.1 had ended after just 1 day! I went and sat in the lounge on my own, had a cup of tea and just pondered my future and my past. Life on the outside was not easy, just as life on the inside [at the Monastery] had been no bed of roses. I mused to myself that I was completely lost, and I really did not know which direction to turn. I did though have the inclination, that if I was not to be a Priest and help people in the community, then at least I should be doing a type of work that was sociable and would assist other people. I had a notion in my head, that I should not be doing work just in order to earn money. Perhaps at this stage of my life, I was rather naïve and somewhat idealistic, but in the stone hard and cold realities of the real world, it would probably not last for very long.

I was feeling insecure on that Monday and down

in the dumps. I just sat there on my own all day. I was not feeling good about myself and not proud about the way my first job had come to such an ignominious and abrupt end, albeit it was entirely my decision. Suddenly, my brother Mike breezed in. He had just finished work and was full of the joys of spring. *"Hiya Kid"* he smiled. *"How did the job go today?"* Sheepishly, I told him that I had not been to work at all that day. Before he could answer, Mum and Dad arrived home together, having both done a full day's work. I decided that it was better if I told all of them the story at once. The family looked shocked when I told them my news! I think they were all disappointed in me even before this, so their reaction was no surprise. Even so, I explained my reasons for not continuing at the company and I believe that they understood my explanation for not staying on, under those circumstances.

My younger brother Mike was by this stage a trainee Supermarket Manager with Spar Supermarkets and he was very highly thought of. It seemed that he was destined to become a Manager himself. He was five years younger than me and was still only seventeen, but was No. 2 to the Manager, Jim Lyons. Normally, I would not have even considered supermarket management as a career. The job was way out of my comfort zone, but when Mike asked me if I fancied joining him at the Spar Supermarket in Marple, it did not seem

such a bad idea, working with my kid brother.
Being honest, I did not see it as a lifetime career,
but I was in such a vacuum at the time, that I would
have considered almost anything. Mike said that
he would put in a good word for me with his boss,
as they were looking for a new trainee manager.
Mum and Dad thought it was a great idea. I would
be working with my brother, we would both be
very local in Marple, and if nothing else, I would
be earning some money. If it was offered to me,
how could I say no? I had been back at home for
well over a month and up-to that point had not
contributed a penny to the family coffers. I was
feeling very guilty about not being in work. I had
never had these feelings before, when I was in the
Monastery. I contributed nothing at all to the
Redemptorists, at least financially, in all the years
I had been there, and yet I had never felt that way
before. Yet, I was now in a very different world.
My parents had both worked hard all their lives
and now it was my turn to do some work as well.

I did not say yes to Mike immediately, I merely
pointed out that it was an interesting idea, but that
his manager may not offer me a job if he felt that
I was unsuitable. I just suggested that we take one
step at a time and see what transpires. That night
in bed, [that was where I did most of my thinking];
I thought to myself, that it may be better if a job
with Spar would not come to fruition. It was not
something I had ever considered, and it was not in

my "master plan", if indeed I had one, for a future career, but perhaps it could act as a stop-gap job, until something more suitable presented itself.

The next day, Mike came home from work at 6pm and beamed at me! *"Say thanks to your little brother, Steve; you've got an interview at 10' O Clock tomorrow morning"*. I said: *"Hey! Thanks Mike!"* but although I was pleased to be going for the interview, I honestly did not fancy working in a supermarket as a career. Even so, I knew that I had to get myself into work, and I had to bring home some money. I put on my best black suit the next morning and went with Mike to the Spar Supermarket in Marple High Street. I felt somewhat conspicuous and overdressed, as Mike was just in his working clothes. It was after all a job interview for me and I had to look my best. The job on offer was a for a trainee manager's position. Well, at least that was the official title, but from what I quickly gleaned, it was a rather inflated description of the job on offer.

The Manager Jim Lyons, was a likeable and positive person and totally committed to the work he was doing. The manner in which he described the job was way beyond what it was in reality. Although it was advertised as a job for a "trainee manager", in truth it would mean starting at the very bottom as a shop floor worker and stacking shelves. It was not quite what I had in mind. That was something for a sixteen year old, but I badly needed the money. It did my confidence no harm whatsoever when Mr. Lyons offered the job to me, but I am not really sure what he made of my qualifications in Latin, Philosophy and Church History. They were not exactly essential qualities for stacking supermarket shelves, but perhaps he considered that my education, albeit classical, would be beneficial as a future supermarket manager, should that ever come to fruition. So, job No.2: I was a "Trainee Supermarket manager."

In all honesty, although I was pleased to be offered the job, it was not what I has in my mind as a long term career move. I started the job the following Monday and I did my best working really hard to impress, but although I made all the right noises, I knew that it was just going to be a stepping stone to something else that I felt better suited to. Therefore, just a few months later, when I was offered an assistant Manager's job in a smaller store, about five miles away, I was not sure if I was heading in the right direction, but of course I took the job. At least there was a small increase in wages. At the Spar in Marple, I recall, with no pleasure, getting my first week's pay. I was on an emergency code, as I was, at that stage, unknown to the taxman. Out of my £8.30 shillings per week wages, the tax man took about £3.10 shillings, then National Insurance had a dip into it as well, followed by the Shop worker's Union 5 shillings.

As a result, my take home pay was the princely sum of £3.16 shillings, out of which I gave my Mum £2 housekeeping. That left me just £1.16 shillings to live on for the rest of the week. It seemed little money for a lot of hard work, over a six-day week. This was life back in the real world.

It was not essentially about the cash! I had never been motivated by money, particularly as I had taken a vow of poverty just a few years earlier and money had played no part in my life whilst in the monastery. I sat at home that Friday evening with the miserly sum of less than £2 in my pocket. I quietly mused to myself how much my life had changed in such a short space of time. Yet the decisions had all been mine, albeit I had frequently been controlled and maneuvered into the type of positions, where those decisions practically made themselves. Even so, I knew one thing for certain. I knew that the work I was doing, was not what I wanted to do as a long-term career. I was feeling unfulfilled and needed to do something more creative. The truth was, I was back in something of a rut. Granted, it was largely of my own making, but it was mainly fueled by the necessity to earn a living. That was something that I had never had to do in the monastery and it was a brand new and unusual experience for me.

Over the next few weeks, I spent a lot of time thinking decisions through. After all, I had spent a good ten years of my twenty two years thus far, in quiet thought and contemplation. It must have been what I did best. However, it was not enough for me to be a thinker. I desperately needed to be a doer and I needed to do something quickly or else I would be unable to support myself.

People would say to me*: "Steve, are you alright? You are quiet!"* They seemed to equate being quiet either with; there being a problem, some sadness, or unhappiness, but this was not necessarily the case. It was just what I did and how I was.

That weekend after finishing my work, I just had an inner feeling that I did not want to become a supermarket manager. Not that there was anything wrong with that fine profession. It was a good and honest job, challenging and ideal for the right sort of person, but that person was not me. In my heart, I thought that I was cut out for something different. My entire life thus far, had been all about high ideals, and doing something exceptional during my life. Yet, if I was unable to live an exceptional life, then at the very least, I wanted to do something really useful, and not merely in the pursuit of money. I genuinely wanted to live a life that would be beneficial to others in some way. My life in the Monastery had been all about prayer, meditation and helping other people. I wanted to help people in any way that I could and at that period of my life, the pursuit of money and possessions, were well down my list of priorities. I was highly idealistic and perhaps I did not fully understand the genuine realities of life in the real world outside of the monastery.

For the remainder of that weekend, I mulled things over and over in my mind. I slid back into my quiet mode again and when my brother Mike asked me: *"Is everything alright Kid?"* I just had to tell him that I would be leaving the Spar supermarket job, just as soon as I could get the work I wanted. My kid brother, Mike, had been good enough to get me the position with the Supermarket and I was grateful to him, but that was not a good enough reason to stay any longer than necessary.

One day Mike asked me what I was going to do next. *"You won't believe me if I tell you, so I'll keep it to myself for now"* I told him, in a demonstratively positive manner. *"Go on, Our Kid" tell me what you're going to do next"* he smirked. *"No, you'll only laugh if I tell you"* I replied somewhat sheepishly: *"No Our Kid, I promise I won't laugh "he* said:" trying to reassure me, but failing miserably, I blurted out; *"I'm going to be a Nurse."* The amazed look on his face said it all and he belly laughed for fully a minute before smirking again and saying out loud"
"A Nurse! That's a girl's job you big Jessie".

Despite his promise not to laugh, I suppose that I

had been expecting exactly that response. This was after all, 1971, when men were men, miners went down the pits and women worked in offices or became nurses and secretaries. Equality of the sexes had yet to be invented and attitudes died hard into whatever camp you were entrenched in.

As I sat there on my own, deeply absorbed in my quiet deliberations, my thought process went something along these lines:

"I want to do a job that is really useful in society, but not just for me, but also for the benefit of other people. Of course, I need to be paid, but the money is of secondary importance. I just need enough to live on and get by, as I will be happy with that."

Only a short while ago, I had been in love with a nurse who had taken great care of me while I was seriously ill in hospital. I had become deeply and emotionally involved with her and she had made a lasting impression on me. At that time in my young life, I was a very impressionable person. Margaret had given me the strength of mind to make the biggest decision of my life. That decision was to leave the Monastery, even though she was not the reason for me taking the decision to do so.

For me, there could be no greater role model than Margaret. She and the other Nurses had done a fantastic job showing me love and care, when I was hospitalized for several weeks and in a fragile state of mind and body. She had made a lasting impression on my young, impressionable and naive mind, due to her compassionate nursing.

I could not think at that time, of any job that would be more suitable for me. I knew that there were male nurses, albeit they were few and far between, but that did not put me off. In that moment, my idealism was so high, that I could quite easily overlook the many potential difficulties of embarking on this unusual career path for a man.

While I was scouring the "Situations Vacant" columns of the Manchester Evening News, I had given a passing glance to adverts at a major Hospital in Salford and Manchester for *"Trainee Student Nurses - Male or Female",* it stated. It was really Avant-Guard! There was still very much a gender divided segregation in the jobs market, where men usually did men's jobs and women did women's work. That was how it was then, but it was at last, in the process of changing. The Seventies must have been one of the most dramatic decades for change throughout the entire century, so perhaps my move into Nursing was not such a *"bold leap for mankind"* after all. That said, my brother Mike did not seem too impressed! Notwithstanding, I decided that I would press ahead, ignoring the appeal of male dominated business, to the idealistic career of Nursing. I was

64

a people person, and one who wanted to do something to help other people in the process, or so I thought at that time.

Immediately, I put pen to paper and tried to put together a "curriculum vitae". It was a difficult task for me. At least, having done Latin for many years, I was acutely aware of what was meant when an employer wanted a C.V. It is a Latin phrase literally meaning a "list of life".

It did not take me very long to put my first C.V. together. It contained a brief description of my schooling and then my time at the Monasteries in Perth and Hawkstone. I then listed my two jobs to-date: One day as an encyclopedia salesman, with an explanation as to why I decided to leave, and then three months as a trainee and then assistant supermarket manager. I read it to myself and had to confess that it was hardly an impressive C.V. As I read it back to myself, I wondered why an employer would be impressed enough to even grant me an interview. Still, I sent it off, more in hope than expectation and was more than pleasantly surprised when, about a week later an official looking letter, bearing the NHS symbol, dropped onto the doormat at home. As I tore open the envelope, I fully anticipated a polite refusal and was delighted but highly surprised, when the letter from the Hospital Matron asked me to attend an interview at a Salford Hospital a few days later.

It seemed that my good education, my ability to write a convincing C.V and letter, and perhaps my intriguing life up to that point, was sufficiently interesting to earn an interview with them.

Mike thought that I was just plain crazy, not just because I was considering becoming a Nurse, but because I had been living away from home since I was eleven years old. Now, I had only recently been re-united with my family, back at home, just a few short months ago. If I was given the job, I would again be living away from my family in a Nurse's Home. I think that my brother had a point, but I chose to ignore it. I was mixed up, somewhat confused, and seemed unable to make correct and sensible judgments at that juncture.

 On the day of my interview, I took the day off work from the Supermarket, to go to the Hospital. At that time, I could not drive. I had been taking lessons and was doing alright, but my test was still a few weeks away, any anyway, I did not own a car. I took the train from Marple to Manchester Piccadilly Station and then another train out to Salford, close to the Hospital. I was smartly dressed in my one and only dark suit, with a white shirt, but at least I now owned a flowery "kipper" tie, so I imagine that I was then in the height of fashion, or something close to it. The new tie was bought due to the teasing of my brother, Mike!

I had never felt so nervous, as I sat in the Hospital corridor outside the Matron's office. I was not alone. There were two young women also there. They were both to be interviewed before me. *"What chance have I got?"* I mused to myself. They were two young and pretty girls, who sounded bright, and they seemed really keen to be Nurses. We talked nervously together before they were called in to their interviews. They looked the part, and at that time, as I sat alone waiting for my turn, I wondered just what I was doing there? I did not even have the answer for myself, so how could I possibly convince the panel, that I was the right person for the job? I was sure that both of the girls would be selected for the Nurse's job ahead of me.

As my turn arrived, I tentatively entered the interview room, and sat before me, were four very stern looking ladies. I felt as if I was facing a firing squad, so piercing were the eyes that were focused so intently upon me. *"Hmm, a very unusual C.V. Mr. Nearey!"* said the obvious leader of the firing squad [I mean, the interview panel!] *"What exactly is it, that makes you want to become a Nurse? It is a little different to being a Monk in a Monastery, is it not?*

My reply was: *"My only experience of Hospitals and Nursing is the six weeks I spent in Hospital just over a year ago. I was amazed and full of admiration at the work the Nurses did and I would*

love to do the same job as them, and be a nurse. "
Despite my poor C.V, my education at Erdington
Abbey and at Hawkstone, had stood me in good
stead. I had been trained in public speaking and
preaching. I was able to put forward an eloquent
and strong case for the Hospital to at least give me
a chance, even though I must have been the least
qualified and most unlikely, of all the applicants
they had interviewed. During my interview I told
the panel that I would be really keen to learn,
hardworking and that my major strengths would
be my relationships with patients and staff.
Without giving anything away, the Matron asked
me when I would be free to start, if I were to be
selected. It was not a "yes" but neither was it a
"No", and so I went away relatively happy in the
knowledge that if I was offered the job, I would
most certainly accept it.

Some three weeks later, when I had not heard a
word from the Hospital, I had almost given up
hope of landing the job in Nursing. Then one night
when I arrived back home after work, Mum
handed me a letter franked by the NHS. Eagerly I
ripped it open and scanned the contents. As soon
as I saw the words: *"delighted to offer you",* I
knew that the job was mine. I just felt inside me
that it was the right job for me. It had everything
that I wanted: A genuine career with prospects and
a caring profession, working with and for people.
The salary was nothing to write home about, but it

68

was much better than the job I was in and there
was the prospect of decent money in the future, if
I progressed up the career ladder. I was invited to
report to the Hospital in six weeks' time. As was
the norm in those days, all student nurses had to
live in at the hospital in the nurse's home. I must
have been the only one in my family to be pleased
with my new appointment! They had a good point!
I had lived away from home since I was just an
eleven-year-old boy, and now within a few weeks
of being back with my loving family, I was going
to live away from home and my family yet again.

My mind was made up. I had become so idealistic
as a result of my extended stay in hospital and my
close relationship with my nurse Margaret, that I
had become totally infatuated with the nursing
profession. There was a very real danger that I
would completely ignore the many downsides to
this new career. I could only see the benefits and
my blinkers were well and truly on! I was looking
only straight ahead, but not looking to either side,
and there were indeed several downsides!

I duly worked my notice at the Spar Supermarket
who did not want me to leave. I then prepared
myself for moving into the Nurse's home at the
Salford Hospital. My parents, brothers and sister,
all made it clear that they did not want me to go,
but as I had already lived most of my young life
away from home, this did not faze me, and I was

looking forward to an exciting new chapter of my topsy turvey life.

So began my 3rd. job, as a Nurse at the General Hospital. It was a 5am start to the day, but I was used to an early start. After a train journey and then a bus, I finally arrived at the Hospital and attended the reception area, where I was greeted by staff and told to wait in a reception room where there were already some sixteen or so eager young girls. Most of them could only have been seventeen or eighteen at most, and I was all of twenty two, so quite ancient by comparison. We all waited around in small groups for the full complement of new student nurses to arrive by 11am. It was with some trepidation that I realized that I was the only male in the group. The young female nurses were eagerly chattering, as they do, and I must confess that I felt well and truly on the fringe of things and completely outside of my comfort zone. A fish out of water, would have been a more suitable description of the way I felt that Monday morning.

I had never been good with small talk. I was brought up to speak mainly when it was necessary or useful, and not just for the sake of it. Neither was I comfortable with idle chit-chat and my years in the monastery had not taught me any of these social skills. I could not believe how nervous and self-conscious I felt and so when the last new trainee entered the room, my relief was almost tangible! It was a man, among a group of women, but it was a relief to see another male and I made an immediate beeline towards him. It seemed incomprehensible that a young red bloodied male would be petrified to be in the midst of seventeen young and lovely girls, and yet I was absolutely terrified and nervous beyond belief.

The young male student nurse was called Mark and he had come fresh from college or university and was about 23 years old. Straight away I felt more at ease, perhaps because I was used to many years of male-only company. I knew how men ticked, what they talked about and somehow they seemed less threatening. Girls seemed to me like a totally alien species and I did not know how to deal with and socialize with them. No doubt, in time I would learn how to associate with them and speak confidently with them, but at that time, I was a bumbling and nervous young man.

The leader of the student nurses assembled us all on chairs in a circle around the room and one by one we had to introduce ourselves to the assembled group. Going around the circle anti-clockwise, I worked out that I would be the tenth out of seventeen to speak, so I knew I had about five minutes or more to prepare what I had to say.

I have never been more nervous in my entire life.

I had given many sermons and practiced public speaking and yet this was something entirely different. It felt like waiting for something really unpleasant to happen, like having a tooth extraction and the waiting was even worse than the tooth extraction itself. Most of the girls, being under eighteen, gave a brief rendition of their education and their family background and sat down quite quickly. And then it was my turn.

I stood up very slowly, playing for time, and told the group that I had left home at eleven, entered a monastery at eighteen, became a monk, trained to be a priest and had finally left at the age of twenty two. Then followed a brief account of my career to-date: One day spent as an encyclopedia salesman and all of five months as a trainee supermarket manager. As I sat down, I could hear whispers and the shock around the room was almost tangible. I doubt I would have received a more shocked reaction, if I had had told the group that I was a mass murderer with two heads!! Talk about making a first impression! Yet I had to tell the truth, and anyway, all of this had been discussed at my interview. I was not sure what affect this would have, but I would no doubt find out quite soon.

It is strange how a person can get an entirely different perspective of life when one is on the other side of an equation. As a patient in a hospital,

I could see a somewhat glamorous and idealistic view of what being a nurse was all about. Looking at it from a hospital bed, particularly when I was ill and hospitalized for six weeks, I had a totally jaundiced view of what was involved in being a nurse. I even surprised myself, that I was attracted to joining the nursing profession. After all, I had been brought up in an all-male environment for well over ten years and then I decided to be involved in an almost totally female dominated profession. A psychiatrist would have had an absolute field day with me. I must have seemed unpredictable at best and totally crazy at worst.

My first day at the General Hospital was a complete blur. I was not used to the intensity of group learning. It was all about getting to know one other and the other members of staff. My mind was in a complete whirl. Without being sexist in any way, I was finding it difficult to relate to so many women at the same time. I had been so used to dealing with only men for so long, that I found it hard to understand the different ways and thinking of our fairer sex! Being referred to as "Nurse Nearey" just sounded plain weird, but I suppose it made a pleasant change from being called "Brother Nearey" all the time. In reality, I would have been happier just being called plain old "Mr. Steve Nearey", nobody in particular!

Our first day there was something of a blur. It took

me a long time to remember the names of all my new student nurse colleagues and I was finding it really difficult to relate to the girls. Don't get me wrong! Who would not enjoy being only one of two male nurses, surrounded by another fifteen young and pretty female nurses? My problem was that I did not fully understand the complex minds and workings of the girls. This was never more apparent than when the student's tutor arranged for all the new nurses to be kitted out with their uniforms. The girls were all busy talking fashion, checking that their uniforms fitted well and that they looked good, and they most certainly did!

Mark, my one and only male colleague and me, were presented with our own version of the male student nurse's uniform. It consisted of a pristine, white, stiff and starched uniform, of white trousers and top. I must confess, that in an instant, the proverbial ugly ducklings, had turned into glorious swans! Within minutes, this motley crew of female and male students, had to all intents and purposes, been transformed into what appeared to be, experienced and true nursing professionals. It was an illusion of course. Being newbies, most of us knew little at all about nursing.

For me, it took me straight back to that first September day in Perth, about four years earlier when a similar group of sixteen young men were all transformed from being a similar motley crew, into a young and fresh faced group of trainee Monks, as we changed from our civilian clothing into the robes of the Redemptorists. I could still recall that day and the great pride I took in wearing that black habit. Similarly, in an instant, I was transformed from a civilian to a completely new person. That day, it gave me a status and respect that was instantly given, but later on, that status and respect had to be earned.

On that first eventful day at the Hospital, for a few hours at least, I completely forgot my nerves and inexperience and basked in the reflected respect and status, that wearing the nurse's uniform of a major Hospital, gave to us all. At that stage, none of us had even been let anywhere near to a ward, let alone a patient. Before that landmark, there were an intensive few days of training to be endured. It was just the start of a strict and difficult three years of training, if we were finally to be confirmed as S.R.N.'s – State Registered Nurses.

The next few days were spent mainly in the classroom. There was so much theory to be learned just to understand the very basics of nursing, before being trained for some of the practical aspects of the job. After my lengthy education at Erdington, Perth and Hawkstone, I had no fears about the theory and learning that needed to be done, in order to qualify for the job. I was confident and well used to schooling, so it held no particular demons for me. My problems were in forming my relationships with other people. In particular I struggled with the female of the species. I was still painfully shy, completely lacking in confidence and a blubbering mess when it came to holding a conversation with women.

I remember with horror, the first day of our practical nursing experience. Our tutor had decided that first, we needed to learn the way that a bed should be made, hospital style. If anybody had any preconception that making a bed was easy, then they had never had a lesson from our nursing tutor! Two nurses had to make the bed together, with or without a patient in it, and every corner had to be precise and equal in length. Talk about precision engineering! Woe betides any nurses that made a sloppy bed with her around. She was just like Hattie Jacques, the actress from "Carry on Matron" but mush feistier. Of course, a bed without a patient is only half a bed, so imagine who was selected to play the part of the patient? *"Stephen"! You can be the patient and the nurses have to lift you and move you around the bed, while they make the bed around you"* the Nurse's tutor instructed: I just hated being the centre of attention and I was so embarrassed to play the part of the patient. I think the other nurses enjoyed taking the mickey out of me, particularly as I was still desperately shy and lacking in confidence, whenever it came to dealing with other people.

They used to tease me all of the time, which made me even more uncomfortable in their company.

The mickey taking went on for quite some time. I think the girl nurses quite liked me due to my shyness, and they would take every opportunity to tease me, but I just took it in my stride and hoped they would pick on someone else next time. Of course, it didn't happen. I fell for the oldest hospital trick that had been doing rounds for years, to newbies in the nursing profession. The ward sister told me to go to the "stores" and ask for "a long stand". Talk about being naïve! I just took the instruction at face value and went to the stores: I said to the storekeeper: *"I've been asked to come for a long stand, by Sister on Ward B5."*
"That's fine" he said, keeping a straight poker face: *"Just wait there and I'll get one for you.*
I waited patiently and totally without question, for all of twenty minutes. When he did not come over to me with the long stand, I went over to him and said politely: *"Excuse me, I'm still waiting for a long stand!"* He looked at me with a semi-smirk and said: *"No, you've had your long stand; I gave it to you about twenty minutes ago."* *"No, I argued"* slightly agitated, *"I haven't had it":* Then like a bolt out of the blue, the penny finally dropped! "Clang!" I sloped off back to the ward with a mixture of annoyance and embarrassment and did not say anything to the Ward Sister. A few minutes later we passed in the corridor and as she

walked past me she kept a straight face and just said: *"Nurse Nearey, did you get the long stand I sent you for?"* I turned, flashed a shy, embarrassed smile to her and carried on down the corridor. I had been well and truly had!

Most certainly, there were some moments of fun and frivolity and I liked most of the student Nurses and life in the Nurse's home, but after the first few weeks, I was beginning to feel uneasy about the work. After the first flush of eagerness, the idealistic part of the job, helping patients and making them get better, seemed to fade a little and the more menial parts of the job seemed to come to the fore. The long hours and the anti-social shift patterns took their toll and I was also finding it difficult in coming to terms with the female dominated environment. Of course, I had Mark, as the only other male nurse in the student group, but there were very few men in the hospital, barring the Doctors and Porters. I was sharing a room with Mark but after initially feeling pleased to be rooming with him, I then began to find it hard to share a room with anybody. In the Monastery I had been used to rooming on my own for several years. The peace and quiet and good order had been a major part of my life. I was very tidy, whilst Mark was extremely untidy. I used to like to spend leisure time quietly in my room, whereas Mark was always chatting, usually about nothing, and I was no good at all with small talk and tittle tattle.

He was very likeable, but he was somehow too friendly and I was a very private person. He was also too "touchy-feely" for me, but I put that down to me being a very private sort of person. At that stage, I kept myself to myself, but it was all part of my natural reserve and my upbringing. If I did not have much to do with the female nurses, it was just that I was shy and lacking in confidence and not that I was not attracted to any of them. We did not talk about the girls when we were together, but perhaps Mark was aware of my Monastic background and was not very sure where I stood when it came to women. It never crossed my mind for one instant, that Mark had not made a play for any of the girls. He was a much more gregarious person than me, he was good looking and I expected that he would mix well with the girls, but it did not ring any bells with me, when he did not.

Mark and I had been sharing a room together in the Nurse's home for nearly three weeks. It seemed perfectly normal, even though I hated having to share a room at all. I just kept myself very private and I was always the first into bed, having changed in the bathroom. It was just a part of my natural shyness and reserve. As soon as I got into bed, I would just say: *"Goodnight Mark, see you in the morning"* and I would then turn over and go straight to sleep.

One particular night, whilst in our room, I went

through my normal ritual and got into bed, turned over and closed my eyes. After a long shift I was extremely tired, but just as I was dropping off to sleep, I felt a face close to mine and was aware of somebody breathing lightly, very close to me. *"Can I come into bed with you?"* He whispered. Immediately, despite the dark, I recognized that it was Mark's voice. I sat bolt upright in bed and said loudly: *"No you can't Mark, what are you playing at? Go and get back into to your own bed!*
He seemed completely taken aback. It was as if he expected a totally different response! What on earth could have given him any inclination whatsoever, that I was even slightly interested in that type of relationship?

I didn't know what to do. I leapt out of bed as he just stood there motionless, unsure what to say or do next. Immediately I threw on my clothes and bolted out of the room as quickly as I could without uttering a word. I headed straight for the exit door to the hospital, past the security guard and out of the hospital grounds. I was still in shock and just wandered around the local streets aimlessly. It was about 1am and I did not want to go back to the Nurse's home for fear of a confrontation. I did not want to see him again. I would not have known what to say. I had not seen this coming and I could not imagine why he would possibly make such a move. If it had been because I had shown little or no interest in the female nurses, then he was barking up the wrong tree, he was well wide of the mark. Looking back, I had not noticed that he had not shown any interest in the girls, but apparently, for a completely different reason. Perhaps he had interpreted my time in the Monastery, in an all-male environment, in an entirely erroneous and different way. How wrong could he possibly have been?

Whilst aimlessly walking the streets of Salford in the early hours, I saw a neon sign with a clock, and noted that it was 3.30am. On the corner of one of the major streets, [I did not know exactly where I was], I saw what appeared to be an all-night café. I fumbled around in my coat pocket and felt some change. By this time I was feeling cold and damp as the drizzle and mist were becoming heavier. I just wanted to get off the streets and get dry and warm. I went into the café and ordered a hot chocolate and some comfort food. I sat there on my own and fondled my mug of hot chocolate in the cusp of my hands until it was empty. Not knowing what to do next, I ordered a second mug and spent the best part of an hour mulling over it, just going over and over again in my mind what had caused this to happen. I examined my every action, word and movement that I could remember since I had arrived at the hospital and I could find no rhyme or reason to explain why Mark had made such an unwanted move. I was absolutely positive I had done nothing at all, even subconsciously, to encourage such an approach and I could find no reason for him to make such a massive mistake.

I stayed at the café until almost six O' clock in the morning, having drink after drink, eventually followed by toast and marmalade in order to justify my prolonged stay in the café. I realized that I would have to go back to the Nurse's home at some time. Eventually, I plucked up the courage, paid for my food and drink at the café and headed back. It was almost dawn and was just becoming daylight. I was tired and mentally exhausted as well as feeling physically shattered. I nodded in the direction of the security guard on the gate and flashed my security badge to him before heading back towards the Nurse's quarters. As I scurried along, I was rehearsing exactly what I was going to say to Mark when I arrived back at our room. I was not looking forward to this. I was not comfortable with any type of confrontation. It was completely new territory for me and something I had never experienced in my life to-date. As I neared the door to our room, I could feel my heart thumping in my chest and I was extremely nervous, not knowing how I was possibly going to deal with this situation. It had suddenly changed everything. I was already becoming disillusioned with the life and the job and now I knew that everything would have to change. I did not want to face this situation or have a confrontation, but I was ready to do so if I had to. I entered the room ready for conflict, but after scanning my surroundings, I quickly realized that the room was empty. I soon came to the conclusion that Mark had more than likely gone straight on to the early shift that we were both due to be working on that day. I was more than relieved.

From that moment on, I knew precisely what I had to do. I did not want to have to face the situation at the Hospital or with Mark. It had all gone so horribly wrong. I was no longer feeling enamored with life as a Nurse, and I now had a situation that I did not know how to deal with.

On a sudden instinct, I collected all my belongings and threw them into the bags that I had arrived with. I soon cleared the room of everything that I owned and then headed straight out of the Hospital once more, past the security guard again, but this time, I walked straight to the bus stop, took the first bus into Manchester and then a train back home. At Marple train station, I needed time to collect myself. I decided to walk all the way from the train station, about a mile and a half, and back to my home, where I knew that I would have some explaining to do, to members of my family.

As I put my key into the front door, Mum was stood in the hallway. *"Hello Steve"* she said: looking surprised. *"I wasn't expecting you home this week."*

Sheepishly and with huge embarrassment I said: *"Mum, I've left the Hospital! I'll explain it all later. Is it alright if I come and live back at home with you and Dad?"*

Later, that day, I knew that I had to phone the hospital to explain exactly why I had suddenly gone "AWOL". They would be wondering why I had not turned up for my shift that morning. I spoke to the Nurse's tutor and told her that I had left without telling anybody, because of what had happened the previous night. She too was shocked, but she did not want me to leave. I told her that I could not cope with this situation, and that I was terminating my employment immediately. I informed her that I felt unable to continue working in such uncomfortable circumstances. She asked me to return and told me that I would make a very good nurse and that they would be able to sort out the sensitive situation concerning Mark.

"I'm sorry Sister, but I've made my mind up. I don't want to face Mark again, and there are other issues and reasons for me wanting to leave. I would normally give you notice, but in the circumstances, I just want to leave immediately. I really can't come back and work there. It would be far too difficult for me. I am not coming back and I am going to find another job. I hope you will give me a good reference in the circumstances!"

I knew that, as I was still in my trial period, either party could terminate immediately, so I just told her that it would be better all-around if I did not return. There was no way that I wanted to confront Mark and now that I had told the tutor, I also told her that there were other issues and that I had not settled into General Nursing. I told her that despite the issue with Mark, I was finding it difficult to adjust to life in a practically female environment. I did explain that I had been living in an all-male community for more than ten years and the transition was just too difficult for me to make at the present time. I needed more time to adjust. I think that she understood, particularly after I told her of my time spent in the monastery. I asked her if I would be given a good reference, and thankfully, she indicated that she would.

I never did explain to my family why I had suddenly left the Hospital without working my notice. I found it impossible to tell them the truth. I was unable to tell them what had happened that night. I would never talk about such a personal and sensitive topic to the family. I was horrified that it had happened and I did not want to tell people the truth, and how it had brought about the end of my nursing career. All I could tell them was that I could not settle into the hospital environment and that I decided to leave straight away. Despite wishing that I could tell them the truth, I never did explain to them what had happened that fateful night and it must not have looked good. I wondered what they thought about me. They must have despaired that I would ever settle down to a normal life again and once more I was back to first base in my struggle to adapt to life outside of the monastery. It was to be a long and difficult road in my attempts to settle back into civilian life.

Chapter 5

Once a Nurse

So job No. 3 had come and gone in double quick time! It was back to the drawing board once again. I sat at home and all I could think of was: *"What on earth do I do next? My life is in turmoil."* I had not expected this job to finish quite so quickly and dramatically. I had no answers at all, to my own questions as to why it had all gone so badly wrong.

Another issue for me was that I had no money and I would not be earning any income for the near future. In the Monastery I had become used to being cared for and not having to contribute to my own keep. Although I had lived there for some years, I had not reached the point of contributing financially to my upkeep and to the finances of the Monastery. Even though I had taken a vow of poverty, I had not wanted for any of life's essentials. Back home though, Mum and Dad rarely had any spare income and frequently lived from hand to mouth. There was no way that I could live at home without contributing financially to the family coffers, just like my brother Mike was doing already.

By this time, my sister Kathy was living away

from home at Bath University. My elder brother Arthur, was already at the Catholic Seminary at Ushaw College in County Durham, training to become a priest, while kid brother Mike, had also been training to become a priest with The Sacred Heart Fathers in Newport. Mike stayed for about two years, before returning to secular life at home.

Already I had borrowed money from Dad who did not really have it to spare and I felt really bad about it, but that's what Mums and Dad's often do. It was just a few pounds, but I hated borrowing it, and I had not been able to repay it up to then. After three jobs had been and gone in rapid succession, I had not managed to earn sufficient money to pay my way, pay my debts and contribute financially.

Even worse, I had borrowed money from a friend that I knew from the Church where we went to Mass on a Sunday. She was called Rose, a young girl in her late twenties, pretty and a sweet person. I had only known her for a matter of a few weeks, but we struck up a friendly relationship after seeing each other at Mass. After the service we would chat to each other and drink tea, while our parents were talking among themselves. Besides the fact that we were friendly, she gradually gave me the impression that she would like to be more than just friends. The truth was that we had rather more than just a friendly relationship in common. I had quite recently left the Monastery, whilst

Rose had likewise, left her life as a Nun in a Convent, just a few years earlier, and she was still single. It was Mum who really let the cat out of the bag. In her motherly fashion, she informed me one Sunday, that she thought that *Rose "was sweet on me!"* [Mum's expression not mine!]. I didn't have a clue about that. In those days, I would not be able to notice a girl making a pass as me, if she hit me across the face! I thought that we were just good friends. It was a clear sign that I was not very worldly wise. A girl was giving out clear signals that she fancied me, and I didn't have a clue. Clearly, that's what spending several years in a Monastery can do to a person.

The truth though, was that despite being a very nice, friendly and pretty girl, she just did not attract me in that way! That was down to me, not Rose. Maybe I was not ready for a relationship, or perhaps Rose was just not the kind of girl for me, yet, I really had no idea why.

When I thought about what Mum had told me regarding Rose, "being sweet on me", I did lie awake at night and thought it all through. Strangely though, and without even knowing her that well, or taking her out, I was clear in my mind that I did not want to be anything other than a good friend to Rose. We were just too similar in many ways, due to our recent backgrounds. I had been traumatized by the final years I had spent in the

Monastery and who knows what sort of anguish Rose had gone through, to reach her decision to leave the Convent after her life as a Nun. It felt clear to me, that when I did eventually have a relationship with a girl, that she would be completely different to me and to the type of background that both Rose and me had lived through. Two people something like me, were not going to be the right mix and it would not work out. I did not discuss our relationship with Rose, and neither did I encourage it to change. Our connection did not develop into anything further.

Even so, Rose and I remained good friends. We would often talk to one another and strangely she seemed to understand me really well. She was very interested in me as a person and she was curious about my years in the Seminary and the Monastic life. She wanted to know how I was coming to terms with life in the big wide civilian world. Amazingly, she had gone through a very similar life path to mine, although it had been about five years since she had finally left the Convent and returned to Civvy Street. By this time she had adjusted well to her new life. I confided in her that I was having serious problems in making the transition from my quiet monastic life, to the hurly burly of life in 1970's Britain. I told her that I had already managed to get myself into financial trouble, by not being able to manage money and my own finances. I was just being open and honest with her. It was unlike me, because I was the sort of man who kept private matters to myself and generally confided in no one, yet her friendly and easy going style caused me to relax and open up. I had not intended to ask her to lend me any money so when she did offer to, by her own volition, I was somewhat taken aback.

"Steve, I can lend you some money if it would help you?" she said to me. *"Rose, I wasn't asking you for a loan, I was just telling you that I was in a bit of a "pickle".* I was embarrassed, but when she thrust some money into my hand, all I could do was accept. *"Thank you, Rose, I will repay you just as soon as I get paid again, but I'm not sure exactly when that will be, as I've just lost my job."*

It was just £20, but in 1971 that was a sizeable chunk of money by today's standards, particularly as I had been earning the equivalent of just £8.50 per week before stoppages for tax and such like. In my eagerness to get life started on the outside, I badly needed some money, but I was not patient enough to earn it. Call me naïve and you would be spot on. Yet I had never had any experience of handling my own money and there I was, a twenty two year old man, and completely useless at dealing with money and any sort of finance. My kid brother Mike had already bought his own car and had money jingling in his pockets, which allowed him to have a great social life. He had bought himself a Ford Classic, a terrific car in the 1960's, [not new of course!], but it had class, style and it certainly made Mike a pull with the girls. Very few girls had their own car in those days, and a young guy with his own set of wheels was still something of a rarity and a big attraction.

I just had to have one, not to pull the girls! I was nowhere near to that stage, but I knew absolutely nothing about cars, and even less about girls and I must have been a used car salesman's dream, gullible, inexperienced and very easy to sell a clapped out old banger to.

Mike's Ford Classic was a really smart car. It was big, very spacious and with long front and rear wings, featuring a smart light cluster at the rear. It was very much like the flashy American cars as seen in the 1950's American movies, at the start of the Rock n Roll era.

Mike told me that I could buy my own car with just a small deposit and a manageable weekly payment. It was HP, [Higher Purchase] but in those days it was called the "Never, Never", possibly because it seemed that you would "Never" end up paying off the debt!

I had recently passed my driving test, first time would you believe? I had taken weekly lessons with Mr. Rutter, the same instructor that had instructed Mike. Right up-to the final lesson, just two hours before my test, I could not reverse a car around a bend to save my life. For some reason I always ended up on the far side of the road instead of keeping close to the kerb. The test was just over an hour away and my instructor was not confident that I would pass. In fact, he even asked me if I wanted to postpone the test and have more lessons. It seemed that "failure" had become my middle name over the past few years, so I was determined that I would buck the trend and pass it first go.

The time of my driving test arrived, and I had only had about twelve lessons. I could not afford to have more, especially as I was then out of work again, so it was imperative that I passed first time, not just because of the money, but for my own self confidence and esteem, which was at a low ebb.

My nerves were jangling right from the start, but the test was going pretty much to plan. The handbrake procedure on the hill start, the emergency stop and all the driving procedures, were going along just fine, but I knew that I still had my "nemesis" still to come; the dreaded "reversing around a corner". I knew that we were close to the end of the test, and it must have been the very last manoeuvre that he asked me to perform. I was parked up, close to the kerb on a housing estate, having just driven past a left hand turn. *"Now, Mr. Nearey, I would like you to reverse around the corner safely and park the vehicle around ten yards from the junction".* I started to panic, I had come so far, I was so close to passing my test and I just had to perform one final manoeuvre and I would have a full driving license. I checked my rear-view mirror, and slowly but precisely reversed the car, watching my mirrors all the time, and did not stray more than six inches from the kerb at any time during this final manoeuvre on my driving test.

The instructor said without looking at me; *"Turn the engine off Mr. Nearey!"* I did so, and despite believing that I had not made any errors, I expected him to say: *"Mr. Nearey, I am sorry to tell you that you have failed!*

I guess that failure had become deeply ingrained into my psyche during my recent life and I expected nothing else, so when he turned to me, unsmilingly, and said: *"Mr. Nearey, I am pleased to say that you have passed"*, it took several moments for it to sink in. I said to him in a stuttering manner: *"I've p-p-p-passed? "Yes"* he replied, *"you drove very well, but this is just the start of your driving, so please drive carefully."*

I practically skipped all the way out of the test centre and went to meet up with my driving instructor who had come to meet me. It was my first real success at anything since I had left the

94

Monastery and it gave me a great feeling of confidence. My instructor could see my beaming face. *"You've passed haven't you? I honestly didn't think you would this time" "Neither did I"* I responded. *"but I could not afford to fail."*

Fresh from my driving test success, and flushed with my newly found confidence, the following day, I traveled all the way to Prestwich on the far side of Manchester to the used car dealer where Mike had bought his Ford Classic car.

4. Steve's Ford Classic 1962

"My brother recently bought a Ford Classic from you" I told the salesman. *"Yeah, I remember him"* the salesman replied; *"Well, I'd like a Classic too"* I told him, much too eagerly. He showed me a gleaming, shiny blue Ford Classic, it had been around the world a few times and was far from being new, but to me it looked and felt like a passport to a new life. The leather interior smelled of real leather, albeit there was a bit of a musty smell inside. He told me that it had been stood around for a few weeks and that was why it smelt a tad musty. Of course, I had been brought up to believe everything that was told me, so I took it at face value. My brother Mike had paid £189 for his car and the price for mine was £239, [Remember this was 1972]! Despite this, I really wanted to be independent and rather unwisely, I paid a £20 deposit, there and then, and signed an HP agreement for credit. A big, big mistake!

I collected the car a few days later when I had arranged for tax and insurance. On the way home I noticed that the gear changing mechanism was a bit on the stiff side. It was not like the floor mounted gear lever I had taken my test in. It was a dashboard mounted lever and I had to struggle to change from gear to gear. I thought it was a little stiff from lack of use and I imagined I would get used to it, as it was different to the normal floor mounted gear shift.

However, after a few days more, it started getting really difficult to change gear at all and it was grinding and crunching, as I tried to do so. My brother Mike was no mechanic either, nor was he particularly handy; it must be a family trait as Dad could barely knock a nail into wood and his inclination to D.I.Y. was non-existent. The fact was, he never had the time for jobs at home. He was far too busy working a six day week, doing overtime and looking after his family.

Mike tried the gear change in my Classic and he said: *"That's not right, our Steve"*. It wasn't exactly a world shattering diagnosis of the problem, but it confirmed my worst fears. I decided to take it back to the car dealer which was easier said than done, because the gears were almost impossible to use. When I arrived there, his attitude was decidedly different to the smiling, smarmy salesman that had eagerly taken my money, not many days earlier. His attitude was most unfriendly and unhelpful and he looked me straight in the face and told me that it was *"bought as seen"* and that it was my responsibility to have it checked out before I bought it. Unhelpful as he was, he was right because my sales purchase receipt clearly said: *"Bought as seen"*. In those days, used car lots did not offer warranties and it was a case of *"buyer beware"*. Many buyers would take a mechanic or someone who had a good knowledge of cars with them. They would inspect a vehicle before they committed to buying an older car. If only I had been able to do the same.

That was another hard lesson I had learned in the big wide world, but I then found out that I was stuck with a car with a dodgy gearbox which may cost more to mend than the car was worth. I did not know what to do for the best and I felt completely out of my depth and this had been purchased using borrowed money. I had used the £20 I borrowed from Rose, as a deposit and then taken on the £239 hire purchase. In desperation I asked the salesman to take it back, but all he was willing to do was accept it back if I bought another car from him. Very conveniently, he had another Ford Classic which had just recently come into stock and he said that he would give me a six months parts and labour warranty, but it would cost me £289 instead of the £239 I had recently paid. That put up my HP payments quite considerably. Dad agreed to be a guarantor for me for the HP, which was not a very wise and secure thing to do, as my finances were by then in free fall and I had just lost my latest job. I promised Dad that I would earn the money, somehow, even if it meant doing the most menial of jobs, to earn enough money to pay my bills and pay him back for his loan. How life had changed from my relatively carefree days in the Monastery, where despite my unhappiness with the life, I was at least free of such menial matters as money and debt, that I had now to learn to cope with.

Thankfully, even though my naivety had cost me a lot of extra money and trouble, the new car turned out to be relatively trouble free. I say "relatively", because it still gave me problems from time to time. At least it wasn't just me though. Mike also had difficulties with the starter motor on his Classic on a regular basis. In those days, starter motors, points and plugs were nowhere near as reliable as today's cars which nearly always start first time. Back in the seventies, particularly with the older cars, like ours, bump-starting the car was often a daily ritual.

At home, Mike and I used to share a bedroom. Often he would leave home in the morning before me, as he had to be at work by 8am. I cannot remember the number of times that Mike would shake me out of my slumbers at 7.15am and whisper loudly: *"Steve, can you get out of bed and help me to bump start my car; it won't start!"* Wearily, I would drag myself out of bed and go down to his car. Mike would push the car while moving the steering wheel from the driver's window and I would push the car from the back. Easier said than done! The Ford Classic was a big, heavy old car and it took some shifting. When we had built up a head of steam, Mike would jump into his car, put the gear into 2nd, and bump start it into action. He could then drive to work, waving his undying thanks to me out of the driver's window! This procedure would happen with alarming regularity and it always seemed to be me, that had to get out of bed to bump start his car. Still, I guess that's what elder brothers are for.

Well, surprise, surprise, the day dawned when it was finally my turn to ask for the favour to be returned. I had to be out of the house early for a job interview and by chance, Mike had a day off work and was looking forward to a lovely sleep-in, especially as he had spent a late night at his "local", the Pineapple Pub in Marple, where he had downed around six pints of Robinson's Best Bitter with his mates.

My beloved Ford Classic did not want to wake up that morning and it point blankly refused to start. I think I must have flooded the carburetor in my vain efforts to get it to start. I was becoming agitated and started to panic, as I did not want to be late for my interview. I needed the work and arriving late for the interview was not the best way to land a new job. I practically ran back to the house, flew up the stairs two at a time and without any niceties, I shook Mike out of his drunken stupor! *"Mike, I'm late for my interview, can you help me to bump start my car?"* Reluctantly, he dragged his beer-sodden, weary and sleepy body, down to the car. Fair play to him, he did not even complain once. I don't think he was even awake.

He must have been doing this act of brotherly love and support, in his sleep. Now normally, when either of us had to jump start each other's car, it usually lurched into life after about a twenty yard push, and away it would go, chugging and puffing out blue smoke as it got moving. This would be after two or three attempts at the bump start. Mike was absolutely shattered and so was I. It was not a great way to head off to work early in a morning.

Fortunately, I had a bright idea. We pushed my car another twenty yards to the "T" junction, pushed it right onto the main road, and then up a small hill to the top of the bridge that went over the local canal. From there, we could let it roll down the hill and as it gathered momentum, I could jump-start the engine and away we would go. That was the theory! Would it work in reality?

It sounded a great solution, but we were both shattered and I was dressed in my best interview suit and getting all hot and bothered. Mike was still in his night-time "Jim-Jams and dressing gown! Notwithstanding, we pushed and pushed, inches at a time, until the "Classic" reached the brow of the canal bridge. With a huge sigh of relief, I shouted to Mike who was pushing hard at the rear of the car: *"Mike, you can let it go now, I'll jump in"*.

As the car started to roll slowly down the road from the top of the canal bridge, I was standing outside the driver's door, steering and pushing at the same time. The car started to free wheel down the hill, slowly gathering momentum. *"Jump in Steve!"* shouted Mike; *"I'm trying to"* I screamed back at him. *"The car door is jammed".* I was in a blind panic! The car was slowly picking up speed, going down a steep incline on the road. Mike was stood aghast, still in the middle of the road, at the top of the hump backed bridge in his Jim-Jams, with traffic building up behind him. It was just like a farce, only this one was being played out for real.

By this time, I was running alongside a driverless runaway car, hanging onto the steering wheel for dear life, desperately trying to yank open the car door that was stubbornly stuck and did not want to open. Mike was still on the bridge watching the drama unfold and yelling at me to jump in. I soon realized that the door would not open and at this stage I was running at full speed with cars overtaking me and vehicles passing in the other direction in wide eyed amazement. It was just like a scene out of a Keystone Kops film.

Finally, the end of the road was in sight. I had to do something right then, or there was going to be one almighty crash. My runaway car and me, then went around a tight bend and down the hill. Without thinking, I did the only thing that sprung to mind. I threw myself headlong into the car through the open window and went head first onto the footbrake. With my legs now hanging out the driver's door window, the car was then out of control and in freefall. Desperately, I pushed hard with all the strength I could muster onto the foot brake with both hands and bit by bit the car came limping to a halt, without actually hitting anything, other than mounting the kerb and ending up on someone's driveway. Strangely, none of the cars or people who passed by, stopped to see why there was a guy with his legs hanging of the car window. Phew! That was a close call! I picked myself up, dusted myself down, and waved to Mike who was still stood on the bridge at the top of the hill in his Pajamas! *"Go back to bed Mike,"* I yelled from about 200 yards downhill. *"And thanks for the push"*. With that, I put my Ford Classic into gear and headed for my important new job interview.

For the next few weeks I was pretty much on a "downer!" The job interview had not been a success and I was still without work, but not without money problems. I had borrowed money from Rose, and from my Dad, and he was acting as guarantor for me to repay the car loan. I could not be late with the payments as they would charge very high interest payments. If I defaulted on the loan, the HP Company would come to my Dad for the money or then take the car back. Under no circumstances could I allow that to happen. To add injury to insult, I was not contributing to the family coffers and I knew that Mum needed the money and that I had to provide some cash pretty soon.

I desperately needed a temporary financial fix. I remembered that a few years before, when I was at Erdington Abbey, I had worked for the local council in the summer holidays. The work was not what I wanted. It was really hard, dirty and the pay was pretty awful. Still, I had emptied dustbins before for a living, so why not do it again. Fortunately, the Council Manager who had hired me back then, remembered me from the work I had done before. To my huge relief he offered me temporary work, covering for council workers who were off work, due to illness or on holiday.

It was quite a come down for me, as I had set my targets quite high again, but for now, I just needed a job, any old job, and more importantly, I needed regular money. I was working full time Monday to Friday, and Saturday until lunchtime. The weekly wages I earned, just about covered the H.P. payments on my car, the running costs, and a contribution towards living at home.

To my shame though, I had still not repaid the £20 loan from Rose, and I was suitably embarrassed when I met up with her at Church and she asked me to repay the money. She knew I was working again and probably thought [quite correctly], that I should have repaid her earlier. She did not know that I was up to my eyes in debt, but that was no excuse. It just showed how much I had failed to come to terms with life in the real world, after my sheltered existence in the Monastery. I told her, to my huge embarrassment, that I had no money at all, and that I would pay her the following week. I think I even had to borrow money from someone else to repay Rose, but it had to be done. I was in a financial mess and I needed to find the solution.

I really had to get myself some genuine work. I was grateful to the Council for giving me the temporary job, but I had to start looking for a proper career. I asked them if I could not work on Fridays so that I could go for interviews and kindly they agreed. I spent all my spare time at weekends writing to companies, applying for work and trying to get job interviews.

I could see my life getting more and more complicated and I seemed unable to settle down to anything at all. I spent a large chunk of everyday looking for jobs, that I thought I may be suited to. Most of the time I concluded that I did not have a "cat in hells chance" of landing a decent job, due to my lack of experience and my unusual background. It was hardly going to appeal to most employers and my three jobs which had ended in abysmal failure, did not auger well for my future.

Suddenly, my eyes were drawn to a job advertised in the Manchester Evening News classified section. A Hospital on the outskirts of Merseyside was looking for Male Nurses. This was of course before the times of job sexual discrimination and employers could still ask for members of a particular sex. There is no way that I should have been even considering this job. After all, I had just left a nursing role in the most acrimonious of circumstances. This was a very similar job, and surely, this was in no way, the right one for me?

I circled the advert in black pen and continued searching. I was still very much in idealistic mode. I was not trying to find a career where money was the over-riding factor. I was still looking out for a role where I would be people centered and able to do something that was largely for the benefit of others, whilst paying a decent salary. A big ask!

I had already applied for a job as a Fireman. In the seventies, this was a job almost exclusively for men, and tough men at that. It wasn't a job that women would even be considered for, due to their perceived lack of height and strength. I got as far as meeting with them, but during my interview it became clear that I did not fit the bill! I came across to them as academic, quietly spoken, not very worldly wise and not the tough guy image that they were clearly looking for.

Even so, I was not put off, though I seemed to make the mistake of applying for jobs that were not very suitable for me. I did not recognize it at the time and I kept making the same old mistakes.

My next job application was successful in achieving an interview, to join the Prison Service. Once more, I was unrealistically idealistic and my knowledge of the real world was sadly lacking at that time. In my mind, I honestly believed that being a Prison Officer was pretty much like that of being a Social Worker. I considered that the job was more about treating prisoners kindly and helping to rehabilitate them back into society! Big mistake! In my interview, it soon became clear that the primary job involved locking prisoners up, controlling them and punishing them for their misdemeanors. At the same time, the idea of rehabilitation was nowhere near to the top of their agenda. It was a rough, tough business and again, they decided that I was not the type of person that they wanted. With the benefit of hindsight, I reluctantly agreed with their assessment.

Due to the lack of any other suitable vacancies, I kept harping back to that advert for the "Male Nurse," that was being advertised at a Hospital close to Merseyside. This one was significantly different, and despite my torrid time at the Salford Hospital, I had the impression that this job was somehow different. For a start, this was not a General Hospital. It was a Mental Institution, a top security hospital for the criminally insane. I still had an inkling that this would be the role for me. Even though my fledgling career had gone horribly wrong at the General Hospital, I was still in love with the idea that Nursing was the job for me. One difference to the Nursing job at the General Hospital, was that this job, was in a mainly male environment. The large majority of Nurses were men. It crossed my mind that I may have a repeat of the incident at Hope Hospital, but I shut that out of my mind and put it down as a one-off event, which would never be repeated.

Most definitely, I was not gay, nor chauvinistic, and neither was I anti-feminist. It was just that my background at the Monastery had been one hundred per cent male, and at that time, I just felt much more comfortable and at home, in that type of mainly male environment.

The Hospital was solely for the criminally insane. All of the prisoners, or patients, however they were viewed, had committed crimes against people and had to be locked up for the good of society. In many cases this was for their own safety too. In the main, the patients did not have physical illnesses, although many of them were medicated up-to their eyeballs. Quite a number of the patients, especially the older inmates had illnesses, just the same as would be found in a general hospital, but they also had mental issues and the public had to be protected from them.

Despite my misgivings, I sent off an application form. If there was one thing that I had learned how to do, during all my years of education, it was to be able to write a good letter and a convincing one at that. While keeping precisely to the truth, I put together an application form that exaggerated my strong character traits and experience, whilst at the same time minimizing some of my shortcomings, weaknesses and lack of relevant experience. It was a slight manipulation of the truth, but it had to be done. Despite that, I was flabbergasted when I received an invitation for an interview at the Merseyside hospital.

The interview day arrived and I prepared myself really well for the barrage of questions that I knew that would be thrown at me. I knew that my C.V. would be my biggest enemy. Even before I could start any employment, I knew that to get past the first post, I would have to convince the interview panel, that a 22-year-old ex. Monk could do a satisfactory job, even in the most trying of circumstances. After that, I had to give a solid explanation of my reasons for leaving the General Hospital so suddenly. I have to say, that I did myself proud. I was so determined to land this job, that I gave the performance of my young life, whilst never at any time deviating from the truth. I convinced the doubting panel that I had all the strong and necessary characteristics, needed for the job, and more importantly, I had the strength,

109

will and determination to succeed in that role.

During the interview, I learned that the job of Nurse at this hospital would be something entirely different to the previous one and that the title of nurse was something of a "euphemism". Despite that, I was so elated to be offered the job, that I had a mind to overlook the deficiencies of the role. It ticked sufficient boxes for me, that I felt I just had to take it. Certainly, there was a degree of desperation about accepting the post. Yes, I really needed to work and I desperately needed that job.

Although it had never been at the top of my priority list, the job paid a lot more than the previous nursing position I had left. It put me back in a male environment once more and I genuinely believed that I would be helping the patients to get better and become well again. Hopefully they could at some time be returned to society.

When I arrived home once more, I was so pleased about landing the job, that I was not expecting the type of response I received from the family. They were much more skeptical than I had expected. I suppose it was hardly surprising, particularly after the farce surrounding my sudden departure from my last nursing job at Salford. I had been away from home for so many years, and although I was now an adult, my family wanted me to come back to them. Yet again I was planning to move away

110

from my family. I told them that I was living much closer now, and that I would be able to come home when my shifts permitted and on my days off.

I packed my bags once more and headed for Merseyside. The Hospital was a daunting place and I was soon to realize just how greatly it differed from a General Hospital. On arriving there, I was shown to my quarters, which were adequate but not that comfortable. Yet, I had been used to much worse than that. The feel of the place was totally different to a normal hospital. At the "General" it was all white, starched aprons and pristine, with a constant smell of disinfection. The nurses were all bedecked in their smart blue and white uniforms and it was staffed largely by girls and women, with just a spattering of men.

Here on Merseyside, it was a completely different scenario. The "patients" were mentally ill, but many had medical conditions too. Although the nurses were there to look after the patient's mental and physical problems, it had to be acknowledged that the greater part of the job was more akin to that of being a Prison Officer than a Nurse.

These patients were mentally ill, but they had all committed significant criminal acts and they were so dangerous that the public had to be protected from them. Within my first few days there, it became clear that the greater part of the job, was that of "patient" control and ensuring that the patients were securely held in the Hospital.

The nurse's uniform was a complete give away. It was practically the same as a Prison Officer's. There was no pristine white uniform. We were kitted out in a two piece officer's uniform and instead of a nurse's temperature gauge, the nurses had to carry a large bunch of security keys. Everywhere they went, from room to room, inside the building or in the secure grounds, the doors and gates had to be locked behind them. This was indeed a prison, in all but name.

The patients in this "special" hospital were exceptionally difficult to control and violent in varying degrees. Some were just too troublesome to control in society, whilst others may have committed violent assaults and murder. In this special hospital, they were to be held at her majesty's pleasure and many would never be rehabilitated into society again. Their patient care would mainly consist of drug control. Whilst some of the drugs may have been designed to help the patient return to health, other drugs were clearly there to enable the Nurses to control the patients during incidents of violent outburst.

It was at this special hospital, that I met my first girlfriend, since my nurse Margaret, while I was in Hospital in Shrewsbury. Margaret had ended our

112

relationship because she felt she did not want to be held responsible for my leaving the monastery.

Nora was also a Nurse, somewhat different to Margaret, as she was a psychiatric Nurse and she lived in the Nurse's home in Merseyside, where I was stationed. Again, it was Nora who made all the running. In fact, she finished with her existing boyfriend in order to go out with me. I really had no idea why. My problem was, I was still not at all confident with girls and my slowness to respond and to take the initiative, must have come across as a lack of interest, which was definitely not the case. I was extremely slow in making any advances and as a result, Nora told me that she was thinking of going back to her former boyfriend who still wanted her. If I had been a bit sharper on the uptake, I would have seen this as a chance to put things right. However, I didn't respond and our relationship was very short lived, lasting just a matter of a few short weeks.

I spent several weeks of my probationary period learning the methods of care and control as taught by the seniors, but as time went along, I became more and more uncomfortable and disillusioned with some of the methods used. Before joining, I was aware of the basic role for the job i.e. caring for the criminally insane. I knew it would be difficult and that the patients would not be easy to look after and control. It would be a big challenge.

However, I expected that, given time I could make a difference. I felt confident that once I had learned the routine, that I would enjoy the caring side of the role and that it would compensate for the time we would just spend acting as a "jailer." However, it was not to be. One evening something happened that sickened me to the pit of my stomach and it was to change my entire view of the institution and some of the people who were called Nurses there.

One of the long term patients was a young man in his early twenties who was nicknamed "Yogi" by the staff. He was a giant of a man, perhaps 6 foot 6 inches tall, extremely strong and well built. He was nicknamed "Yogi" because he always carried around with him a Teddy Bear and was dressed in a one piece boiler suit, due to his incontinence. The problem with his condition was that although he was a man, he had the mind of a child. In the outside world he had killed a man, because he became angry and he responded in the only way he knew how, by lashing out. The result was that another person died, but the patient was not criminally responsible and that is why he was housed in the hospital for the insane.

On one particular day, "Yogi" had been minding his own business, just quietly doing what he did to pass the time of day. Another patient ran up to him and snatched his beloved Teddy Bear off him. Yogi and the Teddy Bear were inseparable! He went berserk! He started shouting and yelling, just like a child would, and then he ran up and down the room tearing at the curtains, pulling them down and throwing the furniture all over the room in his fit of temper, just like a child.

Suddenly, something happened that I had never witnessed before: A whistle sounded [it warned of some type of incident]. About four burly male nurses all descended on Yogi. I was stood on the perimeter of the room. As a "Rookie", I was unsure quite what to do and so I just stood, did nothing and observed. One of the nurses shouted at me to come and help. Yogi was throwing one almighty tantrum and clearly needed to be calmed down and brought under control, but I was not prepared for what happened next. The four experienced Nurses piled on top of him and despite Yogi kicking and flailing, they managed, albeit with some difficulty, to bring him under control. Not content with that, they carried him away, two by his arms and two by his legs and took him into a side room. I had not seen this type of room before. It was completely padded, including the floor, so that the occupants could not harm themselves. If that alone was needed in order to calm him down, then that would have been sufficient, otherwise given the temper that Yogi was in, he could have severely harmed himself. Yet not content with controlling him, the Nurses "got stuck in". I stood back in total shock and

115

bewilderment, as he was thumped and kicked by four burly nurses. Then, out came a syringe and he was injected with Paraldehyde, a strong drug used to control and calm patients down. Even that was not enough. He was then bundled into a straight-jacket and left on the floor in a state of distress. None of them seemed to check if he was alright and they all left the room, followed by me and left him to cry and whimper himself to sleep while the drugs took effect. There was no lasting damage.

I was deeply shocked and upset by what I had witnessed, but I felt too young and junior to even pass a comment about it. One of them said to me: *"That's how you have to do it!"* and then he carried on as if it was just part of the normal daily routine. There was no sympathy or care shown for the patient, who was after all, a human being with feelings, albeit he was a troubled human being.

I never really recovered after that. I felt that the episode should have been reported, but I felt too inexperienced and unsure of myself to dare to take it up with the senior officers. I lay in bed that night and my sole thoughts were about that incident and how that patient had been treated. I was 100% certain that the level of force used, was in no way necessary to bring the patient under control, but I felt that I could do nothing about it. Although this had been the first violent incident of this nature that I had witnessed, there was a general undercurrent in the establishment, that did not feel right to me and I could take only one course of action while I was in that state of mind.

 Job No.4 was about to come to an end. It had lasted barely a few months and yet there was no way I could remain in that environment. I felt somewhat inadequate by leaving without doing or saying anything, yet I did not feel strong enough to do what I felt was right. The following day, I handed in my notice to the Governor and I was heading straight back to square one, yet again.

I was still a probationer at the time of the "Yogi" incident. On tendering my letter of resignation, I was summoned to the office of the head nurse. It was a strange experience. While waiting to discuss my resignation, I thought back to the all-female environment at the General Hospital where I had felt so ill at ease. Yet here I was in a largely male establishment and I felt even more uncomfortable. This time, I was not centre-stage and my reason for quitting did not revolve directly around me, yet there I was, leaving yet another job, before it had even got off the ground. I searched my own conscience deeply. I had been used to soul searching at the monastery and that character trait had clearly stayed with me. It must be all about me, otherwise how could anybody work in four jobs within a two year spell and leave them all so quickly. Was I being over sensitive and too idealistic? Was it all about my principles? I was totally unsure and yet three of my jobs I had left as a matter of conscience. Would I ever be able to adapt to my new life and to the real world? At that time, I still had no adequate answers.

In my resignation interview with the head nurse, I was asked why I wanted to leave so early into my employment there. I desperately wanted to be honest and open, as I believed it was the right thing to do and yet when my big chance came to speak out, I bottled it! I could not do it. I confess to feeling intimidated and so unsure of myself, that I could not honestly give him my true reasons for leaving. I felt that nothing could change the methods and procedures at that establishment, as they seemed deeply rooted into the very fabric of the building. And so the truth would never out! I gave him pretty lame reasons for my deciding to leave. It did not make me look good to anybody. I most certainly did not feel proud of myself in any way and yet I felt certain that it was a better and more honest decision, than staying on and being party to a system of procedures, that I did not approve of. My 4th job had come to a final and sudden conclusion. With hindsight, it was as well that my short romantic relationship with Nora had not taken off, as I was on the move, yet again.

My life was gradually turning into a nightmare! After years of agonizing about whether to stay or leave the monastic life, I had painfully but eventually made my decision. Yet now, my life seemed to be in even greater turmoil than it had been back at Hawkstone. When would this trauma ever end? It seemed that it would be, no time soon.

It appeared to me that I would never be able to settle into anything and that no job would ever be the right one for me. It seemed that the transition from Monastic life into Civvy Street was one that was to be littered with obstacles, even though many of them may had been of my own making. I left the Hospital without having another job lined up. That is certainly something that few people would dare to do now. I was fortunate that during the seventies, jobs were still relatively plentiful, at least in some occupations, so there was some hope.

119

Chapter 6

Finding my niche in life

My poor family must have despaired of me. When I arrived back home they could not believe that I had left my 4th job in such a short time and that I was back in the jobs market. At least they said they understood the reasons for my leaving and were as shocked as I had been, at the way this patient had been treated. Yet deep down, they must have been deeply concerned at my inability to return to the secular life. It was turning into a dramatic saga.

At home, there was effectively a family conference every day, with the only agenda being: *"How to find a suitable career for Steve"*

For a couple of weeks, I was mostly in a state of confusion. I just moped around at home without any real direction in my life. As always I did a serious amount of thinking. I was pretty good at that, as I had been doing it for years. Believe this or not, it even seriously crossed my mind, and dallied for quite some time, that I should return to the monastery. I reached a conclusion that my seeming inability to adapt to civilian life, was perhaps a sign that I had made a mistake and that my true calling was indeed, to be in the monastery. At least I had known what to expect when I was at

Perth or Hawkstone. I had an orderly life and organization. I had a daily routine and regular tasks that I was familiar with. Although far from perfect, it was perhaps more bearable than I was experiencing back at home in Civvy Street.

During all my time at the monastery, many of my colleagues had left, but I was not aware that any had ever returned there after leaving. It seemed that once the final break had been made, then it was final, and final meant not going back. Whilst musing about the slim possibility of me returning to the monastery, my mind quickly reminded me of the long dark days I had spent agonizing about returning to civilian life. As if to bring matters back into sharp focus, my mind jolted me back in time, by remembering the brief moments, when I had considered the long drop from the top of the 120-foot monument at Hawkstone Park, so deep had been my depression at that time. This incident had been the catalyst for reaching my final decision to return to civilian life. Thinking back to that moment, rapidly made me realize that a return to monastic life was not a genuine option, despite my numerous problems.

Back at my home, everybody seemed to have an opinion. Of course, I listened, but in the end it was my life and I had to do whatever I thought was for the best, even if, inevitably, it turned out not to be right. I just had it fixated in my mind, that I needed to have a life where I could do a sociable job, people centered and a job that was for the benefit of others. Perhaps my thinking would have to change, if I was ever to get back on the right track.

It just seemed that every single career I was attracted to, involved living away from home. This was not at all what I needed, but if that was what the job entailed, then I knew I would probably take it. I had been reading in the paper that there were vacancies for social workers. My mind went into overdrive. Perhaps this was just the occupation I had been searching for? Helping others in society is just the sort or work that I wanted, or at least I thought I did. All seemed well, until I read the job requirements in the local newspaper.

It asked for: "University educated, fully trained in suitable social work", and the like. Somehow my Latin, Geography and Church History seemed a little inadequate. In hope, I took the step of telephoning the advertiser, Social services, and finding out if I would be suitably qualified. The answer was a resounding "No". I could of course have taken the requisite training courses, but I was already a late starter and to spend several additional years of studying, did not hold any attraction for me at all. I was trying to play catch up already and did not want even more education.

The one glimmer of hope, was that the person I

had spoken to in Social Services asked me if I was interested in becoming a Residential Child Care Officer. She told me that if I was interested, then the vacancy was only a few miles from where I lived. Surely this had to be of interest. Yet "Residential" meant living in at the Home. At least I would be fairly close for visiting my family when I would have time off work. Of course, at this stage I did not have the job, so it was irrelevant. I called the Children's Home and spoke to the manager. He invited me to the Home for an interview. Quite how I managed to convince him to offer me the job is still a mystery. Although I had only been in the jobs market for a few short years, I had already clocked up four jobs and left them all very quickly. My credibility was rapidly disappearing and if I was not careful, I would soon become unemployable. Fortunately, I was quickly becoming expert at interviews and had the ability to persuade employers of my ability, even though I had lived a checkered career and a somewhat "different" lifestyle. Perhaps my background was intriguing to potential employers. It was certainly a most unusual one for any employer to consider.

Edward Burnell was the Child Care Officer in charge of the children's home. He was a big and brusque character, extremely precise and well organized. I had him down as an ex-Forces Man, probably an Officer. His organizational skills were ideally suited to running a tight ship and the

124

Children's Home would no doubt be well run. His character however, showed no great warmth. He may have run a well-organized children's Home, but I wandered about his lack of warmth with the children. His presence reminded me of Captain Von Trappe, the fictional character from *"The Sound of Music"* who ran his home with military precision, but was distant and over-strict with his children. His wife was suitably sharp, but came across to me as distant, very frosty and an over strict disciplinarian.

At my interview they told me how well run the children's home was. I never doubted it for one minute, but I did wonder whether the children, who were from broken homes, would find the love and happiness that they were already missing from the dysfunctional homes they had come from.

The wardens warned me that I would need to be strict with the children and extremely well organized. In all honesty, I really should not have accepted the position, because I already had strong preconceptions that this children's home was run with a rod of iron and too strong a discipline, instead of a homely and warm environment. I believed that they needed loving surroundings and that eventually the children would either be adopted or fostered by caring, would be parents.

My problem was that I was somewhat naïve, far

too idealistic and trusting. But here I was with a brand new career. It was job No.5! Child Care.

I accepted the job even though it entailed having overnight sleeping at the children's home, for a few nights each week. At least I did get to go home, and I was working just a few miles from where my family lived.

The wardens were strict with the children and I thought that they were just too controlling. I suppose with my lack of experience, I should have listened to them and believed them, when they told me that some of the children, were very worldly wise and that they would take advantage of any sign of weakness. I thought I knew better, which turned out to be a big mistake on my part.

In addition to the two Wardens, there was also a young Houseparent called Pamela. We got along really well together. She was a lovely girl and full of life. Like me, she lived in at the children's home on the nights of her shift, just returning home to Macclesfield on her days off. I remember that she was not that keen on the Wardens either. At least, with Pamela, I had somebody else to talk to and in my own age group, otherwise I would have found it hard to work with the Wardens. Pamela was one girl that I could really relate to. She was a good houseparent, caring and related well with the children. She was bright, funny and a really strong minded girl. I took to her greatly and we had a terrific friendly and platonic relationship.

One day, the wardens instructed me to take a small group of six children on a day out to the Countryside. It sounded like a lovely outing and I thought that the children would really enjoy it. I was trying hard to get the children onside and to know and trust me. I wanted them to like me and particularly, I wanted them to feel wanted and cared for. I believed that the children would all be easy to get along with and that they would all respond to kindness and fairness. However, unbeknown to me at the time, some of the children had already been conditioned to a certain way of behaving, whilst others had already become streetwise early on, and beyond their young years. It was not going to be as simple as I had imagined it would be. I thought that I knew better than the wardens, and I was very wrong. The wardens had been correct, and I had not listened to them.

We had taken the train from Marple railway station to Hayfield. This was the first time that I had taken the children out on their own. Although six children was not a huge number, it was not all that easy to control them and to keep an eye on all of them, all of the time. This was especially so, when two or three of the kids decided that they wanted to do their own thing and be mischievous. It was a cold winter's day and we had taken a picnic and hot thermos flasks of tea. At first, we went into a type of Adventure Park. I expected that they would all enjoy the rough and tumble of the park and burn off some youthful energy before we stopped for a picnic. I had a ball and I arranged a bit of a "kick around" on the field. Two of the boys though, did not fancy this and said they were not going to join in with us. They said that they wanted to go home.

I told them politely but firmly: *"Well you can't go home just yet. I'm going to play with the others, even if you don't want to. Go and play on the adventure swings and then we'll have our picnic all together in a few minutes time."* They both wandered off in the direction of the adventure park, albeit with a rather sullen, moody attitude.

I didn't take too much notice of them and put it down to a bit of a tantrum on their part. There were plenty of other things to do in the park, which was just a few yards away and so I let them get on with it, while I played football with the others.

After about ten minutes I glanced around to check how the two lads were getting on. I could not see them, but not being unduly worried, I had a quick tour of the park and around the other pieces of equipment, but to my dismay, they were not there. The other children said that they had not seen them and only then did I start to wonder where they were. Half an hour passed by. I told the children playing ball to stay exactly where I left them and not to move. I started asking around, but they were not to be seen. Only at that stage did I begin to go into panic mode. I ran back to the other children and told them to get their things together and come with me. We practically ran to find the park keeper and he said that he had not seen them, but he along with two or three others, scoured the park, while I stayed put with the remaining children. This was during the early nineteen seventies, and mobile phones, the internet and instant communication were just events for the near future, so contacting the wardens quickly, was not something that could happen very easily.

By this time, the two boys had been missing for about a half hour and I knew that the next thing to do was to notify the police before telling the wardens at the children's home.

I found a telephone box and there was a couple inside the box talking, and another person waiting. Becoming more and more concerned, I was pacing up and down outside the call box. Exasperated and finally losing patience, I burst into the phone box and said in an agitated manner: "Look, I'm sorry, but this is an emergency, can you finish your phone call please" Somewhat relieved, they were fine with this, and after explaining the nature of the emergency, they just handed the phone to me.

I quickly telephoned the Children's Home and the warden answered my call. I was in a blind panic and talking in a heated and staccato fashion. I was really nervous and afraid of telling him that I had lost the two boys. I just blurted it out and talked and talked, just trying to explain what had happened in the adventure park!

"Stephen", he said, in a calm and controlled manner. *"Just get on the train and come back home. Make sure you bring the rest of the children with you."* I was taken aback and could not understand why he was taking this so calmly and seemingly unworried. He seemed very cold and distant and in no way animated as I had expected. There was a short silence down the telephone line and he said again: *"Stephen, get on the train with the children and come straight back home. The two boys are here!"* With that, he just put the phone down and the line went dead. He left me deeply worried about what had happened. Needless to say I was really concerned, and brooding about what would happen when I returned to the Children's Home.

I could not understand why he had not explained the situation to me. Nor could I believe that the two boys were back at the Home. They had arrived back so quickly and had gone without telling me anything. How did they manage to return home and why, I wondered to myself?

On the train journey, the other children must have noticed that I was quiet and distracted, although I had been trying hard not to show it. I just told them that the two boys had already gone back to the Children's home and that we were returning there too. The children never did get their picnic and were very hungry, so we ate food on the train.

We arrived back at the Home. As soon as I reached the front door, the rest of the children ran back in. I walked in somewhat tentatively and the warden was standing there to greet me with an icy cold stare. The two boys were stood a few feet behind him. They looked sheepish and did not look me in the eyes. I said to them: *"Boys, why did you come home on your own?"* They did not answer and just looked down to the floor and avoided my gaze. At that, the warden told the boys to go to up to their bedroom. He told me to go to his office and wait for him there. Some minutes later he came to his office with his co warden, his wife, by his side.

Without so much as asking me for an explanation, as to what had happened earlier that day, he just lambasted me: *"What the hell did you think you were doing, telling the boys to go home!"*

I was absolutely flabbergasted! *"Is that what they told you?"* I said, still in a state of shock. I did not know what to say: I just replied: *"Well, it's not true; I told them just the opposite. I told them they* *could **not** come home. I told them they had to wait, that they could go on the swings, and that we would all be going home together after the picnic."* The boys were blatantly lying to the warden, but either he did not, or would not believe me, when I told him the truth. The boys seemed accomplished at not telling the truth and just stuck to their story. The warden took the stance that even if he didn't believe the boys, he was still not going to accept as truth, as I had just told him.

"Warden" I said, in a voice full of exasperation: *"All I think I have done wrong, is to take my eyes off the boys for a short while, but I believed that they had gone to play on the swings, just close to where we were playing ball with the others".* They were after all, aged ten and eleven. I could not believe that they would take it upon themselves to take the train home on their own. Apparently, the boys had just got onto the train without paying, [they had no money] and somehow they managed to get off the train and return home without being asked for payment! The boys were certainly streetwise, and perhaps I was just extremely naive? They had well and truly taken advantage of me, as I was new and far too trusting.

I could accept that I had taken my eye *"off the ball"* for a few minutes, so to speak, but I was inexperienced, I had only been in the job for a few weeks, and yet I was out on my own with six children and two of them had disobeyed my instructions and gone home alone.

The Warden was clearly in an unforgiving mood. No matter how many times I told him that I had not told the boys to go home, he seemed to want to believe them. The Warden clearly had the overall responsibility for the safety of the children and he did not want this to reflect badly upon himself. He had to lay the blame with somebody else, and that somebody was me. I was not sure what more I could have done or how I could have handled matters differently.

In the circumstances, I could not see how I could possibly stay any longer. There was clearly an impasse, and it seemed that we both came to the same conclusion at the same time. Just as I began to speak, he also started speaking. *"Go on"*, he said! I continued; *"Look, I may have made a mistake and I am responsible, but I did not tell the boys to go home. Why would I? But you obviously don't believe me, so as there is no trust between us, I am giving you my immediate notice, I resign! "Good,"* he replied, in the sternest of tones, *"I was going to sack you anyway!"*

As I was still in my probationary period, and under these intolerable circumstances, I suggested that there was no point in my working a period of notice. At least we had agreed on something, and so I collected my belongings straight away and I left the home immediately.

Before I did so, I spoke again with Pam who was shocked at the sequence of events that had led to my untimely departure. Like me, she did not get along with the Wardens and she said she did not know how she was going to stay there without me, as our being there together, helped to make life at least tolerable. She did not want to stay on her own. We had become very close friends in my short time at the Children's Home and she was heartbroken when I told her that I had been forced to resign. Our relationship had been purely platonic and yet I was very close to her. We continued to remain very close friends after my departure, and eventually, she also resigned, being unable to work for the people at the helm. Our friendship continued beyond that point, even after I had moved to other jobs. Pam eventually married, and settled down in Macclesfield, but we remained as soul mates. One of the saddest days of my young life, was when Pam's new husband, Dave, called at our home one day, but on his own. It was unusual, as he and Pam were always together. I could feel that something was very wrong. He told me that Pam had been sitting on the sofa watching TV. when suddenly, she developed a blinding headache, after which she collapsed unconscious. She had been attacked by a massive brain hemorrhage and had died instantaneously, aged just 23 years. I was so shocked and saddened for Dave's loss, but also devastated for my own, as we had been exceptionally close, despite being just platonic friends. This followed soon after Margaret, my nurse at Shrewsbury Hospital, had lost her husband while sitting alongside him in a fatal car crash. It was a lot to take in at such an early age.

After saying farewell to Pam on that awful day at the Children's Home, I headed for the bus station and tried to prepare myself on the journey home.

So that was my 5th job, come and gone, within a matter of weeks. What on earth was I doing wrong? I was trying so hard to adapt to life on the *"outside"* and to build a new life for myself, but it was all going very badly wrong and I seemed not to be able to do anything to rectify it.

As I took the short bus journey home, I was in dread of facing my family yet again with my terrible news. I just wanted the bus to go slowly or even to take a long detour, so that I could put off the evil moment! Job number five had come to an abrupt end, in less than two years since I had left the Monastery. It was with a very heavy heart, a degree of anxiety and severe embarrassment, that I put my key in the front door and prepared to confront the family. I just felt like a complete failure. I perceived my leaving the monastery as a huge letdown, after nearly ten years on the long road to becoming a priest. I know that I had let my family down then. Now I felt that I was doing it to them all over again. How could they ever be proud of me? It was just one disaster after another. After not achieving my main goal in life, there I was again failing to make the grade, in every other job that I had attempted so far, all five of them, and I had left them all, within a very short space of time.

I had been mentally practicing my *"leaving speech"* while I was on the bus home. Mum, Dad and Mike were all there, as well as my sister Kathy who was visiting home at the time. She was on leave from her work at Bath University. Unlike me she was happy and settled in her work and building a very successful career there. Mum cheerfully welcomed me home, as I had not been expected back at Marple for a few more days. I stuttered and stammered, but couldn't get any words out! Mum could see something was wrong in my face. Mum's have that sort of inbuilt intuition;
"Is everything alright at work Steve?"

"I've resigned Mum, I'm finished and I won't be going back"! "They didn't want me anymore, and I don't want to stay. I just couldn't get along with the wardens" Mum just looked at me in disbelief and said: *"Oh Stephen! What are you going to do? What are WE going to do with YOU?"*

I looked over to my Dad, searching for support. He never had very much to say. He was an extremely quiet man and he always let Mum do the talking for him, but they were usually in broad agreement. Yet I could see it in his eyes, the disappointment and the worry. I knew how hard it had hit him when I decided to finally leave Hawkstone. My becoming a priest would have meant so much to him and he was still getting over that setback, so he did not have anything to say on this matter. He didn't have to! The look on his face said everything that needed to be said. Kathy and Mike were younger than me and to them, it was just a matter of another job and not that important in the scheme of life, but to me, it was just one more setback after another and my pride and confidence had taken a severe battering. I made my excuses, said that I was tired and I just went to my room to lick my wounds and be on my own. Effectively I had been sacked, but I had saved them the trouble and resigned before the warden was able to do so.

My life was spiraling into a fast and steep nosedive and everything I did seemed to go dramatically wrong. My last year at Hawkstone Monastery was an unhappy and miserable time for me and now it seemed that my return to civilian life after ten years, was equally traumatic. I began to wonder if I really had made a very big mistake in leaving the monastic life, for the big wide world outside.

That night, I sat alone in my bedroom feeling sorry for myself. I just wanted to be on my own and not in the company of the family. I think it was because of the embarrassment of it all and I could not face any of them. I felt such a fool and worst of all, such a failure. Mike came up to our shared room. It had been his room after all, before I had returned home unexpectedly from the Monastery.

"Hiya Kid" he affectionately called me. He was full of the joys of spring. He never seemed to have a worry in his life. *"Oh the joys of youth!"*, and I was all of 23 years old, and feeling much older.

Mike had also once been training to be a member of a religious order. Like me, he had been exposed at a very young age to the persuasive powers of the Catholic Church, and the pull of the monastic life. Just like me, Mike had gone to live away from home at an early age, to join The Brothers of The Sacred Heart in Newport. He also lived away from home, so at one point all three brothers were training for the religious life, albeit at separate establishments. Mike had joined the religious order, aged just 13, though he soon made the decision that the life was not for him. He decided before he was sixteen to leave and return home to a normal lifestyle, while still a young teenager.

In doing so, at such a young age, he escaped the years of indoctrination that I had been exposed to.

As such, he quickly returned to civilian life and the usual teenage lifestyle, without being scarred as I was. For Mike, his short episode in the religious seminary, was but a fleeting moment in time, whereas for me it had been a major chapter of my young life. It had left an indelible mark on me and almost certainly, for the remainder of my life.

The cheerful Mike that bounded into our bedroom that day didn't seem to have a care in the world, and who could blame him. He had a beaming smile [he always did!] and he didn't even want to ask me about my failed job and what had happened. Such matters were of little consequence to Mike at his age and he said: *Come on our Steve, let's go and belt a ball around on the "Rec".* I didn't really feel like it, but I went anyway, to keep him happy. I took all my frustrations out on the ball and felt much better for it. Football had always been my escapism. I had been a Manchester City supporter ever since my elder brother, Arthur, took me to Maine Road to watch City play United in the early 1960's, when I was about 10 years old. Arthur was a big United fan and was shouting for his beloved Reds. Now whether it was merely sibling rivalry, I am not sure, but more likely, it could have been that City beat United by 3-0, at Maine Road and from that day forward, I became a committed Manchester City supporter. I still have to thank my brother Arthur for that!

It disappointed me greatly, in later years, that Mike also chose to be a fan of that other team that plays in Red! Both my Brothers were always at friendly loggerheads with me over my choosing the Blue half of Manchester over United, and that remains the case up to the present day. Some things never change, and supporters never change their colours.

It had been good to have a football interlude to take my mind off my troubles for a short time. Surely matters would improve for me soon, but it would not to be for quite some time and there were plenty of disappointments piling up in the wings and waiting to snare me, just around the corner.

Chapter 7

"Ernie" – The Cheshire Milkman.

Having recently experienced three disastrous jobs, two spent in Nursing, and an even worse experience as a Child Care Officer, I was seriously evaluating if my desire to do work which would benefit others, was the right thing for me to do. Perhaps I should be looking for a career where I could just earn money, as most people do. Certainly, my good intentions and high ideals were being tested to the limit and maybe social and caring type jobs were not the type of work I should be trying for. It was certainly food for thought. In the meantime, I decided that I just needed to get a job, almost any old job in order to earn more money, pay the bills and pay off my debts. I was still young and had time to build a career but for now, I needed a job and some cash, and quickly!

Again I began scouring my local newspaper, the Manchester Evening News. There were thousands of jobs, but none at all that asked for skills involving theology or philosophy, so the only alternative was to go for a job that required absolutely no qualifications or experience at all.

And there it was, staring me straight in the face

141

from the Situations Vacant pages of the paper. It read: *"Milkman / Trainee Manager wanted. No experience required, as will train. Must be honest, hardworking, and be able to get up early in the morning!"* I thought to myself,

"That's just me. Well, at least for the time being"

Honest and hardworking, that's the minimum that was required and I had no problem with that. *"Must be able to get up in the morning!" Well! That was exactly me!* For the past ten years of my young life, I had been rising from my slumbers somewhere between 5am and 6.30am, so that was not going to be a problem either.

I cut out the advert, while thinking to myself: *"I can do this job, not too much brain power required, and the money is quite good!"* That was going to be good enough for me.

I telephoned the number in the paper and spoke to the Depot Manager. The advertiser was The United Co-operative Dairies, based in Hyde, near Manchester. It was only four or five miles from where I lived in Marple, so that was a definite positive. Eagerly I spoke to the depot Manager. I told him all about myself, at least the good bits and that seemed to be enough to earn an interview with him at the Milk depot the following week.

Keeping to my tried and trusted principles, I arrived at the Co-op depot the following Monday, at 10am. As was my wont, I was always early and was knocking on his door, bang on the stroke of 10am as requested.

I arrived in my best interview suit, shirt, tie and highly polished black shoes. As the Manager opened the door, he looked me up and down, from head to toe and asked me to come in; he commented;

"You haven't come for the Managing Director's Job, have you?

I think it was meant as a joke, but clearly he thought that I was somewhat overdressed for the occasion and the position I was applying for. I responded that it was *"still an interview"* and I liked to maintain my high standards, even though I wasn't planning to wear a best suit on the milk – float, if I was given the job. At least, the initial banter broke the ice somewhat:

Again, despite a dodgy CV, which looked as if I never stayed at anything, and despite my unusual past, the Depot Manager offered me the job. That made it job number six. I got the distinct impression that there were hardly hordes of jobless people banging down the doors to have an interview. The fact was, that there were not that many jobseekers that wanted to get up at 4am in the morning, working six days a week and being paid entirely on results. Even so, I quite fancied a job, that involved working entirely on my own, and being responsible for how much money I could earn. I was offered a milk round starting at Hyde Depot, and taking in Ashton-Under-Lyne and parts of Oldham. It was a large round and the poor electric milk-float just about made it around the 5-6 hour round trip, before limping home at about five miles per hour, up the steep hill and back to the Coop depot in Hyde.

What on earth was I thinking of? How many years had I slid reluctantly out of my bed at what could only be described as a "Godless hour!" I soon realized that to get the float loaded up and then complete my round, I would need to start about 4.30am. If I started at that time, I could finish about 2pm and then get some sleep. Some of the other Milkmen started later, maybe 7am, but they were still delivering milk at about 3pm each day.

So, day one dawned. In fact, it was before the dawn. I set the alarm for 3.30am. What on earth was I doing? I crept downstairs, had cereal, toast and hot strong coffee to wake me up. Then it was outside in the dark to the Ford Classic! Each morning, especially in winter, I would intently pray every night, before I went to be bed, that the car would start in the morning. What could be

144

worse than having to scrape ice and snow off the car at 4am, turn the ignition key and then just pray that it would fire up first time and then start? I arrived at the depot at 4am, and several of the other Milkmen were already there and loading their goods onto their floats. Each Milkman was responsible for loading his own float with milk, bread, butter, potatoes, cheese, yoghurt and fruit juices. They would earn money on every bottle of milk sold and for the food products, which paid more. Some of the Milkman had a young helper to drop the milk quickly on doorsteps and thus speed up the delivery process. They would pay the lad or girl pocket money to help out, occasionally before school, on the Friday evening collection and all Saturday morning when they were off school.

I did not have a helper, so it was entirely down to me. On day one, I loaded the float with the quantity of goods that the previous rounds-man had normally carried. My first round was an absolute nightmare! I was given a book with the "round" details in it. It showed the customer name, address and what their daily order usually contained. Many of the rounds-men had been doing their jobs for years and they could deliver the round by memory, without even consulting their delivery book.

As I was a new on the job, I had to check the book for every single customer, i.e. what goods they ordered, on which day, and this could vary. But the worst part of it, was learning the actual round and delivering the correct goods to the right address from day one. The most difficult part of the job was finding the correct house. At 4.30 am in the morning and during winter, it was pitch black, especially during February. The end result was that instead of getting back to the depot at around 2pm, I arrived back at the depot, the last man home at 4.40pm. This meant that some customers were getting their milk deliveries at about 4.15pm which caused a lot of complaints to the depot.

The depot manager was waiting for me when I finally got back to the warehouse after my first delivery round. It had been my first round and it had been a nightmare. Most "newbies" had a helper to show them the job, but not me. The Manager had to wait for me, so that he could check-in the stock on my float and put the vehicle onto electric charge, ready for the next day's first delivery at 4am.

"We were about to send out a search party for you"!, he said, with a semi-smile on his face.

I wasn't sure if he was being sarcastic or maybe it was just his poor attempt at humor, but I think it was the former. Either way, I was cold, tired, hungry and feeling very stressed. It had been a horrible first day. The main reason that I was so slow, was that it was difficult to find the customer's property. In addition, I had to find the precise place to leave the goods. The descriptions in the book were not good at all, if indeed there were any. For much of the time, the last rounds-man had been doing this by memory. In truth he had left the round book in a terrible mess and with insufficient delivery information for a new person.

Each customer had varying requirements. Some wanted deliveries to the back of the house, some preferred the front, whilst others had a kind of "hidey-hole" where the dairy products were to be hidden. Often, the customer would change what they wanted from day to day. They would cancel, or change the order, so that I would have to return to the float. It meant, I would need to return the milk and goods I had taken to their house and start all over again. The previous rounds-man had been delivering it from memory, as he had been doing the same round for years and knew it all by heart.

While I was out on my new round, there had been three complaints telephoned to the depot from my customers. One complained that it had been left in the wrong place. Another said that their order was incorrect and the third one said that I had left the milk and produce on the doorstep, instead of inside the porch. They complained that I was three hours later than the previous man. How was I to know? Hardly anything was recorded in the book, and there was very little information there to help me deliver goods on the round correctly.

Local knowledge was everything. The previous incumbent on the job, had been working the milk-round for some eight years. As a result, he no longer bothered to enter the correct information into the book, which was supposed to be his "Bible." It was meant to enable anyone else to take over while he was on holiday or ill, or in this case because he had left the job for new horizons. He had become so familiar with his round over the years, that he did it all from memory and instinct and the Round Book was nowhere near up to-date.

As the song title goes: *"Things can only get better!"* Well perhaps so, but I very much doubted it. I could imagine that it may well get a whole lot worse, before it began to get better. Really, I ought to have had one of the depot staff accompany me on the round, on that first day, but there was nobody available. I was left to do it all on my own but with not enough information to do it correctly.

As dis-spirited as I was after that first day, I was determined to be a success in this job, even though I had no intention of making it my life's career. Over the next few days and weeks, I still had plenty of problems and complaints, yet slowly but surely, I began knocking the round into some type of shape and things were starting to get better.

148

However, the acid test was yet to come. At the end of each month there was a complete reconciliation of stock sold, money collected and stock still on hand. That would determine how much money I would earn. I had been warned by one of the friendly rounds men, that there was theft and pilfering to watch out for. The stock was all mine [it had been charged out to me] so any stock losses, would be my losses. He also warned me that the theft was not just while I was out on the round. He had a quiet word in my ear and warned me to be careful about theft from inside the depot. I was told to watch out for the person checking goods out to me. It had happened that a higher volume of stock was being charged out to a rounds-man, but that a lower amount of stock was actually put on the float. That stock loss would be mine. Believe it or not, theft from Milk Floats was a lot more common than I or most people would imagine. The Milk Floats were just slow electric vehicles and they were completely open, other than a roof, with no sides and without any real security. It was extremely easy to steal from them. The value of the total stock was very high and therefore attractive to many passers bye or anyone who had a mind to steal from it.

While I was away from the float delivering my produce, I would leave the vehicle unattended, for up-to two to three minutes. That was more than enough time for any would be thief to come and help themselves, and they often did. However, the worst case of theft, was when I was delivering milk and produce, to customers in a block of high rise Flats on the outskirts of Ashton-Under-Lyne. I had several customers on the top few levels of the flats, which was not at all good for me. Firstly, I was not at all keen on lifts. I was nervous about using them. I had a fear of enclosed spaces and I would worry about being trapped in the lift. Whenever I was able, I would walk up the stairs rather than risk the lift and I always breathed a huge sigh of relief when the lift doors opened.

When delivering to these customers I would need to use a trolley on wheels, to deliver the milk in one drop. That was tough enough and even worse if anybody changed their order, as frequently happened. If so, I would have to hot-foot it down the sky-scraper and back to the float. Even worse, I would worry about leaving the milk float unattended, as this was the most dangerous situation from a security point of view.

It was as early as my second week, that my worst fears began to be realized. Certain parts of the day were relatively safe, as thieves were unlikely to be out and about between 5 and 7am of a morning, but late morning, afternoon and Saturdays, when youngsters were off school, were the most vulnerable times. On one such occasion I was at the top of the flats in Ashton, delivering milk from my trolley. As I looked out and down to the milk-float a long way down, I could see youths helping themselves to milk and other products. I shouted down at them, hoping that it would scare them away. No such luck. They knew that it would take me minutes to get down the stairs or lift, so they casually took as much as they could carry and hot-footed it back to wherever they came from. They even had the nerve to give me the "V" sign, laugh at me, and then sauntered in no off in no particular hurry, back to where they came from.

Of course, when I arrived back at the float, out of breath and panting, there was no sign of them. Clearly they lived in local housing, but which and where? I had no chance of getting my stock back. Missing was milk, potatoes cheese and butter! I was seething with anger and indignation. The stock loss was all mine, not the Diary's. Maybe I could now understand the reason why the previous Rounds-man had left! Later on and feeling quite dispirited, I contacted the Police, yet all they did was to effectively shrug their shoulders and ask what they could realistically do? They said they would keep a watchful eye on the flats at key times, but no-one was ever caught and I never once saw the Police keeping a watch on my milk float.

In my first month, I just knew that there had been several instances of theft from my float. It was when I was away from it delivering milk and unable to keep a watch on it. There were many areas of the round, when I knew that it would be safe and secure, but there were other areas, when I felt it was vulnerable. I was sure it would cost me money and that people would steal from me.

Later, I realized the reason why Rounds-men had a young helper with them, as often as they could. Not only did they have a young and fresh pair of legs to do the running, but they also used the helper as a look-out on the float, while the Milkman made his deliveries.

It was only when I arrived to the end of the month and the stock reconciliation had taken place, that I realized just how difficult it was to make a decent living in this job. After taking back the remaining stock for counting, the difference between the stocks I had sold, and the amount of money collected, was vastly different. There was a significant stock shortage which came to light when the money I collected was totaled at the depot. I was crest-fallen when I realized just how little money I had earned for a full month of hard graft. It seemed so unfair that the Dairy took no risk at all with the stock, yet the Round-man took the entire risk and all the subsequent financial losses, even though it was mainly, not their fault.

There was worse still to come. Included in my takings was money owed for stock delivered, but which had not been paid for by the customer. Most of my customers were as honest as the day was long. I used to go out on Friday evenings between 6pm and 9pm to collect my money. Many would let me know if I had not charged them enough by mistake. A large number would know exactly how much they owed and would leave the money in an agreed place, for example, in a milk bottle, in a secluded place. For the rest of the honest people, I would collect it every Friday night.

The problem was, that whereas most of my customers were good people, there was a small minority of customers who ordered the products, but had no intention of paying for them. When I was new on the job and a bit green, I allowed customers to keep getting their milk and produce, but they never seemed to be at home when I called for the money. Sometimes, customers would send their child to the door, with a message that they would pay me the following week, but some never paid at all. I had allowed a significant number to get away with this for about four weeks and some as much as six weeks. Eventually, I toughened up and told customers that they would no longer get products delivered, until their bills were cleared. With some, it worked to a degree, but others had no intention of paying me and just changed to another dairy. It meant that I would never be paid, and I would have to write it off as a loss to my account. It was disheartening for me as I was working for very little reward.

After about six months, I took a close look at myself, the job and my life and reluctantly concluded, that I would soon have to leave the Milkman's job. The truth was, I was earning a pittance, from a job where I worked six days a week, and very unsociable hours including Friday nights and Saturday mornings. It was not much of a life. I wasn't earning much and I concluded it was not much of a job either. If only people would pay me! If only others would stop thieving from me! If only I didn't have to worry about Depot staff cheating me! The amount of money I had left at the end of each week, was just not worth the time and effort I was putting into it. There was no point in carrying on any longer. I could see why so few applicants had applied for my job.

It was such a shame, because although being a milkman was hard work and very anti-social, there were certain aspects of the job that I quite enjoyed. I liked being my own boss. No-one was telling me what to do and I liked most of the customers. The role of the Milkman has often been likened to that of a social worker. He would look out for people and help them if he could. This was certainly true of my round, where there were many old people who loved to see their Milkman and have a daily natter with him. This would slow me down a little, but I felt good about it and I enjoyed the chatter and the sociable aspect of the work.

Although it did make the round quite a bit slower, I enjoyed doing it for the pensioners. I would often be asked to come in for a cup of tea. Really, they wanted a bit of company or someone to talk to, so for me, it was all worthwhile. Sometimes, when the old people could not get out because of the winter, they would give me letters to post for them and I always obliged. I must confess that there were occasions when old people said they could not afford their normal order and wanted to cancel it. I am sure that they were genuine. I would sometimes write off their bill and just give them the goods. Even when they eventually had some money, and offered it to me, I would often refuse it. I used to scold myself for doing it, but then I reasoned with myself, that they were much poorer than I was, and I was happy to let them have it.

I became fond of many of the older people on my round and I would often call in on my route every day, just to make sure they were alright. I would often end up making a cup of tea for them and would have one myself before moving on.

Despite my unscheduled stops on the round, I still earned the reputation of being;
"Ernie, the Fastest Milkman in Cheshire!"
It was 1973, and Benny Hill had a famous hit with his hilarious rendition of "Ernie", which went to

No.1 in the charts. It was a massive Christmas hit back in 1971, and was still fresh in people's minds. I was as fit as the proverbial butcher's dog. I used to be the first into the depot each morning around 4.15am and I would practically run around the whole of my five to six hour milk-round. Many was the time I would hear people calling me "Ernie," as I flew around my route and dropped off their milk at top speed. I don't think I ever walked the round, at best it was a sprint and at worse it was a "power walk", but it enabled me to stop off and see my pensioners, as well as finish on time.

There were other trials and tribulations of the job. One was avoiding animals in order to drop the milk off. Normally dogs were kept inside, but occasionally I would come face to face with a fierce "mutt," at something like five o'clock in the morning. I would be lying to say that it was not scary. On one occasion, at one of the few wealthy properties, I had to open a gate and walk quickly in the dark to drop off the milk on the doorstep. Now, normally the dog was inside the house and would always bark when he heard me coming down the drive. But for some unknown reason, on that day, the barking sounded much closer to me and as I approached the door, I could see the whites of its eyes. The huge dog looked angry, was drooling from its jowls and began to snarl at me. I stopped dead in my tracks, as it was a German Shepherd. I was about ten yards from the door.

Very slowly, I bent down and put the four bottles of milk on the path and then I started to walk backwards and slowly towards the gate.

Suddenly the dog must have remembered that he was supposed to be a guard dog and he came after me like a bat out of hell. I turned, swiveled on my heels and then took off like "greased lightening", in the general direction of the entrance gate.

With the Alsatian hot in my pursuit, I reached the gate, with the dog just a few yards behind me. Unfortunately for me, the gate was on a sprung hinge and had closed behind me. There was nothing else for me to do. There was a privet hedge about four feet high either side of the gate. I had about one second in which to make my choice. It was either the hedge or the dog. It was an easy decision! I dived head first over the hedge and fortunately landed on the soft grass verge on the other side. Fearing the worst, I waited for the Alsatian to leap the fence too. I lay curled up in a defensive position and expected the dog to attack me. I held my breath for a second or two but the dog did not follow. It was literally two feet away on the other side of the hedge, barking and snarling viciously for all that it was worth. I had escaped with my life, or at least a serious mauling, but it was a very frightening experience and one that many other Milkmen could relate to.

The house owners must have heard the noise of this incident and quickly arrived at the scene in seconds. They grabbed the snarling beast away with them. It had not been their intention to leave the dog outside and they were deeply apologetic about the episode. The house owners took me indoors [Once the dog had been made safe] and helped to clean me up. I had landed in a muddy heap on the soft grass verge. They gave me a cup of tea, even a piece of toast and helped me to clean myself up. Then they asked me to rest for a few minutes in the warm, before I did what Milkmen do. I carried on with the round, until it was finished, and everyone had their milk delivered. We were a hardy lot! [Us Milkmen!]

158

Chapter 8

The Monk's re-union

It was while I was a Nurse at the psychiatric hospital on Merseyside, that my personal life began to change quite significantly.

On my frequent journeys to Merseyside, to and from the Special Hospital, I was aware that two of my good friends were living on the Wirral in Birkenhead. They were the McCarthy twins, Declan and Brian. They had been Novices at the Monastery in Perth during the year I spent there in Scotland. Unlike many of the other Novices, they had not progressed to Perth via the Juvenate route at Erdington. This was where young boys would be educated and developed until they were 18 years of age and then ready to enter the Monastery. They had decided to join rather later in life than I had, but also at the age of eighteen, just like I had done, and I got to know the twins very well.

Both the boys, Declan and Brian had left the Monastery at Perth during their twelve months as Novices. Unusually, they did not leave together, Brian came to his decision first, and then Declan decided that the monastic life was not for him either. Twins often follow one another, so I was hardly surprised when Declan followed Brian out of the Monastery gates not long after. I was particularly sad when Declan left after about six months. He was something of a character and a really likeable lad. Brian was quieter and rather more sensitive. I had more of an understanding with Brian, as I was not unlike his personality in several ways. At the time, I wondered if Declan would follow suit, as twins of all types, tend to want to be together and do the same sort of things. I really felt that when Brian left, that Declan would find it especially hard to live without his twin brother, as they had been together all their lives. When that time came around, and Declan departed Perth, I was greatly disappointed, but not at all surprised.

5. McCarthy Twins Declan left, Brian right - 1966

It was a huge blow to me and a massive loss, as their leaving the monastery really knocked my confidence. I saw so many of my fellow Novices [and friends] leave and I felt that I too, would not be able to continue there until the end of my one-year term. In the end, I did eventually complete my full year as a Novice, but not without much soul-searching, and afterwards, I lived for almost three more years at the seminary in Hawkstone Hall.

When I eventually left for good, I often thought of Declan and Brian, as I did for many of the friends I had made at both Perth and Hawkstone. I use the word friends, but we were not permitted to have special friends. We were encouraged to be the same with everybody, and to have a respectful relationship, but not a special friendship, with any one colleague in the Monastery.

Despite often wondering how the twins were getting along on Civvy Street, I had not contacted them since they had departed Perth, to return to the new exciting world of the swinging seventies. However, I had found out where they lived and as I was traveling to the hospital on Merseyside one day, completely off the cuff, I decided to call on them. They were thrilled but greatly surprised to see me stood on their doorstep with a beaming smile. We were all excited to meet up together again, after nearly five years. We spent hours over a few drinks re-living the times we had spent together, some of it good, and some not so good. Strangely, at this stage, I did not have anybody in my life that I could truly call a friend. In the Monastery we had not been allowed to have friends as we know them, and now that I was living in the civilian world, I still did not have one single person, that I could genuinely refer to as my friend. The only other person was perhaps Nora, a brief ex-girlfriend. As it has already been documented, I was not particularly good with girls, especially as friends!

Brian and Declan invited me to stay and have a meal with them. They were still living at home with their parents. Their Mother was a lovely woman, extremely welcoming and friendly and very typical of many Irish people of their era. I stayed that evening and enjoyed a meal with them. As I had downed one or two pints of Guinness, they asked me to stay over. It was great, and very therapeutic to re-live the times we had spent together in Perth. As good as it was to catch up with them, I also needed to rid myself of many demons relating to that period of my life. As much as anything, I needed, for my own sanity, to understand how they felt at the time they left the Monastery. They had both, albeit at separate times, left the Monastery "like a thief in the night", as the saying goes. One day they were there, and then the next day, they were gone. The Novice Master did not offer anything by way of an explanation, other than to say that they had left of their own choice and we must pray for their happiness, on their return to normal life. It was difficult to lose people so suddenly. It was not like losing a work colleague. We had lived together twenty four hours a day and seven days a week in a very close and almost closed community, with a singleness of mind. It felt like a huge, sudden loss.

During our reunion, Declan told me that he was shortly to be married. I was well and truly delighted for him. He had been back in the outside world for close on five years and he had met a lovely girl. *"You'll come to the wedding, Steve"* Declan ordered and of course I was pleased to accept his "invitation," even if it had sounded more like a command! *"Are you bringing anyone?"* he asked. *"Err! No, I'll be coming on my own, if that's alright, Dec!"* *"Sure it is"* Declan quipped: *"We'll fix you up with someone when you come!"* He wasn't joking! I think he already had a girl in mind, but he wasn't letting on who she was.

A couple of weeks later, I received a letter from Brian and Declan's Mother. It was an invitation to Declan's wedding. It was to take place at a Catholic Church in Birkenhead the following Saturday and it was addressed to: *"Steve and Friend."* Naturally, I replied that I would be attending. It was great to be back in touch with them, the only current friends I had. They were also my most recent connection to Perth and The Redemptorists, where I had spent a considerable part of my young life up-to that time. Strangely, I still felt the need to talk about those days, even though it was nearly five years since the twins had left there. I told them that I would be coming on my own. I was not close enough to anybody in my life, to ask them to be my companion at that time.

On the morning of Declan's wedding I was working at the Mental hospital, but I was given a dispensation to finish work at lunch-time, so that I could attend the 2pm function. I quickly changed from my Nurse's uniform and into my new wedding suit. I was really looking forward to the occasion, as I rarely went to any social gatherings. Family apart, I had no other friends to speak of.

Declan's Mum was a really pleasant lady, very talkative, friendly and easy to get along with. Even more, she was extremely welcoming and made me feel completely at home. In fact, she insisted that I stayed at their house on the night of the wedding and I was more than happy to accept her invitation.

On the big day itself, other than Declan, who was busy preparing for his nuptials, and Brian who was totally absorbed with his Best Man speech, I did not know anybody to speak to. I was hardly an outgoing and gregarious person who could mix with just about anybody. In fact, I was just the

opposite, quiet, very shy and I kept myself to
myself, barely mixing with the other guests. It was
not that I was unfriendly or unsociable; it was just
that I had not learned the social skills of mixing
with people that I did not know. I just sat at the
table or quietly in a corner cupping a pint of beer
to myself and watching others cavorting around
the floor to the music of The Beatles, and Gerry
and the Pacemakers, their local Liverpool heroes.

 Declan spotted me all alone in a corner doing a
decent impression of a wall-flower and popped
over for a quick chat, as did Brian, who by this
stage was looking a little worse for wear, having
been celebrating a little too heartily the wedding
of his twin brother. It surprised me that it was not
a double wedding as the twins were so close that
they were practically inseparable.

I don't think they liked seeing me all alone, and
they felt a little guilty about it. They need not have
worried, as being on my own was something that
I had become accustomed to. They had perhaps
forgotten that I had remained in the Monastery for
about four years after they had left the Order. It
was taking time for me to become adjusted to the
faster and racier pace of life in 1970's Britain.

I told them that I was perfectly happy just sitting
and supping my pint of Boddingtons Best Bitter. I
hadn't told them that it was about my 3rd or 4th pint

and that I was quite content doing just that. I was more than happy just to sit and watch the wedding guests rocking and rolling on the dance floor.

Even so, Declan and Brian seemed concerned, quite wrongly, that I was not enjoying myself.

Coincidentally, Declan's Mum was a trained Staff Nurse at the local General Hospital, where she worked. Well, there were a group of co-incidences! I had been a Nurse, my first two girlfriends' had been nurses, and now I was chatting to the Twin's Mother, also a nurse, about my two failed experiences at Hope Hospital and then a high security hospital on Merseyside. We had a long chat about the nursing profession and I told her that there was absolutely no chance that I would consider joining that profession again. Likewise, it was unlikely that I would ever be offered a job in nursing again. I still had not found my niche in life, so the search was about to continue until I found it.

Chapter 9

Shoes maketh the man

It had been great to see my old Novice friends Declan and Brian at the wedding, but when my psychiatric nursing job on Merseyside abruptly ended, it became clear to me that my honeymoon period back in the real world, was definitely over.

This decision became even clearer when my fifth job at the Children's home had also ended abruptly and I was in severe danger of becoming unemployable. My C.V. was starting to look like a "situations vacant" column in a job centre. Prospective employers would want to know what had gone wrong in each job and why I had changed my career path so suddenly and so often.

Discovering my niche in life was clearly proving to be "Mission Impossible" and I had to do something about it, and soon, or I would be permanently out of work and with all that unemployment entails, i.e. no money, lack of status, and a social life that was heading nowhere in particular.

I decided to have a serious talk to myself. I was very good at doing that, having had plenty of practice during my monastic years. Deep down, I knew that I was better than my employment record had shown thus far. I knew that I had the ability to be a success. I had been given an excellent education at the Erdington Juvenate and then in the seminary at Hawkstone. I was also taught how to behave, how to treat people and relate to them. That was the theory, but I now had to prove this to prospective employers. I had not done myself any justice up-to that point, by going through six jobs in less than three years. A period of stability was essential, and it had to be during my next job.

Despite having a regular routine at job hunting, it was purely by chance, that I landed my new job. Indeed, I really believed that this could be the one for me. It could be a real job with a genuine career.

I was walking through the shopping precinct in Stockport one Saturday afternoon, when I saw an advert in a shop window. The shop was the giant shoe store, Dolcis. I had stopped looking for any type of social work, having come to the conclusion that I could still be a decent person and hold down a job that merely pays me money. The advert in the shop window asked for these qualifications:

"Trainee Manager, Experience is preferred, but will train the correct candidate." It asked for interested persons to apply in writing to the store manager. I stood outside the shop and thought to myself; *"Fortune favours the brave"*, just go and

apply for it. The job is there for the taking. I marched into the store. I was really smartly dressed on that particular day. It must have been the force of habit. I was not greatly into casual or modern clothes and I felt more comfortable, and more like me, when I was dressed in a suit.

I had never been in a Dolcis store before, so I had a really good look around, pretending to be looking for a pair of new shoes. The products seemed to be a very good quality and the footwear looked and felt expensive. I took my time and quietly watched how the staff went about their business. I dallied for quite a long time, handling different types of shoes. The staff must have thought that I was either a store detective or perhaps a shop-lifter. Eventually, one of the lady assistants came over to me and asked if she could help me. I said: *"Yes, I'm looking for black, laced up, highly polished formal shoes in size eight."* I had briefly spotted a very smart middle aged man walking the store and assumed that he was the Manager. I tried on some shoes. I didn't really need them, nor could I really afford them, but if my plan worked, it would be well worth it. I bought the shoes, despite the high price tag and a leather protector and cleaner. It was clear the staff had been trained to sell added value items.

After paying for the shoes, I asked the sales-girl, who had been most helpful, the name of the store manager. She told me it was Mr. Jones. I asked her if I could see him now. She looked puzzled! She asked me if everything was alright. I assured her that it was and asked again if I could see him. She showed me to his office. Straight away, before he could speak, I took the initiative: *"Mr. Jones, I am pleased to meet you"*. He spotted straight away that I had a Dolcis shoe box under my arm. *"Have you just bought some shoes?"* he ventured. *"Yes, I have"* Quickly, he was on the defensive; *"Are they alright? Is something wrong?"* *"No, not at all*," I ventured, growing in confidence all of the time. *"In fact, on the contrary, I am really impressed with the store, your staff are excellent and the shoes are very good quality indeed".* *"Well, how can I help you, Mr. Nearey?"* *"Well, I'm hoping that you can help me, Mr. Jones."* *"I came in to look at your range of shoes. It's my first time inside a Dolcis store. I am really impressed with the shoes, the store and your members of staff. Your sales people were not too pushy, but they were really helpful and good salespeople too. After they had helped me to try on and then buy these shoes, they then sold me shoe cleaner and shoe protector. I tried on five sets of shoes, but the assistant was really patient with me, until I was satisfied."* *I am very pleased with my new shoes.*

He looked pleased with himself. It reflected well on him and his sales team. After all, I was now a Dolcis customer! I could see him glancing at the

170

shoes I had on. Fortunately, I was well dressed that day, as I had been to Church earlier in the morning. My shoes were spick and span and highly polished. There is a saying, I'm not sure where it came from, but it goes that; *"Shoes Maketh the Man!"* As he was the manager of a top shoe store, that comment would not have gone amiss.

I discreetly looked all over Mr. Jones from the tip of his hair to the heel of his shoes, in a manner that I hoped he would not have noticed. His appearance was immaculate, he was well groomed and his hair was slicked down. He sported a dark, three-piece pin striped suit, that was suitably sharp. He had a pocket handkerchief, that perfectly matched his rather loud, but immaculately smart tie. Glancing towards the wooden floor, I was dazzled by his very expensive looking shoes. They were brogues, absolutely gleaming and of the highest quality. I would not have expected anything less, from the Manager of a top-quality shoe store.

While I was looking at his shoes, I looked up at him and said: *", Mr. Jones, while I was looking at the shoes, I noticed that you are advertising to recruit a trainee manager. Well, I am hoping to start a career in selling and I would like to apply for the position, please." "Well, I have requested that candidates apply in writing, but as you are here now, let's have a talk";* He gestured at me to take a seat. He sat back in his desk seat and calmly said: *"Just tell me about yourself, and your C.V. to date, Mr. Nearey"*

At that point, I was beginning to wish that I hadn't taken such a brash and direct approach. I was now speaking completely off the cuff, un-prepared and I felt quite vulnerable, even though I was putting on a front that smacked loudly of bravado. In the circumstances, I felt that I had to be upfront and honest about my CV, even though it may have been off-putting to my interviewer.

I told him all about my background in the Monastery. I was completely honest about the mistakes I had made in my career choice to-date. I explained that all the jobs that had been involved with social work, appear to have been a huge mistake. I thought that I was cut-out for that kind of work. The truth was, that I had a good education and that, this was the type of work that I would be good at. He listened intently, and he didn't say too much, but after a while, he paused and said:

"Stephen, I admire your initiative and the fact that you really seem to want this job. I am going to speak to the other candidates, but I will contact you again quite soon. Let's leave it at that for now and see how things go"

It was left like that and I had to go home and just hope that my ploy had worked. I hoped that I had impressed him sufficiently, to take a chance on me. In the meantime, I completed an application form putting it all in writing, crossed my fingers and then hoped for the best. Meantime, it was back to work, being Ernie, *"The Fastest Milkman in Cheshire"*, but mentally, I knew that it was no longer the job for me. Being a milkman had given me back some self-esteem, because I knew I was doing a good job, but it was always going to be a stepping stone to bigger and better things for me. Onwards and upwards was what I then hoped for.

The tipping point for me was one March morning. I had risen that day at 3.30 am as usual. The car would not start straight away, due to lashing rain and wind, with the rain causing the engine to be damp. After spraying the engine compartment with WD40, it eventually dried out the plugs and to my huge relief, it then started. I arrived at the Coop Depot an hour late, but the rain and hail lashed down for practically the entire round. I was like a drowned rat and despite my winter clothing, I was soaked through to the skin. I must have run around the entire milk-round at a fast pace, partly to keep warm and in part, to deliver people's milk to them on time. In addition, I just wanted to get the job done and go home to a warm fire and relax. On the journey home, the milk float was battling against a fierce and freezing wind. It was struggling to get back up the hill to the Depot. The electric engine battery was becoming very low. I thought to myself; *"What on earth am I doing here? This is not the career for me."* Despite my eventual unhappiness of my life in the Monastery, it was nothing compared to the complicated and difficult life I had lived, since I had returned home and to work in civilian life.

It was a Friday, and my round, due to my late start, had not finished until 3.30pm. By the time I had checked in my stock and got into my car to drive home, I felt really down in the mouth. I did not arrive home until 4.00pm, which meant that I had about an hour and a half to eat, then rest before I had to drive back to the depot and do the round all over again, for my Friday night money collection. That meant that I had no sleep at all. By the time I finished collecting the money, it would be about 9.00pm and when I arrived home, it would be time to go to bed, before the Saturday delivery and additional money collection. It was not that I did not want to work hard, but the stark truth was that it was just not worth the effort, for the amount of money I was earning in the job. In addition, there were no signs that I would, anytime soon, be given a supervisory role which I had been implicitly promised. I was beginning to feel downhearted.

Imagine my excitement then, when I arrived home that Friday afternoon and there was a letter waiting for me. It was a crisp, business like document, which had been franked with the "Dolcis" logo on

174

the front cover of the large white envelope.

I held the official looking letter for a minute or two without daring to open it. It remained un-opened on the table while I made a cup of coffee and toast and then I placed it onto my breakfast tray, sat down in the lounge and plucked up the courage to open it. I felt as if the letter was my *"escape from jail"* card, but what would it say? In truth, I feared it would be a rejection letter, despite my promising interview. I was getting used to disappointment.

I carefully opened the letter and quickly scanned the first paragraph. It started with; *"I am pleased to inform you"* My heart was racing and I could not read it quickly enough. I was anticipating being told that at best, I was going to have a second interview and that I was on a short list. I could not really hope for any more. Then I read the words: *"I am pleased to inform you that your application has been successful, and I am pleased to offer you the role of Trainee Manager with Dolcis Shoes."*

From being down in the mouth, glum and feeling wet and cold, I suddenly felt a rush of adrenalin. For some strange reason, I just had the feeling that this was to be a turning point in my life and that from that moment on, the only way would be *"Upwards and Onwards"*. That day, I didn't bother going to bed, I only had another hour or so before I had to go back onto my milk round again, to collect the week's payments. Knowing in my mind that my decision had been made, I suddenly felt good, and went to work with a spring in my step. Even though I had to do the job for another four weeks, I could cope with that. That evening, I went out to do my collections with a more confident attitude. I was also determined that anybody that owed me money was going to pay up, come hell or high water! My first step was to leave a note with anybody that owed me more than one week's money. The note stated that they would not have any more milk deliveries until they were paid up-to date. Also, during the following week, I left a letter with other debtors, those who owed more than three weeks money, that action would be taken to collect the debt, if payment was not made within fourteen days. The worm had suddenly turned and all at once, the former. *Mr. Nice Guy"* was now *"Mr. Tough Guy"*, and not before time.

The following Monday, I asked to see the Depot Manager after my round. I went to his office when I had put my float away and told him that I was not going to continue. I informed him that I was giving him four weeks' notice of my intention to leave.

"That's a shame" he said; *"With your education I had high hopes that you would become a Manager with the Dairy."* I reminded him that I had joined the Dairy on the basis that it would be a joint

176

supervisory and rounds-man role. I reminded him that in the six months since I had worked there, I had never been given any assistance or training with the round. I told him that I had regularly lost money because of theft from my float, and that in all of the six months so far, he had only ever once spoken to me, let alone discussed the supervisor's position. At that, he said that he would now be willing to discuss the management training, but I told him that I had already been offered a much better position with far greater prospects. So, *"Ernie"* The fastest Milkman in Cheshire, had come to the end of his very long tether.

I worked my round meticulously for the remainder of my notice period and I handed the round over to a new man, in the last week of my employment. At least, the round was almost debt free when I handed it over to him. Also, the round book was completely up to-date, so that he would find it easy to take it over on his own.

 I was quite touched by the comments of many of my customers, when I told them I was leaving. They were really sad. Many had come to think of me as a friend. And so, my sixth job in just three years was about to end, but this time, it was on a much more positive note and with a job well done.

For once, I was able to go back to my family with my head held high. I was not going to tell them how bad the Milkman's job had been. On the Friday afternoon that I handed in my notice, I was able to go home and tell them that I was furthering my career with a much better job and company, far greater prospects and importantly, much more money. To say that they were greatly relieved was something of an understatement.

So, I was about to commence Job No.7 at Dolcis Shoe Store. It was the first day of Spring when I started my new job at Dolcis. It just seemed a very appropriate day. A new season, a fresh start and the dawn of a brand new career?

"The quality of a man's shoes reveals how much he respects himself", as the saying goes. Of all the items in a man's wardrobe, shoes are his single most important element of style. Have you ever noticed women checking out a man's shoes before their eyes rise to scan the rest of his appearance? If so, then you will already know this. The truth is that; *"shoes maketh the man."* If this is true in the world of business, it was certainly true inside the *"World of Shoes"*, and Dolcis was a key player in the shoe business. My new Manager was to be extremely strict on that appearance. After spotting his well healed Brogues, when I first met him, I had also noticed that his footwear shone more than the shoes of a London Guardsman, I knew that he would expect precisely the same standards of appearance from me and in all aspects of my work.

As I walked into the Dolcis Store on my first
Monday morning in the job, I knew little or
nothing about shoes and the shoe market, other
than what I had learned in my research, in order to
win the job. The least that I could do was to make
an impression with my appearance. After all, I was
the new trainee Manager and I had to look the part.
In fact, I had to be the part. I breezed into the store,
but in reality, much of it was bravado. I was
nowhere near as confident as I pretended to be.
However, looking the part, and feeling the part,
went a long way towards it. I had bought a brand
new suit. It was a double breasted three piece suit
in a dark brown pinstripe with flared trousers,
which were very much *"a la mode"* in 1973. My
shoes were the expensive ones that I had bought at
Dolcis in Stockport, when I was trying to bluff my
way into earning an interview with Mr. Jones, the
Stockport Store Manager.

I must have spent about fifteen minutes shining
and buffing my shoes the night before, so that they
would look at least as good as my Manager's.
After all, shoes are what we were all about and
woe betide any member of staff who came to work
in footwear that did not positively reflect the
footwear business that we were all involved in.

I arrived early at the store. Most of the staff had
not arrived by then, but Mr. Jones was already in
his office. We met each other on the shop floor,

face to face. It was like two warriors eyeing each other up before going into battle. He was the King and I was the young Pretender! Instantly, I could see that Mr. Jones was immaculate, like a manikin, and I had matched him, shoe for shoe, shirt for shirt and suit for suit. I was sure that his outfit had cost at least double what mine was worth, but he had a big manager's income and anyway, I knew that I looked the part, so I felt extremely confident.

We went into his office and he outlined my induction programme which was initially to be for three months. He introduced me the staff who were all extremely professional and experienced. He then asked one of the senior members of staff to be my mentor for the day and then to give me a tour of the shop's departments, the products and introduced me to all the other salespeople.

I felt more at ease with Dolcis than I had felt in any of the previous six jobs I had tried. I was extremely grateful to Mr. Jones for giving me a big chance, when, my "Curriculum Vitae" screamed; *"Beware of this Man!"* to potential employers. *"He is not a stayer. He is a huge risk!"*

Even before I had even done any work for Dolcis, I just felt that I belonged there. For the first time since I had been a Monk at Hawkstone, I had a strong feeling that I was a part of an organization that wanted me, I fitted in, and it gave me immediate status, and an adrenalin lift. For the very first time, I felt that I was a part of the company and that I was going to be a success. This feeling was reinforced by the fact that everyone in the store treated me like management, and yet this was only my first day as a trainee. I was aware that I was as green as a cucumber and knew nothing about the shoe business and that I had to learn from the existing members of staff in the store.

I believe that I possibly earned that respect just by the way I presented myself, that is; business like, very smart, friendly but not over-bearing. I tried to look as if I knew more than I actually did. The staff and customers knew nothing about me and for all they were aware, I could have been a really experienced member of management, even though I was a twenty three years old trainee.

The first day went really well for me. It had mainly been a watching brief, to look, listen and learn. What I had seen was impressive. All of the Sales people were extremely well trained, well presented and professional. The entire set-up at Dolcis was slick and of the highest quality.

The following day Mr. Jones had arranged for me to go on an induction course to their Head Office. It was a very professionally run course. Dolcis was a huge Shoe Chain with branches all over the UK. The course at their Head Office was an induction

181

for all new Dolcis staff, irrespective of job or
seniority. There were separate sessions for trainee
managers, and there were four of us in this group.
It was very slick and there was a really competitive
edge to the sessions among the four trainee
managers. I knew I would have to be on my toes
and the tutor was deliberately pitting the trainees
against each other, to see how they would cope and
react to pressure. It was obvious that they were
looking out for their next Managers and I knew
there would be fierce competition for the next job
vacancy, due to Managers moving on, promotion
or new store openings. I was not a naturally
competitive person, and I had not been used to
competition, so I had to work extra hard to show
that I had the drive and ability that was demanded,
in order to become a Dolcis store Manager.

Back at the shop it was a case of starting right at
the bottom of the ladder, but that was alright by
me. I was a novice in the Shoe business and keen
to learn. I was initially asked to go on back room
duty. That meant selecting the footwear from
stock for the sales staff, that the customers wanted
to try on. It was a good way to learn about the
hundreds of different styles and sizes of footwear.

After working for a few days in the stock room, I
was anxious to work on the shop floor. Despite
their juniority, the sales staff knew much more
than I did. The sales people were extremely slick

and professional. They were taught techniques that helped them to achieve a sale, come what may, and then to sell added value, by making sure that customers bought accessories, to increase the value of each purchase. Each salesperson had to record each of their sales and value. It was competitive to see which person would achieve the highest numbers over the period of a week.

First, I was asked to work in in the Men's Shoe department. Due to my all male background, I was very much a man's man at that stage of my life. By that, I mean that I was always more comfortable in men's company than with women. Therefore, I was pleased when Mr. Jones told me that the next part of my training was to be in the Men's shoe department. Men shop in a completely different manner to women. Men seem to know what they want before they go shopping. They look around and quite quickly, if they see a pair of shoes they like, they try them on and if they fit and look good, then they would buy them, pure and simple. Also, selling them accessories, was generally a logical thing to do and happened in most sales. I spent a full week in the Men's Shoes department and felt perfectly at home. Even better, I was the top Shoe Salesman that week. That was a relief, particularly as I was the Trainee Manager and was expected to do somewhat better than the other sales staff.

Week two was not such a good week for me. I was

asked to sell in the ladies Department. As I admitted, I was not at ease in the company of women. I was just plain awkward and rather shy, but I was not sure why. It must have been everything to do with living in my all-male environment, at the Monastery for 11 years. What I did learn quickly, was that women shop in an entirely different manner to men.

This was before self-selection became the norm. A woman would walk into the store and when I would ask her what type of footwear I could show her, a typical answer would be: *"I don't know"* or *"I'm not sure, or I will know when I see it."* Perhaps she would not know what she wanted or maybe she just wanted to look and then try on.

I would then go through the process of guessing what she may want to buy. Based on the sparse information I was given, I would then go to the back store and select up-to three pairs of shoes for her to try on. This process of elimination could mean showing and trying on up to a dozen types of shoes. Even at the end of the process there was no guarantee that a sale would result. A normal sale time for purchasing a pair of shoes would be five to ten minutes for a man, and fifteen minutes to thirty minutes for a woman. In truth, I did feel ill at ease in the ladies department and it showed in the sales figures. I think I came second to bottom in the sales list that week. It was not

184

impressive for a management trainee, but I was not surprised. I did not feel that I was on the same wave length as women, when it came to be selling them ladies footwear.

One of the main fashion items for ladies during 1973, was for white, knee length, stretch polyurethane boots. They complemented the mini skirts that were in vogue at the time. Sales of the boots were amazing and just about every woman had at least a pair or two in her wardrobe. I must confess to feeling uncomfortable in helping ladies to try on their footwear. In truth, I think that the ladies would have preferred a female sales assistant and would generally feel more comfortable with a member of their own sex. A lady salesperson has a much better understanding of what type of shoes a woman might want. It may well have been one of the reasons for my poor sales figures in comparison to the sales ladies.

To say that I was pleased to finish my stint in the lady's shoe shop was a gross understatement. It was however, by far the biggest department in the store and so it was essential that I had a good understanding of it. Women buy a lot more shoes than men and it is a far larger market.

All in all, I was really pleased to be working at Dolcis. It was a professionally run company and at long last, I began to feel good about myself. I was a trainee manager, dressed like a businessman and I had the prospect of managing my own store within a couple of years. It should have been just what I wanted to do for the next ten years or so, and yet, there was something unusual about the job that said to me that I was not quite settled, that I would not be doing it in the longer term.

One day, Mr. Jones told me that the assistant Manager at a smaller store had left and that they needed someone to act as the under Manager. The store was in Burnley, Lancashire. At first, I was reticent about traveling that far to work every day and yet, it meant promotion, so I could hardly refuse. It seemed a big step upwards for me.

I spent almost four months at the Burnley store as Assistant Manager. It stood me in good stead because I learned a lot more and made more progress at the smaller store, than I would have done at Stockport. It was however, a tough and difficult job. It was a long drive every day, meaning that I left home at 7am and I did not leave the store until after 6pm. That meant that I did not get home from work until after 7pm. It included working Saturday too, so I did not have too much time left for myself or in fact, anything else.

I was not afraid of long hours and hard work but there was one particular aspect of the job that I found it hard to come to terms with. Going back to my monastic days, I had a condition that may well have started in the Monastery. I felt confined and enclosed, a type of claustrophobia. At the Monastery in Perth, my life was practically encased within the Monastery building and grounds and there were times when I felt physically confined and wanting to be outside in the wide-open spaces of the countryside.

As good as my job was at Dolcis, I was working from 8am each morning until 6pm at night, for six days a week. So what was the problem? For most people, that is the norm. Millions of people are doing that every day. And yet for me, spending ten hours a day inside one building gave me a distinct feeling of confinement and deep down, I knew that I could not do that for a substantial portion of my life. It was not just a case of my wanting to be out and about more. I actually started feeling ill. My breathing became labored, I would become restless and anxious and would then become agitated if I spent too much time indoors. This is a condition that I still have until today, decades later on. Whenever I have to spend too long at home or in one place for several hours, I just have to move, to go outside and breathe fresh air into my lungs. I am in need of open spaces in the great outdoors.

Ultimately, my days at Dolcis were numbered for this reason alone. It was going to come to an end because of the necessity of working within a shop environment with long retail hours being a pre-requisite. I had to have freedom to roam outdoors.

There was one particular episode that proved to be the catalyst, and meant that I would yet again have to move on in my stop-start career.

It was when my temporary spell at Burnley came to an end, that I returned to my position as Trainee Manager at Dolcis in Stockport. I had made significant progress there, because I was second in command and I had learned much more quickly, because of the extra responsibility.

It was towards the end of the year in 1973. The day was December 24th, the last working day before Christmas. It had been a very busy Christmas Eve and trade had been really brisk. Like everyone else I was tired after the long festive period at work and was ready for my Christmas break at home. It was almost 5pm and the Manager had just let the staff go home a little early as there were no more shoppers left in the store. That day I had come to work on my Scooter. I had a *"Vespa Vega"*. It was very trendy and I liked the feeling of freedom when I was riding it. In addition, it was easy to park and did not cost me anything to park it, unlike the car. I used to bring it into the building up the rear delivery lift and leave it at the back of the warehouse. As usual, I made my way up to the rear delivery lift and put my Moped inside it. I was going to take it downstairs and then pop back into the store to say goodbye and wish Merry Christmas to Mr. Jones, my Manager.

I pushed the button to take the lift, me and my Scooter, to the ground level. The lift started moving downwards, but then with a definite jolt, it suddenly stopped, and everything went deathly quiet. As it did so, the lift lights went out. I waited, breathless, for a few seconds expecting it to start again, but it did not. For somebody with a genuine dislike of confined spaces, this was my worst nightmare. I waited a few more seconds and kept pressing the button. Nothing happened. I was in complete darkness. I could not see anything and was fumbling around in the dark for an alarm of some type. It was the old type lift with a concertina type sliding door. I felt a state of panic welling up inside of me. I did not know if anyone was aware that I was in the lift. I had no idea if anybody knew it was stuck. Then came the dawning realization that this was Christmas Eve at 5pm and that I could be there all over Christmas and nobody would know anything about it. I began to think that I could be in the lift until December 27th when the Store opened again. I wondered how I would survive all that time with no food and water. Who could possibly know that I was in the lift? Surely they would think that I had gone home. I had not said goodnight to Mr. Jones. Did he think that I had already left? All these questions and fears

189

were coursing through my mind, when suddenly there was a loud clanking noise, a period of deathly silence, and the light came on again in the lift. It must have been about fifteen or twenty minutes out of action, but to me it had seemed like an eternity. Without me having to do anything, the lift moved downwards and with a massive relief, I opened the door and stood outside for fully a minute, deeply gasping in, the cold fresh air. At that, a security man came around and asked if I was alright. He could see that I was badly shaken. He was aware that the lift had stopped working, but he had not known that anybody was inside. At that point, my Manager Mr. Jones arrived and asked if I had been locked in the lift. He was already in his coat and ready to go home. I was still in a state of shock, but with huge relief, I wished him a very Merry Christmas and set off on my scooter for home, telling him that I would be back for business as 8am on 27th. December.

Whilst driving my scooter home that Christmas Eve, I came to a definite decision. I did not want to continue working much longer in a single place. My problem was nothing to do with Dolcis, my employer. I actually loved the company and very much enjoyed the work, but I knew that I had to work in a totally different and open environment.

I needed to do work where I could move around in the open and move from place to place. It was an illogical conclusion, it made no real sense, but I knew that it was going to happen sometime soon.

It was to be food for thought for me, over the Christmas period and I would have to do something about it in the New Year. For the time being, I just wanted to forget all about the horrible lift episode, and just enjoy my Christmas break.

As far as lifts were concerned, this incident was to be the catalyst for a lifelong fear of elevators that carries on into my life today. Since that awful Christmas Eve, I have always avoided lifts at almost any cost, even if it means having to climb up several floors on foot, to reach the higher levels of a building. On the credit side, it was good exercise for me, so it wasn't all bad.

191

Chapter 10

Up the career ladder

The New Year duly arrived. I had already returned to work at the shoe store on 27th December after an enjoyable Christmas, and I was feeling suitably refreshed and ready for the challenges that lay ahead. I had no problem at all with my employer. Dolcis was a fine company and it was a very good job. My only problem was that I could not imagine me working there year after year in the same building. It was irrational, but it was brought on by my desire to be able to work outdoors. It all stemmed from my feeling of claustrophobia which developed in the Monastery at Perth and had been with me ever since then, and up-to the present day.

At the start of the new working year, it was at the forefront of my mind that I would be seeking different employment. It was not something I really wanted to do, as I loved the job and I was aware that my CV needed to be much more stable. It seemed insane that I should be looking for different work at a time when I should have been showing more stability in my employment record.

Back at home I talked to my brother Mike. He was doing very nicely, still with Spar Supermarkets, where he had worked his way up-to Store

Manager. During the short time I was working with him at the Spar in Marple, I must confess that it had never been my ambition to be a Manager with the food Supermarket. Perhaps it had subconsciously been for the same reason, which was an irrational dislike of being confined indoors for long periods of time.

While I was working at Spar Supermarkets, I would sometimes notice the smartly dressed, suave salesmen who visited the store, selling their company's products. To my way of thinking, they had an interesting job and lifestyle. It seemed attractive, challenging and they drove from place to place in their company cars. They seemed to be their own boss, solely reliant upon themselves and their ability to sell. More so, they were not confined to a single place of work. They would travel around the country, driving from business to business. It looked like an ideal solution for me.

I began to review the way I was approaching my job searching. After leaving the Monastery, I had it fixed in my mind that I should follow the same path that I had, when I was training to be a priest. I thought that I would be best suited to doing the sort of work that would be for the benefit of others.

 Up until that point, my career in caring jobs for the community, had been an unmitigated disaster. Other than my very brief spell as an encyclopedia salesman, [remember I left that company because of their unethical selling techniques!] my previous jobs in Nursing and Social Care were clearly not suitable to my qualities and ability. All my previous employment, had come to a short and abrupt end within a very brief period.

Hopefully, I could still be a decent person, and hold down a useful job in the community, without being a Priest, Monk, Nurse or Social worker?

I mused over all those possibilities, then I slept on them. It was absolutely essential, that my next move had to be the correct one. It had to be an employment in which I could settle down and begin to forge a successful and long-term career.

When we were both working at the Spar, Mike used to deal with some of the sales reps. I didn't say much to Mike about my motives, but I asked him the name of the Nestle "Rep" who visited the store. I had chatted to the "Rep" on a couple of occasions, asked him about his job, and it had a genuine appeal to me. It seriously crossed my mind, that this could be the sort of job that I could be suited to. Whether it was a job that I could get, and more importantly, be good at, was entirely a different matter? Mm mm! It was food for thought.

There were no job vacancies, as far as I knew, so I just took a chance. I wrote to Nestle and told them a little bit about myself and asked them about a job with the company. In truth, I wrote much more in hope than in expectation and so when I received a brown coloured envelope, franked with the Nestle logo, I was more than surprised, but even then, my expectation was that it would just be a polite rejection letter. Imagine my surprise then, when I carefully opened the letter which thanked me for my interest and advised me that the company were recruiting for Sales Merchandisers in my area. My C.V. looked more like a shopping list than a curriculum vitae, but strangely, it did not seem to have put them off, as they wanted to interview me at a local hotel within a couple of weeks.

I had always been an excellent letter writer and skillful in selling myself, but I was afraid that they would be deterred by my life in the monastery. I feared that it would give them a wrong impression of me. Although I honestly detailed all my seven jobs within three years, I did not tell Nestle about my time in the Monastery. I was not being completely upfront and honest, but neither was I telling any untruths. Instead of detailing my life at Erdington, Perth and Hawkstone, I merely put down on the application form, that I was involved in further education and listed my qualifications. It was of course the truth, but with a few notable omissions!

Two weeks later, I attended an interview at a hotel

196

near Manchester. I had no experience, so I tried to make up for it by planning my interview to the "nth" degree! I did comprehensive research on the company, its products and their history, and despite being extremely nervous, I practically bounded into the interview room. I looked absolutely immaculate in my smart new business suit, and I was the image of somebody who was ultra-confident, enthusiastic and determined to get the job. My public speaking at Erdington and Hawkstone, had stood me in good stead, and during the interview I could actually feel that they were impressed with me, despite the job record that was in front of them. I defended my choice of social jobs, told them that they were mistakes, and that I was definitely cut out for a career in selling. I asked them outright, to give me a chance and I promised them that they would not regret it. It was all "bluff and bluster" of course. I had experienced so much failure in my short time since leaving the Monastery, that I was absolutely determined to land the job with Nestle and that it would be the starting point of a successful career in selling.

The three interviewers looked at each other and then looked towards me again. I think they were taken aback by my ultra-positive approach to the interview and my seeming confidence. I hoped that they would be tempted to employ me despite my background, rather than because of it. The leader of the interview panel said: *"We will be in touch quite soon, Mr. Nearey"* Despite the words they chose, not being either particularly positive or negative, I hoped and believed that I was going to be offered the job and, so I said to them:

"Gentlemen, thank you very much for interviewing me, and I look forward to hearing of your decision, quite soon."

On leaving, I shook the hands of all three men, strongly, looked them straight in the eye and then marched briskly out of the interview room.

I hadn't told my family about this interview. There had been far too many false dawns. I just wanted to keep it under wraps until I knew the result and then I would let them know, assuming that it was a positive response. I could not endure any further failure and disappointment in my career. I had experienced so much of those since leaving the monastery and I was determined that at long last, I was going to be successful in my next job..

It was better that my family did not know about the latest interview at that time. It could be yet another false start to my crazy career, so until it was a done deal, I decided to keep it under wraps and wait until I had a signed and sealed contract with a new employer.

Chapter 11

Best Man Blues

My secret interview for a job in a totally different market, I kept a closely guarded secret. My family had been completely supportive, but I did not want them worrying that I had now gone totally insane. I desperately wanted to land my big job and then tell them all about it, if and only when, it became a done deal. The suspense was killing me. I had already been waiting a whole week, but I had still not heard a thing from Nestle. I just had to be patient for a little while longer.

Meantime, my little brother Mike, five years my junior, was about to take centre stage as Groom. The date for his forthcoming nuptials, at the tender age of just eighteen, was earmarked for the following weekend and he had chosen me to be his Best Man. I felt deeply honoured. This was to be my first public speech. Goodness knows I had years of practice, by preaching sermons in the Monastery. Mike and I had always had a close relationship and it was more than a coincidence that he too, had once been on the road to joining a religious order. He seemed to follow in exactly the same footpath as me. I had gone to an exhibition of Religious Communities in 1959, which resulted in me signing up to join the Redemptorist Order of Monks in 1960, at just 11 years old. Some five years later, Mike and the family went to an exhibition of Religious Communities, just as I had done. Mike, was just a kid at thirteen, but he joined The Sacred Heart Fathers, who were based at Woodcote Hall, Newport. At that time, I was still with The Redemptorists, so Mike would not have learned from my experiences, that it was not a good idea to leave home at a very tender age to join the Church. He was two years older than me when he joined, but still a youngster who did not know his own mind. Even so, he did make up his own mind most definitely when he was fifteen. He had become very unsettled at Newport and with the religious life. He yearned to be back home with his family, and the lifestyle of a normal young teenager. Whilst he had the decisiveness of mind to tell them he was unhappy there, I had just soldiered on and let matters take their own course.

With Mike's wedding looming, I was a nervous wreck. Even though I was pretty confident at public speaking, due to my preaching practice at Hawkstone, I was not used to public speaking on social occasions, nor was I feeling very confident because of the difficult times I had experienced since leaving the Monastery. My seeming inability to adapt to the civilian world, after my monastic journey, was badly affecting my confidence in just about everything I attempted to do and it had showed up in many of the poor decisions I had made in just about every aspect of my life.

I had been attempting to write my speech since the day after he had given me the good news, but there was a big difference between sermon writing and speech writing for a wedding. In fact, when I read back the initial draft of my best man speech, it sounded much more like a sermon than a wedding speech, so I had to scrap it completely, and start all over again. While I was re-writing my speech, I was trying hard to remember my duties to Irene, his bride and her bridesmaids. I also had to say pleasant things about my brother, which was not too difficult, and to tell various humorous stories about him during his bachelor life. This was rather more difficult, as I was not about much during his teenage years at home. I was trying to make it humorous as well as being very sincere, so as to entertain the wedding guests.

When the big day arrived, it turned out that my best man speech was second in importance to another of my wedding day duties. As best man, I had two main duties to perform. Number one, was my speech. My other responsibility was to look after and produce the wedding ring during the marriage service, which was not that difficult, or at least, so I thought!!!!

On the morning of the wedding, the Nearey

household at Marple was a buzzing hive of activity. People were flying here there and everywhere, in an effort to be ready in time for the wedding. They had to be dressed in their best bibs and tuckers. Neither Mike nor I, were at our sharpest, courtesy of the late stag party, the previous evening. A trip into Manchester for Mike's favorite hot curry, followed by a night club visit and copious amounts of Boddingtons best bitter, had left us both feeling "fuzzy headed." We were feeling under the weather and well and truly hungover. We were not *"bright eyed and bushy tailed,"* as we needed to be, on the morning of the wedding. That was a big mistake!

I managed pretty well to make sure that Mike, as the groom, was properly dressed and attired and that he looked as smart as he possibly could. I checked that he had everything he needed, and then made sure that his groom's speech was securely tucked safely into his inside pocket.

After that, I set about the task of making myself presentable. I had bought for myself, on H.P of course, a brand new three piece suit. It was a dark brown pin-striped suit, with a white shirt and a flowery kipper-tie. It was hardly my place to say so, but looking in the mirror, I did look extremely smart and was very much, the part of the best man. It was then Mike's turn to make sure that nothing had been forgotten. He went through the order of service with me, the wedding plan, the timings and then he carefully opened a small jewelry box and handed to me the bride and groom's wedding rings. *"Take good care of these, our Kid"*, said Mike: and he exaggerated and emphasized every single one of the seven words he articulated, looking me straight in the face as he did so.

"Just give them to me Mike! I'm putting yours into my left waistcoat pocket and the Bride's into my right waistcoat pocket". Just like him, I emphasized each and every word and patted my pockets to show him where they were.

"There! are you happy now? They are safe and sound!" Once the job was done, he seemed happy and more relaxed and he scurried off to badger somebody else about the wedding arrangements.

Minutes later, I came skipping quickly down the stairs. Time was running very short and I met one of the visiting guests head on. He was coming quickly up the narrow stairs. The problem was, he was carrying a hot mug of coffee! He wasn't looking ahead, and I couldn't stop in time. Smack! There was a head-on collision. I bowled him over and landed on top of him. The hot coffee went just about everywhere, and all over my suit, waistcoat and shirt. We both ended up in the bottom hallway in a heap and we were both very wet and stained. It was a best man's worst dream.

We had something like ten minutes to get into the limousine and to get to the wedding. I flew into my bedroom, Mike was busy elsewhere, and I didn't want to worry him, by telling him about the accident. I looked in the mirror and concluded that not only was all my clothing wet, but it was also badly stained by the coffee. There was nothing else that could be done. I just had to change my entire wedding outfit at the very last minute.

Mike shouted from downstairs: *"Hurry up Steve, we'll be in the car."* From our bedroom I yelled back! *"I'll be with you in two minutes, Our Mike".* I didn't want to tell him about our "slight mishap" on the stairs, as he was already feeling agitated and he would have gone into panic mode. Anyway, it was my job to make sure everybody was calm!

Fortunately, I still had one more presentable three piece suit in my meagre wardrobe, so I did a quick change, made sure that I had my best man's speech in my inside pocket and raced downstairs. I flew down the steps to the car, and jumped into the back seat. Mike was already sat in the front and he did not even notice that I had changed my wedding outfit. I was not going to trouble him. He had enough on his plate; after all, he was the one about to become married!

The limousine set off for the church at Sale, in Manchester. Mike turned around and said to me:

"Steve, have we got everything?" Using both hands I gestured to him to calm down; *"Take it easy Mike, everything's OK."* At that, he turned around, sank back into his car seat and just relaxed. He took out his speech and silently read it to himself for the rest of the journey. Feeling tired, and somewhat stressed, I had my own speech to worry about, I put my head back on the seat and closed my eyes for the thirty-minute journey.

6. Bridegroom Mike, left - Best Man Steve right.

Once we arrived at the Church, I was feeling refreshed and more relaxed after my power nap in the car. Mike seemed nervy, but reasonably chilled, as we took our place at the head of the Church and then awaited the arrival of the beautiful Bride along with her attendants.

The big moment then arrived; the bride walked down the aisle looking as pretty as a picture and took her place next to Mike, with me just to his right. The priest, our brother Arthur, came to the part of the ceremony where the bride and groom were to exchange rings. Still, nothing rang a bell with me. I was in complete and blissful ignorance. Then, Father Arthur, looked in my direction, Mike also looked at me in an expectant manner. Then it twigged! *"Oh right, the rings!"* I muttered to myself: I put my hands into my waistcoat pocket! Nothing there! I tried the other waistcoat pocket, Nothing! I searched my other two jacket pockets more in hope than expectation. Next was my last throw of the dice! I tried my trouser pockets and they were all empty. In desperation, I put my hand into my inside pocket and took out my best man speech. There was nothing else in the pocket! Then, after a few moments of stunned silence, my heart slowly began to sink. I looked at Mike and Irene and I then glanced towards Father Arthur. There was a dawning realization within me and it must have been written all over my troubled face.

I felt as though every person in the church was fixated on me and peering in expectation and anticipation. There was nothing else to be done. I turned to Mike and whispered in his ear:

"Mike, I've not got the rings! I had to change my suit and the rings are still in my other waistcoat

pockets!" The congregation started whispering to one another. Mike then whispered into Irene's ear and she passed it onto Father Arthur. I could hear low sniggers and tittle tattle from the inquisitive congregation!

I told Mike that it was too far to drive back home to Marple to get the missing rings. In desperation, we came up with the idea of borrowing a ring just for the ceremony and we could do the real exchange of rings at the reception! Brilliant!

It was a botched up solution but it was all we could muster in that moment of panic. At least it meant that the wedding ceremony could continue. I quickly went to Irene's sister and asked her, in a whisper, if we could borrow her wedding ring. She slipped it off her finger and gave it to me. I then took my wedding ring off and there you have it, we had bride and groom wedding rings, after a fashion! I passed them to Arthur and he continued with the ring ceremony. Approaching the bride he said: *"With this ring, I thee wed"* and he slotted the wedding ring onto the Bride's finger. The ring was huge! Irene's sister was much bigger than the Bride and it slopped around on her finger like a large washer. Irene looked around and whispered: *"This isn't my ring!"* *"Just put it on, I'll tell you later"* Mike whispered to her. In all honesty, she took it extremely well. Many brides would have been horrified if their wedding had been spoiled in

207

this way, but she took it all in her stride and never held it against me, as she had every right to do. The day had been saved, but only just! I knew I would take some stick as a result! Immediately after the wedding service, I asked one of the guests to drive me home. I searched my original, coffee stained wedding suit and there in the waistcoat pockets, were the missing wedding rings. With a huge sigh of relief, I neatly put them safely into a box and back into my pockets

Back at the wedding, I was certain that I was the butt of all type of wedding jokes, doing the rounds. In the circumstances, I thought it would be better to pre-empt them and take the *"Mick"* out of myself. I was certain that others would be going to do it to me, particularly the groom, my brother, Mike. Nervously, I started my speech. This was the first public speaking I had done since my preaching practice in the monastery, so I was really apprehensive and it showed. I began with:

*"This is the first wedding I have ever attended, and despite all the jokes about the best man forgetting the rings, I have never ever heard of **any** best man who has actually done so:* long pause: *"……. until today that is!" I think that Irene has forgiven me, but I'm not too sure about Mike so, rather belatedly, I would now like to present the bride and groom with their **real** wedding rings."*
I then proceeded to relate to the wedding audience

the slap stick episode of the *"flying coffee mugs"* on the stairs at home. It seemed to win them over and gained some sympathy for myself, it certainly had them in fits of laughter. At least, I was able to convince the wedding party that I had not actually "forgotten" the wedding rings, and that the lack of rings at the ceremony, was all down to that awful coffee mug accident on the stairs. Fortunately, the room had gone into roars of sympathetic laughter. It was a great way to start my speech and it took all the tension out of my nervous delivery. I was a mightily relieved Best Man! The rest of the day went like clockwork and to this date, despite all the ribbing I got about the Best Man forgetting the rings, I have never heard of anyone else that has ever done so.

7. Bride Irene, Groom Mike and Father Arthur.

209

Chapter 12

On the Up!

The week after Mike's wedding, I received a letter that was going to put my career right back onto the straight and narrow, for the first time since I had come back into civilian life. I was going in the right direction at long last. Although my previous job as a Milkman was a step in the right direction, it was not the right career for me and had bordered on being yet another bad decision.

My most recent job at Dolcis was certainly on the right path. It was a good selling career and one that should have resulted in me being a business manager with a major company. As already documented, I did not see it as a long term career because it meant being confined to one place. My fears and anxiety relating to claustrophobia would always prohibit me from making a career in that business or any other type of business, where I was enclosed for lengthy periods in one building. I needed a job where I had the freedom to roam and not, like millions of others, must work in a single place or building all of my life.

The letter was from Nestle, the Swiss Food Manufacturer and I had been offered a role as a

Sales Merchandiser. I was absolutely thrilled. I had endured three years of making mistake after mistake and I just knew that I had landed the right job and that I was at last heading in the correct direction. That day, I handed in my notice at Dolcis. I felt bad about doing so, because it had been a good position, a fine company and I could have gone places had I stayed. It was gratifying that they thought enough of me, to ask me to reconsider my decision, but when I explained my reasons for wanting to leave, they understood.

The job offer from Nestle was excellent. The salary was so much more than I had earned in any of my other roles and it gave me a freedom which I had not found in any of my other employment. Even better, there was a company car which went with the role. What a relief! At one stage, I had two Ford Classics and a Vespa Vega Scooter, with all of them on H.P. At last I could rid myself of my debts and the dodgy cars, as my new company car, a Hillman Avenger was brand spanking new and more importantly, all the running costs were paid for by the company. Whew! Free of debt at last.

So my 8th job was finally up and running. I still received a lot of stick and teasing about my frequent job hopping, from family and friends:

"What is your new job today, Steve?" was a typical quip or *"How long before you resign this*

job?" was another. I had to put up with all this banter, but I did not try to defend it, as moving quickly from job to job was going to be a sure fire method of moving up the career ladder and improving my status and income. After all, I had started my career rather later than most. I was 22 years old when I took on my first and disastrous occupation as an Encyclopedia Salesman, so I had some catching up to do in the career stakes.

The Nestle job seemed exactly the right type of work for me. It was challenging, targeted and instead of a Monk's Habit, Nurse's Uniform, or a Milkman's Cap, I could dress in a smart, sharp business suit. A semblance of near normality was returning to my troubled and complicated life.

The actual work, in truth, became a bit mundane after a while. In theory, it involved selling the company's goods to the major supermarkets. It was in truth, not that challenging. It only required filling the supermarket shelves with the Nestle products, counting what had been sold since the last visit, and then putting in a replacement order. It was a simple case of arithmetic! Stock minus sales equaled a New Order! It was hardly Rocket Science, nor was it genuine selling, which required a fair degree of planning and skill.

I spent a large portion of my work just filling shelves with Nestle and Cross & Blackwell products in the large supermarkets. It was a very big part of the job and I had spent rather a lot of time doing precisely that, at the Spar Supermarket, in my first year in work, but for much less money. As such, it was a less challenging role than I had expected. The really pleasing aspect of the work, was that I was not stationed in any one place. I traveled a large geographical area, covering several counties and went from store to store meeting different people all the time. No danger of claustrophobia then! I felt certain that if I had stayed for a significant length of time, I may have been promoted to a more challenging role, but there was no indication that it would happen for quite some time, because of the structure of the company. Nestle was a huge business with a large management and I was a man in a hurry to try to catch up for a slow start to my selling career, after several false starts. I had been just over a year in the job, which for me seemed like a lifetime, but I began to grow restless for a role which was more challenging and so job number nine was looming large on my near horizon, despite having access to all kind of free samples of Nestle Chocolate and other goodies, which were a perk of the job. Perhaps this was to be a good move, as all the free chocolate and additional calories were not doing anything for my bludgeoning waistline.

At least when I asked the employment consultant to find me another job, it was on the back of two reasonably successful roles with the Coop Dairy and Dolcis, and it made my updated C.V. look a little more respectable than the previous jobs.

The recruitment consultants told me that Gillette were looking for Sales Merchandisers in the North West, so I could not wait to apply. I knew a friend who was already working for them and he spoke highly of the company. I had my interview which went well and it seemed to be a good progression for me after my time with Nestle.

I was delighted to be offered a job which was to be Job No.9. This would to be the 1st. of my two spells that I would spend with Gillette. I enjoyed the work, and it was a really professional company. It was very hard work and they demanded a lot from its employees, but then the rewards were also very good. Things were going well for me, but I was still a sales merchandiser and I had my eyes set on a higher target. There was a lot of competition for promotion to the next level. When my friend Gary, who had suggested I came to Gillette, decided to move onto another company, he soon told me of a vacancy with his new company, for a Regional Sales Manager. Despite being happy at Gillette, I could not resist the temptation to gain another promotion, so I immediately applied for the job.

The company was Boden U.K, a thermoplastics company which sold plastic garden products. The

position was for a Regional Sales Manager. It
covered a large portion of Northern England and
was a genuine sales role. No more merchandising
was required. It was to sell and develop a region
with a range of garden frames and cloches to DIY
outlets and Garden Centre's.

This was to be cold selling of a new range and
required genuine selling ability. The job needed
bags of determination. It was most certainly a
tough job, but I was confident in my ability and I
welcomed the challenge after the rather more
cushy sales-merchandising positions at Nestle and
Gillette. The company, Boden Thermoplastics was
a very large UK company and so I felt confident
that they would have the resource to be successful
with this new range of untried garden products.

Although there was plenty of competition for the
advertised job, I felt sure that I had done a good
interview. I had developed a good and impressive
interview technique, which probably made me
come across as more competent and successful
than I actually was. Even so, I was relieved and
very happy when I received a telephone call telling
me that I had been selected and that I was being
offered the position of Regional Sales Manager for
the Northern division of the UK.

In due course, I completed my period of notice
with Gillette and was ready to take on my new

challenge. I was now into double figures with my jobs tally, having commenced my 10th job in just a few years. On the morning that I started my new career with Boden, I took the early train from Manchester to Somerset and arrived at Boden around eleven o' clock. I was to spend two days at the company offices as part of my introduction to the company This was my 10th Job in a relatively short space of time, but I was on the upward curve.

I went through my induction course during the Wednesday and Thursday, and then on Friday, I completed a tour of the offices and factory and then spent time with the National Sales Manager.

Come 1 pm, I had completed my induction and I prepared to drive home that evening before starting work on my Region the following Monday. I thought that I had made a good impression during my time at Head Office and the future was looking bright for me. I was really pleased with my new employment package. My basic salary was good, better than at Gillette, and I had been promised an excellent commission on top of that, assuming that I achieved my sales targets. At that stage, I was feeling really positive and confident in my ability. On top of my remuneration package, I had also been given a very good pension scheme. My company car which was sat outside waiting for me, was a brand spanking new Ford Cortina 1.6 XL, in a flamboyant Daytona yellow paintwork. It was most certainly a massive improvement on the clapped out Ford Classic that I had been driving, just a couple of years earlier. Driving the Daytona yellow Cortina, people could see me coming from a distance. It was pretty difficult not to see and be impressed by, the loud and fluorescent colour!

At 2.00pm, I climbed into my brand new company car. I pretended to be pretty cool about it, as I waved goodbye to my Manager. He said: *"Drive Carefully"* and then I drove off, tentatively at first, until I became used to the feel of the car and the new controls. His words however, would very quickly come back to haunt me!

In truth, far from feeling cool and relaxed, I was really excited. A new job, a new car and after a long and busy day, I was setting off on my long journey home, a distance of some two hundred and twenty miles.

It wasn't my first company car. The Hillman Avenger I had driven for Nestle was very smart indeed, but my bright, new Daytona yellow Ford Cortina was something else. As I set off from Somerset, I felt as if this was the best I had been in years. My career was on a steep upward curve, and life was at last getting better and better for me. I had experienced a series of disastrous personal and employment decisions, but I truly hoped that this was to be the final turning point, the moment when everything would at last start to go right for me, and hopefully, stay right.

It was a dry and very hot day, during the summer months. The road conditions were fine and it was a very pleasant evening to drive. As I was heading North on the M5, I was thinking about my new job and everything that had happened to me that day. I was also glancing around the new surroundings in my new Cortina. I had not had time before I left the office, to become completely familiar with everything in the car. I was quietly checking out the dashboard, equipment and controls. It had a superb stereo radio system, which was top of the range for the nineteen seventies.

By the time I reached the midlands where the M5 joined the M6, the traffic had become really heavy. I was also very tired after my long and busy day and there was all sort of information coursing through my mind. As I arrived at the intersection of the M5 and M6, I moved quickly from the middle lane, into a gap in the outside lane. I had only been in the third lane for a few seconds when suddenly I saw brake lights immediately in front of me. Before that moment, I had been on auto pilot, calm and relaxed, but as those brake lights quickly came nearer, I had an instant rush of adrenalin, which I could feel was searing through my veins. It jolted me into life from my relative slumber and I slammed on my brakes; my wheels locked; I was screeching to a halt, but I just knew at that moment, that there was going to be a collision. In the seconds before the crash my thoughts were; *"Oh No!" What have I done?"*

There was a loud bang of metal on metal, as I drove into the car in front of me. Like me, it had braked and hit the car in front of it. As I braced myself, it jolted me forward and my seatbelt locked. Before I had time to react in any way, I instinctively glanced into my rear view mirror. To my horror, I saw a van careering towards the rear of mine at high speed. There was no way that it was going to stop. There was a huge crash as it screeched into the back of mine, crunching my car between it and the car in front of me. Immediately afterwards there were further bangs coming from behind, as other cars collided with one another. I was jolted badly once more after the second collision. Then it all went eerily quiet and still. I sat for several seconds in profound shock. I did not dare to move. Then, my first thoughts were: *"Well, I am alive"* and *"I think I am alright"*. I was still locked into my seatbelt. It had certainly saved me. I felt all around me. I seemed to be still in one piece, and I could feel no pain. Gingerly, I tried to unclip my seatbelt and surprisingly it sprung open. I could see that there was carnage outside and I just wanted to get out there, help out and breathe some fresh air. I had gone into a massive state of shock and I could barely draw my breath, as I went into a state of panic. I was involved in a motorway pile up and I was partly to blame. My mind was awash with all kind of thoughts and dread, about what would happen next and what would happen to me.

While these thoughts were flashing through my mind, I pulled hard at my driver's door handle, but it would not open. It was jammed tight. My car had been tightly squeezed between the car in front and the van at the back. I leant over and pulled at the passenger door, but it would not open either. I then tried to wind down my driver door window and with some difficulty it opened about halfway down. I was very slim in those days, and somehow I managed to lean through the window and slither down the outside of the door and onto the motorway tarmac, where I sat in dazed bewilderment for some several moments.

It was only when I was on the outside, that I could see the full scale of the devastation. As I pulled myself wearily up onto my feet, I was struck with horror as I saw a man, presumably from the van behind, staggering towards me, seemingly covered from head to foot in blood. The *"blood"* was also covering the back of my car, in stark red contrast to the bright Daytona yellow of my Cortina.

He staggered across to me and with great concern he asked me if I was alright. *"I don't think I am injured"* I responded, *"but what about you?"* I was really concerned about his injuries, particularly the *"blood"* all over his head. *"Oh me, I'm ok, it's just a bruise on my forehead, where the paint tin hit my head!"* Suddenly, and with a huge sigh of relief, it all began to sink in; His van sign said: *"Painter and Decorator"!*

When his van smashed into the back of my car, the paint tins in the back of his van flew forward and a tin of red paint had burst open and spilled all over him. When he got out, he leant onto the back of my car and the paint on him went all over what was remaining of my crushed boot area.

Amazingly, despite the carnage of twisted metal from the collision, involving about eight vehicles, nobody seemed to be seriously injured, although several motorists were taken by ambulance to hospital for medical treatment. At that stage I was beginning to feel some pain in my neck and back but I did not want to go to hospital, so I just kept quiet about it and hoped that it would go away.

After the initial shock, and the sheer relief that there were no serious injuries, came the dawning realization of what had happened and the consequences of it all. Within minutes, traffic had tailed back for miles, in both directions. Ambulances had arrived along with several Police vehicles. As I stood quietly, in shock, at the side of the motorway, the seriousness of my situation began to hit home. My car was an undisputed write off. I had only had a brand new company car for less than three hours and I had written it off! Surely, that must have been some kind of perverse record, but not one that I would ever be proud of. Instinctively, I knew that I was to blame for my part in the debacle. If only I had put more space between me and the car in front of me! But, it was all too late. What was done, was done. I was all alone with my thoughts, standing on the hard shoulder of the motorway, shaking with nerves, aching all over my body and waiting to be interviewed by the Police. Eventually, a Police Officer came to me and took my statement. In all honesty I knew that my position was indefensible. I had been too close to the car in front and unable to stop. I had been lulled into a false sense of security and in changing lanes, had not allowed sufficient space to develop between me and the car in front. I really had no defence at all.

I had been cocooned in my bright and shiny new car and I felt indestructible. I asked the officer what would happen to me and he told me that I would probably be charged with driving without due care and attention or dangerous driving.

In all honesty, I was less concerned about a driving conviction. I was far more bothered about what was going to happen to me, when I informed my

new employers about what had happened to their
brand new car. I still had that dubious pleasure to
look forward to.

After what seemed to be an eternity, a breakdown
truck arrived and managed to separate my
crumpled Ford Cortina from the car and van
wedged into the back and front of it. I only needed
to glance at the wreckage to know that it was not
repairable. It was just a crushed wreck of metal,
instead of the lovely new car it had been, just a few
hours earlier. It would shortly be on a tow truck
and on the way to the scrapyard. The tow truck
took my car to a recovery yard where the Insurers
would inspect what was left of the wreckage. They
said that they could take me to a local hotel from
where I could recover a little and make a phone
call, to arrange for somebody to come and collect
me. Of course, this was before the days of
computers and mobile phones, so telephone
contact was not easy. After the car was left at a
recovery yard, I was left at a hotel on the junction
of the M5, and close to the intersection of the M6.

I did not really know who to call, to pick me up.
Fortunately, my friend Gary Duncalf had already
joined the same company as me, but in a different
division. It was Friday evening around 6pm and I
called him. It was a lot to ask of him, but I had a
lot to carry and I could not get a train home. I was
too dazed, shaken and stressed to get public

transport and I badly needed help. Fortunately for me, he understood my predicament and said that he would come and collect me, but that on a Friday evening, it would not be until about 9pm when the weekend rush hours had subsided.

With huge trepidation, I then plucked up courage and phoned Boden. I was secretly hoping that there would be no answer, that they had all gone home and I could just leave a voice message. Just my luck! It was my manager, Alan, that answered the phone. He was just finishing off work, before getting ready to leave the office for the weekend.

"Alan," I said. My cool and positive stance which had been prominent earlier in the day, was now gone and in a shaking, timid and nervous voice all I could think of to say was; *"Alan, I'm afraid that I've been in a bit of a crash"* It was a massive understatement, but I was trying to build up to it slowly, and try to explain what had happened.

Alan was always ultra-positive; *"O.K."* he said, elongating each of the two letters of the OK.

"First of all, are you alright"? I assured him that I was. *"Right, was anyone else injured?"* He sounded genuinely concerned, and I was grateful for that. Again I assured him that nobody had been seriously injured *"OK,"* he continued, *"And how is the car? Can you still drive it home?*

"Err No!" I stammered. *"Alan, it's a write off. I've been involved in a Motorway pile up".* *"But it wasn't your fault was it?* He asked hopefully. *"Not entirely"* I said, hopefully trying to rescue the situation a little. *"What do you mean, Not Entirely?"* *"Well, if someone else had not crashed into the back of my car, then it would not have been written off, but I'm afraid that they did."*

"Steve, were you at fault?" *"Yes Alan, I am being prosecuted for driving without due care and attention".* A silence followed:

"Steve, the last thing I said before you left Bridgewater was, Drive Carefully, remember?" *"Yes, and I'm really sorry Alan."* I don't know what else to say."* I told him that I had arranged with a friend to pick me up and take me home.

"Look Steve, I'm glad that you have not been injured, but I am not happy that you have written off a brand new company car. You haven't even written your first sales order yet and you have cost us a lot of money on your first day. Get the train down to Somerset on Monday, the earliest train you can, and then get a taxi to the office. I will see you in my office at 11am and decide what we are going to do about it."

I had been on a real "high" while driving home before the crash, yet within a matter of a few short hours, I was back to the lowest of "lows". It seemed that life would never run smoothly for me, especially my life after leaving the monastery. There always seemed to be yet another disaster lurking somewhere around the next corner.

Around 9pm Gary arrived at the hotel. I was really grateful to see him, as he had given up his Friday evening to collect me and take me home. I felt such an idiot, after all, it was my fault for not paying attention and keeping a safe distance from the car in front. I was too smitten with being the proud user of such a lovely new car. I had no idea what was going to happen. Would they sack me? I just did not know. I then endured a very nervous and unhappy weekend and waited to face the music with my boss, at 11am on Monday morning.

I was really miserable that weekend at home, knowing that I had made a very poor impression in the first week at my new company. I was without a car and had to get around on public transport. I was concerned about what my boss was going to say and whether I would still have a job at the end of our meeting on Monday. Anyway, it was a thoroughly miserable situation to be in and I barely slept at all that weekend.

I took the earliest train I could on Monday at 6.30am and got off at the Railway Station. I arrived at the offices at 10.30am. I just had time to compose myself and prepare what I was going to say before going into my meeting with the boss at 11 O'clock. Some of my new colleagues came up to me and said they were surprised to see me again so soon. I think they had heard what had happened and they knew that I had been summonsed, but did not want to say anything to me at that stage.

On the stroke of 11am, [I was always on time,] I knocked on the boss's door and when he replied, I marched in. I always believed that attack was the best form of defense, so I breezed in, looking business-like, but not at all cocky. He beckoned me to take a seat and without being invited to speak, I launched into my defensive tirade:

"Alan, I really am sorry about what has happened. I was careless and I was at fault. It's so much worse because it was my first day out, but I suppose it could have happened at any time. I will make it up to you, I promise."

He didn't seem that impressed, and why should he. I think he had already decided to make me suffer and he knew exactly what he was going to say to me. I awaited his response, but I feared the worst.

"Stephen, I am giving you a written warning as to your future behavior, due to your lack of care with company property. It is a serious matter. You are lucky to still have a job. You have not made a great

228

start to your career with us. I strongly recommend
that you get straight back onto the road tomorrow
and start selling some company products."

I assured him that I would be giving it everything
I had, and that I was out to make a good
impression, albeit somewhat belatedly.

"Good!" He said: *"I look forward to seeing the*
orders flooding in. There is a vehicle in the
loading bay for you and the depot manager will
take you to it: "Be more careful this time" he said
in a stilted and emphatic manner. *"You can be sure*
of it" I replied, and I then left with the depot
manager. The entire meeting took all of ten
minutes, if that. It was just short and to the point.

I went to the warehouse area and I had no idea
what type of vehicle I had been allocated. I did not
dare to ask. I was just pleased that I had not been
sacked and that I was back on the job. When I saw
the vehicle I was given, I was certain that this was
their idea of a punishment, because I had trashed
their new company car, albeit accidentally.

The depot Manager took me to a battered old
Vauxhall van. It must have been used as a run
about by anybody and everybody at the depot. It
was white, quite old, very dirty and it smelt. It was
obvious to me that smokers had been driving it and
it stunk to high heaven. I felt that this was all a part

of my punishment for trashing their new car.

"We haven't had time to clean it for you, so you will have to do it yourself when you can." He told me without apology. He was responsible for all company vehicles and likewise, it felt very much like it was a punishment he was handing out.

All I could do was to take it on the chin. I said nothing more, and after checking all the controls, I thanked him rather sheepishly, and went on my way. I had only been there thirty minutes in all.

Back home, I was left in no doubt that my new employer was not too impressed, but at least I still had my job, so I set about making a much better impression. I cleaned and polished the van and took hours over it, so that it gleamed and looked practically new. My new boss was due to work with me on the following Tuesday and when we met, I knew that he would have something to say about the van, if not the car that I had written off on my first day out! We had a good day on the business front and I said nothing at all about the van, but I was really happy when he commented how spick and span it was and how well organized I had made it for the business. All my files and samples were neat and tidy. I think I must have made a decent impression, as when he was leaving he said: *"We won't leave you with this van forever, so let's just see how you get along!"*

I just got on with the job, kept my head down and did my best to make a lasting impression. About a month later I had a message from the Sales Director that I was to return the van that week and that there was a brand new replacement Cortina ready for me. It was not in Daytona Yellow, thank goodness! Perhaps that was a good omen. It had bad memories for me.

Having gotten the Daytona Cortina out of my system, I set to and concentrated on the job in hand. I had given up a really good job at Gillette to join this company and I knew that it was something of a risk. The main body of the company was excellent and they were a big player in thermoplastics. The new division I had joined was another matter, however. Over the weeks and months, I tried my hardest to gain new sales for the Gardening products, but for some reason, it just would not happen. If I had been alone in struggling to make the range a success, I would have been a worried man, but none of my sales colleagues were having a good time either. It seemed that the new product range was not going to be a winner and I could see the writing was on the wall. I decided that it may be easier to "jump" ship, than to receive the "push" that looked to be inevitable. For once, I got it spot on and shortly after I had "jumped" into the arms of another company, I learned that the new sales division at Boden had been withdrawn and the product was discontinued.

231

That was prematurely the end of my tenth job.

My friend and colleague Gary Duncalf, who had kindly driven to my rescue after the car crash, had also worked for Boden in the main company and he had also recently "jumped ship" to join the Multi-National giant, Gillette Industries. He told me that they were recruiting for a salesman in the North West and he even put in a good word for me, which went a long way to helping me land the job. Otherwise, as a result of my suspect jobs record, I may have had difficulty in persuading them to take me on. As it was, I did a really positive interview and was delighted to land the job back in the mainstream business, with a very major company. It was my 2nd. spell with Gillette. I felt honored as I was told that it was company policy not to re-employ people who had left them. They must have made an exception in my case, which made me feel good.

So, it was hello to job No.11 within just six years. Fortunately, the seventies was a good decade for employment in business and there was a big demand for salesforces and good salespeople. I think I was lucky to be in the right place at the right time and it was great to be back with Gillette.

Gillette turned out be the best company that I worked for in my entire career and it was the most challenging, rewarding and enjoyable period of my time in employment. This was to be my second spell with the company, and I have to say that I was delighted to be re-joining such a good organization. With hindsight, it had been a mistake to leave them in the first place and it was good to be back with them.

I quickly realized when I rejoined the company that they were the real deal. They were a large multinational, worldwide company and with big household products in the UK, particularly well known for their shaving products, and not just for the men. They were just my type of company.

I was given the job of territory Manager in the North West of England. It was a very professional set-up with high standards and great expectations from all employees, especially their sales team. *"Sales"* as they said: *"were the lifeblood of any company"*. The company always promoted from within their ranks and after a successful spell as a Territory Manager, I was duly promoted to Key Account Manager. There were many large wholesalers based in the Jewish Quarter of Manchester, close to Strangeways prison. They had a nickname of "The Swags", which was a credit to their success in wholesale business in the City. I even earned myself the nickname of: *"King of The Swags"* as I spent most of my time selling to and managing their accounts.

233

8. Steve right. King of The Swags

9. King Canute Nea

This period was the longest that I had remained in any job so far, and when I was offered yet another promotion, it was positive food for thought. I had done exceptionally well as a Key Account Manager and I had been offered the position of Area Sales Manager, responsible for a team of six sales people and a large area of business in the country. The problem for me was that the new job was in the South West Region of England. It meant that I would have to relocate home to another part of the United Kingdom, that I had never been to before. On the positive side, it was a major promotion, bigger salary, bonuses, a better car and yet I hesitated. There were serious domestic issues I had to consider, that would not make it an easy decision for me. I had a lot of thinking to do.

The difficult decision, was not really a business one. It was all about having to move to another part of the country and all that the move would have entailed. By this time I had family responsibilities and it would have been a huge upheaval to move home to the West Country. It was such a long way from where I lived and I had family and friends to consider. In addition, I had lived away from home and family for such a large portion of my younger life, that I did not fancy moving so far away. I really wanted to stay closer to my roots, and everything I knew.

With this in mind, I decided with my head and not my heart! Wrongly, I accepted the promotion to Area Sales Manager , whilst knowing that I may not be able to see it through to its conclusion. I had not discussed my domestic situation with my employer, but I agreed to take on the promotion, because it was a natural progression for me. It seemed like the right thing to do, but it was to be yet another big mistake.

I was to live in a hotel pending a move to the West Country. I went to stay for an indefinite period in the Crest Hotel at Bristol, where I stayed for several months, working from Monday to Friday, and just going home at weekends. It was far from an ideal solution and it turned out to be untenable.

Up-to that point, everything had been going really well for me at Gillette. I had already had two promotions and I was really enjoying the job and the camaraderie in the company. Until then, I had been single minded and concentrated all my efforts on my work. It was probably fair to say that Gillette, being fairly typical of an American company, wanted to "own" their employees "lock stock and barrel." The company demanded much more than a 9-5 work ethos. It demanded, unofficially, that the employee did exactly what had to be done in order to achieve the targets which had been set? If that meant working ten or twelve hours a day, then that is what had to be done. If that involved working weekends too, then so it would have to be. In all fairness, when it came to remuneration, they could not be faulted. They demanded total commitment, but they also gave a lot to its employees in return.

Against that sort of criteria, I began to have problems. A new General Manager had recently been appointed and he was cracking the whip. His crackdown coincided with a dip in my performance, due to my domestic issues and working away from home, pending a move to the West Country. Working so far from home for so long, was proving to be extremely difficult. I was finding it very hard to concentrate on the work whilst living and working from a hotel in the far south of the country, commuting back and to, from North to South every week. I was spending too much time traveling the country and not dealing sufficiently with the work objectives.

When I was asked to attend a meeting with the new General Manager, I had a bad feeling about it, and inside of me, I could tell what was going to happen. He had decided to re-structure the salesforce and he was going to use the opportunity to make me redundant in the process. He told me that he thought I was not concentrating on my work, but instead of sacking me, he decided that my position was to be made redundant. It was a bad time for me, but it could have been so much worse. The last thing I needed in my predicament, was to have to relocate to the West Country, so by sheer good fortune, this was a blessing in disguise. I needed a fresh start, but in the North West, so that I could get my life back on track again. Sadly, my 11th. Job of work, my 2nd with Gillette, had come to an unhappy end.

It was quite sudden! Once they had made up their mind, everything happened straight away. From being informed that I was surplus to requirements, I was told to empty my desk, leave all my company equipment behind and close the door on the way out. It was as quick and as final as that. I did get to keep the company car for several weeks in line with my contract and that was a big help. After that, I did not let the grass grow under my feet. Being out of work had always been a no-no to me. I would rather do something, anything, rather than nothing, so I set about finding some part time work, while I found another job. I had heard of a temporary part time job going at a local transport company called "Baker Transport" My 12th job of work.

OK! It wasn't rocket science. It was a security job, working nights. It didn't require great intellect, just common sense and keeping awake at nights. Since my monastery days, I always fancied being a man in uniform. Somehow, it gave the wearer a type of authority. I had already had a Nurse's

Uniform at Hope Hospital, a "Prison Officer" type uniform on Merseyside, and a Milkman's white cap and coat. Now I had a very smart navy uniform and peaked cap. I looked very smart indeed.

I was on the security gate of the company and besides checking around the site for security issues, I also had to check the delivery trucks in and out during the night. This was a twenty four hour business and I was kept busy through the dark hours. It was a tough assignment. I started at 7pm and went all the way through until 6am the following day. Not only could it be "brain-drainingly" boring, but it was exceptionally tiring. Of course, I did what I was expected to do and I did it to the best of my ability. Even so, other than checking in and out the occasional lorry, and doing a security check around the premises several times a night, it still left several hours in the dark wee hours of the morning. If I had gone to bed after breakfast each morning, then it may have been tolerable, but I was not the sort to do that. Anyway, there was no way that this work was going to be for months let alone years, so I set about looking for work, a proper job with genuine prospects.

During the nights at quiet times, I would sit and write applications to prospective employers. I really wanted to get back into business management as quickly as possible.

Instead of going to bed, as I rightly should have done, I spent my time searching for a new sales management position and going for interviews, then I would go back to my security work at night.

The job didn't arrive straight away, and I was becoming increasingly frustrated. In truth, I felt like a fish out of water, but at least I was gainfully employed and it brought in additional income.

One particular night I had gone into work feeling particularly tired. I had worked the previous night, then travelled two hundred miles during the following day to an interview and then back home again. I had not had any sleep at all that day or night. I went back into work at 7pm as usual and I did my routine tasks of checking wagons in and out and then I patrolled the premises. I wasn't too bad while I was busy, but around about 11pm, I made the fatal mistake of sitting in my comfy chair in a nice warm office, looking out onto the security barrier. My eyes were heavy, I gazed straight ahead and slowly my eyelids began to close and it was "Goodnight Vienna". It was bound to happen, I dropped off into a deep, deep sleep. I doubt that a herd of galloping Wilder-Beasts crashing through the security barrier would have woken me up that night, so deep was my slumber. I was effectively dead to the world.

Believe it or believe it not, one of the wagons had

arrived during the night, and the driver had seen me asleep. He opened the security gate himself, collected his load and departed, returning momentarily to close the security barrier. I had known absolutely nothing about it.

Fortunately, for my sake, he had left a note on my desk in front of me, telling me what he had done and he had effectively done my job for me. On the other hand he could have come and gone and taken all sort of goods from the depot and I would have known nothing about it. The next time I saw him, I thanked him profusely for not dropping me in it, as it would surely have resulted in my dismissal. I got away with that one, but it did worry my conscience. I made my mind up that I just had to get that new job, and I had to get it quickly. Night-time work was not for me and I was determined to get myself back into mainstream work straight away. I redoubled my efforts, but I slept most of each day from that time onwards.

241

242

Chapter 13

Fifteen minutes of fame

Fortunately for me, my relationship with the Recruitment Consultants was a very close and regular one. I must have been on their Christmas card list, and they on mine. I certainly had plenty of use for their services and I was never off the phone to them or in their office, cajoling them to find me a position. This time, they came up with an interesting opportunity. It was with a business called Spearhead Sales & Marketing. They were a brokerage company, which meant that they provided a salesforce for companies who either did not want, or could not afford, their own sales force. Spearhead were a "salesforce for hire" and at any one time, they represented about eight or ten companies and sold their products. Again, I had no problem in obtaining an interview, and my wide range of experience was responsible for me being offered a job as Regional Sales Manager for the north west of England. I was to commence job No.13 with Spearhead. The company had a varied and diverse product range. They sold cigarettes for the London Tobacco Company and a Turkish government cigarette. The smell and taste was disgusting! In the product range was German larger, French jams, French toast, Ravenhead glassware and much, much more. It was quite a responsibility, one salesforce representing about a dozen or so companies, who were all desperate to gain distribution and sales in the UK Grocery and DIY marketplaces. If we achieved good sales for the tobacco companies, then the lager companies would complain that we were not doing as good a job for them. It was hard to keep all the clients happy all of the time and to show them equal effort and importance, but we tried hard.

I enjoyed my time with Spearhead. They were a London City based company. I needed to travel there frequently to the office, which I would normally do by train, due to their proximity to the main London Railway Stations. On one particular occasion, I went to a sales meeting at the London Head Office. It was very close to Christmas and after the meeting, the entire company gathered together for a pre-Christmas office party. It was to be my "fifteen minutes of fame," yet I did not know it at the time. Our Christmas office party was held at the Royal Garden Hotel in Central London.

After the main festivities, Tom a friend and colleague of mine, decided it was time for him to go home. We had all had far too much to drink, as is the norm office parties, especially at Christmas time. I decided that I would go and say goodbye to him at the front entrance of the hotel. In any case, I really needed some fresh air. Without realizing it, we both still had our party hats on, festive attire and were blowing toy trumpets at anyone who cared to listen. At the front of the hotel, there were crash barriers on the pavement. We did not know it at the time, but Kensington Palace was a stone's throw away, around the corner of the hotel. There were just a few people outside, and I spotted a couple of police officers close by. I thought nothing of it. Then, as I was saying cheerio and Merry Christmas to Tom, a limousine came from around the corner. To my shock, I thought to myself, "I recognize that driver!" It was none other than Prince Charles himself, driving his Ford Granada. They were leaving Kensington Palace for Windsor that night. In the car seat next to him was Princess Diana, head bowed, as was her custom, with baby Prince William and his Nanny in the back seats, accompanied by their royal security guard.

By this time of night, I was somewhat inebriated after heavy partying, so I had lost most of my normal inhibitions. As his car passed by me, just a matter of feet away, I yelled towards his car, somewhat disrespectfully; *"Hello Charlie",* with a drunken slur, waving madly to him, as he drove by me. He seemed not to take offence. In fact he smiled at me, as did Lady Diana. They both seemed really amused, and waved back to me, albeit with much more decorum than I had shown. The difference was that they were stone cold sober and I was ever so slightly inebriated.

10. Prince Charles, driver, with Princess Diana, waves to Steve, with Fez, on the pavement.

Excitedly, I said farewell to Tom, and went back inside the hotel to tell all my colleagues what I had witnessed and what they had missed. It had been quite an experience, and as a genuine fan of the royal family, I had probably got as close to any of the Royal family, as I was ever likely to.

That night, I stayed at the Royal Garden Hotel and was heading to Euston Station to get the train back home to Manchester the next morning. We had enjoyed a terrific Christmas Party, and I was still feeling the after affects in terms of tiredness and one almighty hangover. I was barely awake, as I went for the train and was feeling queasy and not at all well. I dashed to get an early train. It was only 8.30am on December 24th. It was of course Christmas Eve. I was already excited about going home for Christmas and I wanted to get there early. As I went for my train, I thought to myself that I would try to have a sleep on the journey and catch up on lost slumber from the wild party the night before. As I passed the W.H. Smith shop at the station, I decided to buy a newspaper. It would give me something to read and to pass the time on the two and a half hour train journey. Work was now finished until 2nd January, so a relaxing read of the paper on the journey home, was just what the doctor ordered. I bought a Daily Mail, unusual for me, as I nearly always bought the Daily Express. It was the headline that had tempted me to buy it: **"MP warns the Queen"**, it blurted out: The article was about the Queen backing the Falklands War in her Christmas broadcast. It was fortuitous, as it turned out, as The Daily Mail on that day, was to give me my "fifteen minutes of fame"! I sat back comfortably in my seat, sipping from a mug of British Rail coffee and munching on a sticky bun. I read right through the front cover of the paper. On turning over the page, to page three, I was shocked! Staring back at me from the paper, was a Christmas story and a page of festive items. The Mail's banner headline blurted out:

"There is more than one way of saying it:"

"A Merry Christmas! Party revelers wave Charles, Diana and Prince William off to Windsor." Said the Mail article. It continued;
"They were saying it with party hats and toy trumpets to the Prince and Princess of Wales yesterday: **"Merry Christmas!"** The royal couple, with Prince William and his nanny in the back of their Ford Granada, were leaving Kensington Palace for Windsor. Suddenly revelers from an office party at the nearby Royal Garden Hotel, spotted Charles at the wheel. With a loud toot and raucous waves, they greeted the smiling Prince and his family."

Then, a picture of Charles and Diana caught my attention. Charles was smiling out of the window of his car and waving to someone. There were two revelers, both sporting Christmas party hats and blowing toy trumpets, whilst waving wildly at the Royal Couple. "Wait a minute!" I thought to myself; that reveler looks just like me. I looked again and yes **it was me!** with Tom stood next to me, waving like a wild banshee! I could not believe it. I was in a main feature of the Daily Mail on Christmas Eve. The man sat opposite me on the train was also reading The Mail, and had just turned the front page. He was also reading page three. I couldn't help myself: *"That's me!!"* I said to him: *"I beg your pardon"* he retorted: *"That's me, waving to Price Charles in the photo. I had no idea there was a photographer there!"* He glanced

11. Daily Mail article. Party Revelers. Xmas Eve 1982.

at the paper for some moments and then looked closely at me, scrutinizing my facial features. Of course, I was shorn of my party Fez and Christmas trumpet, but he could still see the likeness. *"Well,*

well" he said with a loud chuckle. *"What's all that about?"* I told him the story and he was really amused. I had not seen any newspaper reporter or photographer at the hotel, as I had gone outside, so I was amazed to see the picture and story as a main feature in the Daily Mail. In fact, I did not know at the time, but it was also in two other national daily newspapers that fateful Christmas Eve.

As I snoozed on the train home, I could barely wait to get home and tell my family and my work colleagues what had happened the night before. Mobile phones had not reached the masses in those days, until the mid to late eighties. As soon as I reached home, my wife had already heard the news. I was a minor newspaper celebrity and this was to be my fifteen minutes of fame! My boss and several colleagues had already telephoned home to tell me that my antics had made a main feature in the National papers. It was as well that I had been behaving myself, inebriation excepted!

The New Year began and it was back to the serious business of work. Spearhead was a young and thrusting company and I really enjoyed my short time there. I never seemed to stay anywhere too long. It seemed to be part and parcel of my make up to come in, make my mark, and then move on. I started late and needed to catch up quickly. On this occasion, I was really enjoying my time with the company, despite one particular negative. We were salespeople for two cigarette companies, and just about everybody in the company was a smoker. I detested smoking. It was mainly the smell and the stench it left on my clothes that I hated. If I was with a colleague in his car, often he would smoke all day, especially as there were free rations and plenty of them. It had an effect on my health as it permeated my clothes and my nostrils, causing me to have a bad chest. I was already suffering from bad respiratory problems.

I recall one particular occasion when I traveled by train to London and I had exactly the same problem in the smoke filled carriages during the three hour journey. Then I went to our London Headquarters for an all-day sales meeting. There were ten people in the meeting and nine of the ten in the group smoked. I was the only one who did not have the tobacco habit. This was not quite the truth. I was very much a passive smoker! The entire room was filled with used smoke and I had breathed in their poison all day. On the train home, it was again the same. When I arrived home, my chest was wheezing, and I stank to high heaven of stale tobacco smoke. The moment I arrived, late that night, my wife said: *"Get those stinking clothes off, all of them and get in the bath."* The 2nd hand smoke had permeated all of my clothing, my body and all my belongings. They were washed and put outside to dry and freshen up. This was just a temporary solution, as I knew that the same thing would happen again the next day, and the next, infinitum!

I think that it was that night, when I had cleaned myself up and decongested my nose and throat, that I decided, with regret, that I could not continue much longer in that job. It was ruining my health. I was not going to put it at risk any longer. I decided there and then, that I would start looking for a job that was less damaging to my wellbeing!

Being Elvis

It was around about that time, that there was an unrelated worldwide event that would eventually have a major effect on my life.

It was 16th. August in 1977, a day that is now etched on the lives of all Elvis Presley fans all over the world. It was the day that Elvis Presley died, the day that the world lost The King of Rock and Roll. I remember driving to my meeting that fateful morning, when the news broke on the car radio. When I first heard the news, I could not take it all in. It had such a huge effect on me, that I can still remember exactly where I was, when the news broke. I was so shocked that I had to pull over on the side of the A560 in Stockport and take stock of what I had just heard. It may have seemed a strange, even an over-the top reaction, because at that stage of my life, I was not an Elvis Presley fan. Like a huge number of people, I enjoyed his music, but I did not realize at that moment in time, just how much I would come to love his music and the man himself, over the decades to come.

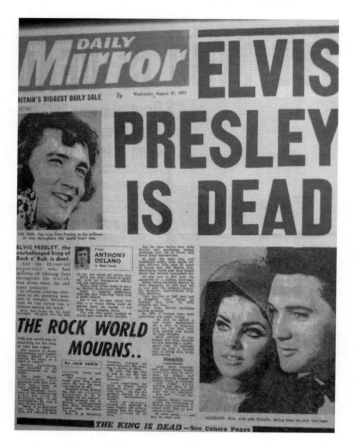

12. Elvis is Dead. Daily Mirror August 17th, 1977

From that fateful day onwards, I became, day by day, a massive fan of The King of Rock & Roll, to such an extent that I began to sing his music and take a huge interest in his life and everything associated with him. The shock of his untimely death influenced me to such an extent, that one day, many years later, I would ultimately become an Elvis Tribute Artist, albeit an amateur performer, not a professional singer.

As a young person, the nearest I would become to be a singer, was performing with the Church choir, in my red and white robes, whilst in the junior seminary at Erdington Abbey. I had a reasonably decent voice for singing in a choir, but I was only among the chorus and not one of the main solo tenors! There was never any inclination at that time, that one day I would become a solo performer and indeed, impersonate the late, great Elvis Presley himself.

Years, and even decades passed by, concentrating on my daily life and work, before, in the twilight of my life, I would eventually become an Elvis performer, albeit, not to earn income, not as a job, but just for the fun of it, or to raise money for charities, and good causes.

Back in the real world, the tough world of business had to be negotiated and there would be no time for such fanciful distractions. My mind had been made up by the constant smoking of my Spearhead colleagues. I was going, with some regret, to start looking around for yet another job.

My previous boss and colleague, Bob, who I had worked with at Gillette had recently moved to another Company based in South Manchester.

Holt Lloyd was a large U.K. manufacturer of automotive accessories. He was the Sales Manager at that time. Fortunately, we had kept in touch and when he wanted a Sales Manager, he called on me. He knew that I had been released by Gillette before joining Spearhead. Fortunately he had not taken my career at face value, otherwise he may never have offered me the job, but he had known me from my time at Gillette and he knew what I was capable of doing. Bob always liked to surround himself with his own people, people that he knew and he could trust. Fortunately, I fell into that category and I was soon underway with my eleventh job of work.

255

Chapter 14

Back with the Big Boys

After my most recent stint working with smaller companies, I was really pleased to be back with the "big boys" the large multi-national companies.

My 14th.job was to be the National Account Controller at Holt Lloyd. I was to manage a portfolio of the company's most important accounts all over the U.K, which was quite a challenge and responsibility. After losing my job at Gillette, I needed a quick pick me up and when Bob came knocking at my door, I was only too delighted to join him. We nearly always worked really well together. It was like Brian Clough and Peter Taylor, Sherlock Holmes and Watson. He was always number 1, and I was always No.2, yet it worked well for us. I was back in the big time and back on the road to being a success.

Holt-Lloyd was an entirely different type of company, similar to Gillette in its ambition and terrific product range, but it was an English Company with English ways and it operated in a much different way to Gillette, with its American methods of business. Bob however had worked for both companies and as Sales Manager he managed his sales team in his own unique style with peculiarities and similarities of both companies.

Bob was a larger than life character. He had a great sense of humour, was easy to approach and with a real sense of mischief. He could be a great boss to work for, well, sometimes, but when it suited him he could be really difficult to work for too! As with life at Gillette, Holt-Lloyd wanted to "own" their employees, in so far as they were giving a first class remuneration package, but in return they demanded their pound of flesh and more. Bob epitomized that work ethic, even more so. He encouraged our work to be our social life too. We worked hard and played hard, but, work was work, play was play and although he could be a friendly, life and soul of the party, type of boss, the next day at work, he could be a cold, ruthless tyrant and the camaraderie of the night before would be a forgotten moment of the past. Talk about a love – hate relationship! He could be a great friend, a terrific boss, and then in the next instant, he could act like Attila the Hun!

I had been continuing to work for many months, whilst suffering excruciating back pain, due to a serious medical condition. I had crushed vertebrae in my lower spine. This medical condition was making it exceptionally difficult for me to drive and to work. I was finding it extremely hard to do my job, as well as I needed to. Driving was really painful and it was a big part of my job. I needed to travel to all parts of the UK, often spending up to eight hours a day in the car, either side of keeping my sales appointments. There were times when I would just need to drive home and lie down flat. There was little relief from my lower back pain. While trying to cope with this, I was feeling huge pressure of work, due to a massive workload, big objectives and a very demanding boss.

Eventually, the persistent pain won the day and I had to succumb to my back problem. I had two crumbling lumber discs and they needed urgent medical attention. It was close to Christmas and I was still working on 22nd December, but when I arrived home late, after an early start and a long drive to London, I just lay on the floor all evening and was in tears, due to the pain and frustration of the condition, which was becoming worse by the day. The orthopedic specialist came to see me at home and when he saw the condition I was in, he asked me if I wanted to go into Hospital on Christmas Eve. Who would even consider being admitted to Hospital on Christmas Eve, and miss Christmas, if they were not in a seriously bad condition?

The next day I did not go into work. It was the first time I had taken a day off work ill, since I had started the job. I never missed a day's work unless I was out on my feet and unable to function. I telephoned Bob who was not best pleased, because we had an important client meeting that day, but at least he said he understood, although I don't think that he did. Reluctantly, I took the specialist's advice and prepared to go into hospital later that day. My wife took me to Hospital as agreed and I was immediately put on traction for several days. Unfortunately, there was no improvement in my condition and Christmas Day was spent strapped up on traction and eating "synthetic" NHS Turkey and "Rubbery" Christmas pudding.

On Boxing Day my back was operated on and despite particularly invasive surgery, I could not feel any improvement and the level of pain was just about the same as before. The specialist decided that yet more surgery was the answer and this was carried out on New Year's Eve.

Come 3rd January, I was starting to feel that the 2nd operation may have done the trick and I was on the long road to recovery. I was aware that the 3rd January was a notable day, because it was in my diary, as the day I was to return to work, after the Christmas holiday. However, I had spent the entire Festive period laid up in hospital. I had had no contact from work, but Bob telephoned the Hospital that day and we spoke. I had to tell him that I had just had my 2nd operation a few days earlier and that it would be some time before I was fit enough to return to work and able to drive.

Bob said all the right things, and wished me a speedy recovery, but I could feel that his main concern was the job that had to be done at Holts and I was not available to do my work. I was feeling under pressure to return to my job, even though I was still very ill in Hospital.

It was to be another two weeks before I was discharged from Hospital and then I needed to recover at home for a few more weeks before I could even be considered for a return to work. In the meantime, I think my boss Bob, must have been missing me, because he asked me if I could do some paperwork from home, as I was still unfit to drive. In these pre-computer days, it was very difficult to do anything meaningful, but at least it was keeping me in touch with the business. Eventually the day came when I felt fit enough to return to work. It was about eight weeks since I had been laid up and I was pleased to be back in "harness," at long last. I went into the office early and had a meeting with the boss. I told Bob that I was really pleased to be back and I was looking forward to getting back to work.

Bob did not exactly welcome me back with open arms. Instead he said:

"Steve, things have changed since you've been away. Your job had to done by someone while you were off, and Mike has stepped up to the breach

*and has taken over what you would have been
doing. He's been doing a brilliant job. You've
really got your work cut out, to get your authority
back and to get your job back!"*

I was taken aback! I had just recovered from a
serious back operation and had come back to work
as soon as I was able, but it felt as if Bob was
punishing me for being ill in Hospital. He had
made it clear that I would not be able to ease
myself back into my job. Instead, I would have to
work like a Trojan in order to re-establish my
position and my authority in the company. But that
was how Bob managed the business.

Although he could be a tough task master, we were
still good friends, but I was soon to learn that work
was for business, and social life was for friendship.
Ne'er the twain shall meet! I was under no
illusions that this was life working for Bob.
Needless to say, I buckled down to the job in hand,
wrestled back my National Account Controller job
from the young 'Pretender' and before long,
normal service had been resumed.

Business in the seventies was not quite as PC as it
is today and relationships between suppliers and
customers were built not only in the place of work,
but also in the areas of corporate entertaining. As
suppliers, we worked very closely with our key
customers and spent a lot of time with these major

accounts. This relationship was extended into the social arena and on occasions we would invite customers to corporate social functions. There was no additional business agenda to these corporate events, but naturally, a good working relationship and trust could be built on such occasions and this was bound to help to cement the business relationship we had with our key clients. Corporate events such as the Henley Regatta and Horse Racing at Chester were always popular functions and a very pleasant way to go to work! It was certainly more enjoyable than lengthy business meetings and although business would naturally be discussed during the events, it was more about building relationships with the key personnel of our major business partners.

One such example of this was a day out with the main buying team of one of our major High Street retailers. We had a £6 million pounds per year business with this client and so they were very important to our company. It was a very effective way to mix business with pleasure and to talk about work, while having an enjoyable day out.

On this occasion, the corporate hospitality was rather different to the big corporate events such as Henley Regatta. We had chosen a popular business event particularly with the younger type of client and most of the people involved, men and women, were in the "thirty-something" age bracket. It was just as well, because the activity involved was the ever popular "Paintball"

This was an interactive sport or game, which is competitive, and requires a decent level of fitness. For those who are unfamiliar with "Paintball", it is basically a War Game, featuring two Armies attempting to "kill" the enemy and reach the target from their respective base camps. Fortunately, the participants who were only using a paint gun, which resembled a Kalashnikov rifle, were only using a paintball bullet rather than the real thing!

The objective was to shoot the enemy and if the paintball "splattered" onto their combat suit or any part of their body, then the victim was "dead" and had to retire from the action. The team that reached their target camp first was the winner.

In theory, Paintball was a terrific activity, good fun and enjoyable. It was great to dress up in combat uniforms, especially for the boys, and to fire paint guns at human targets. It took place in a wooded area and it felt just like the real thing. It was a very enjoyable but nerve-wracking activity.

The problem with the choice of Paintball as a corporate event, was that it was a competition, and a competition to the death at that, even if it was with "pretend" guns. Both sets of team members, from our Sales team to their Buying team, were highly competitive young professionals, fighting for their company, to be the victor. The nature of this type of professional is to win, and to win at almost any cost. This was not a good idea. It was not the kind of social activity we should have arranged with such an important client. The combat became so competitive that no-one wanted to be shot, and therefore to be out of the game. During the action, members of both teams were shot and had paint all over their uniforms, but hastily wiped it off and refused to admit being shot. There were accusations of cheating, flying around and far from this being a fun event with our biggest client, it was in danger of getting out of hand, with personal insults being hurled about by members of both sides.

Fortunately, our new Sales Director was a very calm and much less competitive character. He could see what was happening and could feel that the atmosphere had changed from a fun day out, to a highly charged and not very pleasant battle to be the victors. It was just as well that the event came to a halt at half time for lunch. He took the opportunity to pull all our team together and despite his normally calm and laid-back demeanor, he laid into us with such vigour, that we were left in no doubt about how we had to behave in the second half: In a raised voice, which was most unusual for him, he was shouting: *"Do you realize that you are in danger of alienating or*

*losing our biggest customer? This Paintball is
meant to be a friendly bit of fun and instead you
are turning it into a war of attrition! Well, this
stops right now! I don't care if we win or lose, but
you will behave in a civil and friendly manner,
even if they don't! We are here to entertain them,
and if that means that they win, then they must win.
Do I make myself clear?"*

It seemed as if the competitive nature of the people
in both companies had allowed the entertainment
to get out of hand, almost out of control, and far
from fostering a close relationship, it may well
have done exactly the opposite. In the process we
may have lost our company a massive £6 million
pounds customer.

Needless to say, the second half was a totally
different ball game. I had never seen so many
"home" soldiers lie down and die after being shot
and the customer's team won the event at a canter
in the second half, going home victorious and
winning the Paintball trophy. A lesson was learned
that day. Sport is sport, but business is business,
especially if it meant letting the customer's team
win. As hosts, it was after all, the courteous and
decent thing to do.

A similar socio-business function was held
between our companies some six months later.
This time, the inter-company challenge was their

266

choice and they challenged us to a football match. As the hosts, we selected a match at the ground of Oldham Athletic F.C. At that time, Oldham Football Club were just one of two major clubs that played on Astro-Turf, so during the winter there was no chance of the match being called off due to bad weather. The challenge was rather one-sided, in that the customer played regularly in a league, whereas we just managed to cobble together eleven players from all parts of the company, who barely played football at all. Even so, we would of course have given it our very best shot, and hoped for a win. However, our sales director who was due to play, was barely a player at all, and again he made it very clear that our objective was to keep our customer happy and if that meant losing, then so be it! As it turned out, it was still a feisty affair with plenty of flying boots, more than the odd swear-word, and some bad tempered complaints to the referee. The fact that our opponents ran out 5-1 winners, made it academic, and there were handshakes all round at the end of an enjoyable match. Oh well!

Holt Lloyd was a great place to work. Not perhaps to the same extent as during my spells with Gillette. The two companies worked in very different ways. Gillette was the big, brash American company with a work ethic to match. Holt Lloyd were every bit as professional, but in a very much more English sort of way. Both

267

companies were very inclusive of employees families, particularly on the management side. Holt Lloyd however, were much stuffier in their approach to management, than their American counterpart. Management were more clearly on a different social level to their other workers, whereas Gillette would have allowed all levels of employee to mix and socialize together.

At one particular business function at Holts, my new partner was introduced to the Sales Director. He would normally shake the man's hand, and would then plant a kiss on the cheek of the manager's wife. As my partner shook hands with him, he pointedly said, with something resembling a smirk; *"I won't kiss you today, as you are not yet married to Steve!"*

It was said with something resembling a smile, but he was clearly making a point. He knew we were not married at that time, and the company liked all their management to conform to the norm, i.e. marriage. In due course, we did marry, and at the next official function, my wife who is not normally a vindictive person, was introduced to my Sales Director. On this occasion she could not resist getting her own back. She flashed her wedding ring in front of him and said with a disarming smile: *"You can kiss me this time, we are now married"* I said nothing, but smiled and thought to myself; *"Touché!"* Well said.

In those days of the mid 1980's, political correctness was nowhere as keen as it is these days and business was carried out in a far friendlier and less formal manner. People dealt with people, rather than companies with companies, and business relationships were forged by personal associations.

With this in mind, our company were the sponsors of a major nationwide golf tournament, the final of which was held at the world renowned Gleneagles Hotel and Golf Club. It was a major company function, with key customers hoping to play in and win the Holt Lloyd Golf Tournament. To show the stature of the tournament, dignitaries such as Mr. Dennis Thatcher, and footballer Jackie Charlton were playing in the golf tournament and the famous entertainer, Mr. Roy Castle, was one of the main entertainers after the evening meal.

It was at the evening entertainment in the restaurant, that I could so easily have made a fool of myself. As I referred to earlier, I became an Elvis Presley fan, from the day of his sudden death in 1977. From that time onwards, I started singing, after a fashion. My singing came about because one day, whilst out shopping in Wilmslow, I called into an electrical shop which was proudly selling a new-fangled gadget called a "Karaoke" machine. Remember, this was in the days before Karaoke was even heard of by most. The store sold it as a new machine that plays music backing tracks and the person sings along to it, by reading the words from pre-printed sheets. It was revolutionary at the time, and the store assured me that they were just about the first shop in the UK to have sold these new Karaoke machines. The backing tracks were taped recordings of well-known music. Things have certainly moved on since those early days.

Although the machines were expensive at the time, I just had to have one, and so I bought one of the Karaoke machines. At first, there was a very limited range of music and most of the backing tracks were fairly traditional songs such as Frank Sinatra and other such classics. I used to practice occasionally at home and it felt just like being a real singer. In addition, Sinatra songs were relatively easy to sing and not too demanding. At that time, I did not know anybody else who owned a Karaoke machine. We would often have people round to our house and have a Karaoke singing party. It was quite a novelty. My boss, Bob was one of the friends who had been to our home at one such house party and had belted out a song or two.

In the evening session, after the day's play at the Gleneagles Golf Tournament, there was professional entertainment after dinner, featuring the fantastic Mr. Roy Castle. The following night, there was a splendid meal for the hundreds of guests. There was a five piece band playing sedate dance music, which was pleasant enough, but Bob, my boss had other ideas to liven things up a little.

Bob sidled up-to me at our dinner table and said: *"Hey Steve, are you going to give us a song? "Absolutely not"*, I retorted; *"It's one thing singing at home with friends, and anyway, I've had a skin-full of wine already." "You'll be fine"*, said Bob, as he walked away smiling, in the general direction of the band. My blood ran cold and panic rushed through my veins. Surely he wouldn't do it? But I knew Bob! I saw him speak to the band leader and then walk away and back to his table. He had always been a prankster and I feared the worst! I would not be disappointed!

Was he having me on? I felt sure that he was. Nothing happened for a few minutes and I started to breathe a sigh of relief and relax back into my seat. I had only ever sung in the choir, while I was at the monastery, and I had never sung solo, except within the safe confines of my own home. Just as I was feeling calm again, the band leader strode up-to the microphone and announced:

"Ladies and Gentlemen, we have a special treat for you tonight. In the audience we have a semi-professional Night Club singer from the Northern Club circuit. May I introduce to you Mr. Steve Nearey, who is going to entertain you! Come on up Steve!"

271

I froze stiffly into my seat, with a feeling something betwixt terror and panic. This was just not me. I did not dare to do it. As I sat there, transfixed, the audience began clapping and whooping and the band leader again called; *"Ladies and Gentlemen, let's hear it for Mr. Steve Neareeeeeeeeeeeeeeey!"*

With everybody urging me on, and baying, I stood up so slowly, that it seemed to take an age for me to reach the stage. In the leaden walk across the dance floor, the dread was coursing through my mind as I wondered just what I would do when I eventually arrived at the stage area. Before I knew it, I was there and the band master said to me quietly: *"What are you going to sing Steve?"* I thought I had better try to explain to him that it was all a prank by Bob and that I was really not a singer at all. That is exactly what I did.

The Band leader said to me: *"Well Steve, you've got two choices; you can either go and sit down and look foolish, or you can try your luck up here"* I did not answer him. He thrust a microphone into my hand and I just said: *"Strangers in the Night"* by Frank Sinatra. *"OK."* He said: *"What key do you sing in?"* *"Key!!"* I replied, with a puzzled look. *"Key!!"* I don't know anything about keys, I only ever sing in my bath!" *"Just give me a note and the band will follow you"*, he said: I let out a sound which went something like *"aghhhh"* and

272

the band leader told his musicians, *"play the song in the key of "F""*

At that, before the music started up, I summonsed up something akin to Dutch courage, from deep down inside of me and with the microphone in my trembling hand, I faced the audience full on;

"Ladies and Gentlemen, before I start, I would just like to throttle Bob for sending me up here. Just for the record, I am not a Night Club singer, and this is the first time I have EVER sung in public.".

At that, summonsing all the bravado I could muster, I turned to the band, just like a true pro, I nodded for them to play. The music struck up with the introduction and I went straight into the song, giving it everything I had. At home I had practiced the moves and gestures and I made it sound and look as close to Sinatra as I possibly could. After the first few bars, the audience broke into applause and that gave me extra confidence. At the end of the song there was loud cheering and clapping and before I could make my escape to the safe haven that was my chair, the band master asked if they wanted more. *"Oh no!"* I thought to myself. I just wanted to get back to the safety of my seat next to my wife. Not a chance! The noise from the crowd meant that I had no choice but to sing another song. At first, my mind went a complete blank. I couldn't even think of another single Frank Sinatra song. This was a long time before my Elvis singing had arrived on the scene. I asked the band what Sinatra songs they could play. *"San Francisco"* came the reply. *"OK" Play it!* I hastily agreed.

I sang *"San Francisco"* and, just like *"Strangers in the Night"* it went down a storm. I couldn't believe it! The audience must have been drink-fueled! As soon as it finished, I thanked the band and the audience and made a speedy exit, shaking my fist and glowering at Bob, my boss, as I dived for cover. As I sped across the dance floor, a mouse scurried across the floor directly in front of me, causing me to sidestep it, so as not to tread on it. The question was? *"What was a mouse doing scurrying across the dance floor of a five-star hotel?"* But, that was another matter, and what an eventful evening, but thankfully, it was all over.

I arrived back at my table, took my seat and in about five seconds flat, I downed a large glass of red wine that someone had very kindly put in front of me. It was a welcome relief.

Moments later, my boss Bob, marched over and said: *"I knew you could do it!"* Shame you don't do your job as well as that! That was Bob all over! Five minutes later, our Sales Director sidled across to the microphone to give his end of evening speech and in front of everybody he said: *"Nearey! Well Done! You've managed to turn the world-renowned Gleneagles Hotel, into a ruddy working men's club!*

It was though, a good company to work for. It was a case of work hard, very hard, but also play just as hard. Just like at Gillette, the company practically wanted to *"own"* its management team. In return, the rewards were good and it felt very gratifying to be part of a close knit and committed management. Even so, life at Holts was lived very close to the edge. It was all about achieving tough targets, which were the be all and end all. Objectives had to be met, otherwise people did not stay in their jobs too long. That was the reality of life at the sharp end.

The manner in which the sales team was run had changed significantly when our Sales Manager, Bob, decided that he wanted to move onto pastures new. He was ambitious and it seemed that progress at the company was going to be slow because his next promotion was being barred by a very professional Sales Director. Bob was a man in a hurry and had decided to move to a smaller but growing young company in St. Anne's on Sea. It was a European company trying to get a foothold of business in the U.K. market. Tiger Plastics was a P.V.C. manufacturer, marketing bathroom and household products. Bob had accepted the job of Managing Director, which was a major career step for him, albeit with a lesser known company.

As always with Bob, he was that type of person who always liked to surround himself with his own people. He had already taken me from Gillette to Holt Lloyd, and now that he had moved to Tiger Plastics, he wanted his key team to be made up of people that he knew and trusted, his own personal team. I must admit that I did not expect to get the call, but when it came, I had no hesitation in making the decision. It was a no brainer! Since Bob had left, a lot of the buzz had gone from the previously vibrant team we had at Holts.

I received the phone call at 11pm on a Saturday night. Bob never did anything the conventional way. He would never dream of calling in office hours between Monday and Friday. Calling at 11pm Saturday night, I knew it must be important. Not necessarily though. I recall one occasion when I was on holiday in Turkey and Bob tracked me down to a small hotel in Bodrum, just to ask me where a particular piece of paper had been filed. Nothing trivial then!

When he made that late-night call to me, he painted such an idyllic picture of what life at Tiger Plastics was going to be like, that there was absolutely no way I could turn down the offer to join him. There was a decent increase in salary and my job title would be "Commercial Manager," yet another step up from being National Account Controller. And so, it was going to be a case of

Job No.15 Tiger Plastics, here I come!

It was good to be re-united with Bob again. I knew
for certain that life would never be dull with Bob
at the helm. It was a step up for both of us. Bob
was an M.D. for the first time, and I was
continuing my steady, if unspectacular climb up
the promotional ladder. It was a big step up for me
after the disasters of my earlier career.

It was a fair old drive every day to the Tiger
Plastics offices in St. Anne's on Sea, close to
Blackpool. I knew for sure that it was going to
entail long hours and plenty of pressure in the new
job. I was up and about at 6am every morning and
I would leave home at 7am in order to miss the
heavy rush hour traffic to St. Anne's. It was a good
hour's drive and that was without any holdups, so
I would normally get to the office by 8am latest.
Bob was always in the office before me even then,
but as he only had a 15 minute drive from North
Blackpool, it was hardly that difficult. After a
day's work in the office, there was no point in
leaving until after 6pm, as the rush hour traffic was
just too heavy. I would usually leave about 6.30
pm and have a trouble-free drive back to
Warrington, usually reaching home around
7.30pm. Life at Tiger Plastics was brilliant to start
with. The company was vibrant and thrusting. The
new sales and marketing team and Bob's
enthusiastic leadership, led us all to believe that it

was going to be an unrivaled success. It was a new product range to the U.K. and at first, the signs of success were clearly there to be seen. We even had a real live Tiger in the office to do a promotional photo shoot. OK, so it was just a few month's old baby Tiger, but it was still a real Tiger!

13. Steve with Tiger – at Tiger Plastic

We were trying extremely hard to gain distribution and sales throughout the U.K, but after a year of trying, the breakthrough with the major accounts would not come. The product was a range of plastic bathroom household products. It was a decent range, but it was very similar to branded products of better quality, which were long established in the key DIY, Kitchen & Bathroom chain stores. There was no room for a similar one.

Unfortunately, the product range had few if any unique selling points. As such, it was difficult to achieve the major inroads we needed into the UK market. It started to become difficult and eventually the pressure came down on us from the client manufacturer, who demanded to see sales. The newly built warehouse, which had been constructed on the strength of the anticipated sales, was full to the brim of stock and it was selling out very slowly indeed. The warning signs were ominous. After twelve months of "flogging a dead horse", the day of reckoning was about to arrive. Despite the best efforts of Bob, me and the sales team, it was beginning to fail and heads were about to roll. The question was? "Whose Head"?

Just some nine months earlier, when the prospects were looking much rosier, I had been promoted to the position of Sales Director. It was my first directorship and I was duly proud of it, but, unbeknown to me, it was the start of a slippery slope.

Despite a major effort by all the sales team, the orders did not come in volume, and I could see what was about to happen, as I was head of sales. I was called into a meeting with Bob and the Financial Director. My redundancy letter was already printed out and was on Bob's desk already signed. I think the expression is: *"fait-accomplit,"* as they say in French. I was told that due to the precarious sales position and the size of the potential trading losses, that substantial cost savings had to me made. I was to be the sacrificial lamb. It was understandable. I was head of sales, the most expensive employee after the MD and he would now have to cope with my position as well as his own. At least I was not directly blamed for the poor sales position, although I took the chop!

I could see the letter, already signed, in front of Bob on his desk. After being told the bad news, I said, "I suppose there is no point in discussing this?" He looked at me with a sympathetic half-smile and just handed me the redundancy letter which he had already signed and he told me that it was all done and dusted. He tried to soften the blow by detailing the generous terms of my redundancy package. We had previously been good friends and I think he found it difficult to make me redundant.

Fortunately, but also quite astutely, I had previously negotiated a rolling six-month contract which would cushion the blow, if I was ever made redundant. This was to give me sufficient time to find another job after I was released.

My redundancy was effective immediately. I cleared my desk, returned all my company property and that was that. I did manage to keep my company car for up to six weeks, as it was a part of my redundancy package.

Unbelievably, I found another excellent job within just a few short weeks. Sadly, job number 15 had come to a speedy and abrupt end but Job No.16 was there and waiting for me in the wings.

281

Chapter 15

Last of the Multi-Nationals

So there I was back on the jobs market once more! I had worked for several multi-national companies recently, albeit not for very long. Names like Nestle, Gillette Industries, Borden and Holt Lloyd were all massive organizations in their particular fields. Yet my part in each, had only been that of a cameo, as I had moved on rather too quickly for my liking. On some occasions, it had been at my discretion, and other times at the company's behest.

Having been made redundant by Tiger Plastics [Coram UK], by their corporate name, my generous severance package had afforded me the time and financial ability to quietly re-assess my situation, without panicking about having no money to live on. I was ready to take weeks, even months if necessary, to find exactly the right job for me. Luckily a job landed in my lap within days, and it seemed to be just what I was looking for.

My considered decision, was that I was no longer going to court the big multi-national companies, to ply my trade as a business manager. I constantly found myself to be No.2 rather than No.1. It was similar to my very young days when I most

definitely suffered from what they call 2nd child
syndrome. It was a type of inferiority complex,
and I had lived with it throughout my childhood,
and into the first few years of my business career.
I felt that I could do so much more and that I was
not achieving my potential. My plan was to stick
with the age old adage of:

"Being a big fish in a small pond!"

A friend of mine had told me about a job that was
on offer in the "Car Mat" trade. The Company was
"Contour Car Mats" a new division of Caravelle,
a UK company, based in rural Hampshire. I was
already very familiar with the car accessory
market due to my time at Holt Lloyd, so I had a
head start due to having many contacts in the trade.
I landed the job as General Sales Manager in
August 1990. Once more, the market and new
product range sounded good. I was ready to start
my 16th job, this time with Contour Car Mats.

During the first few months with Contour Car
Mats, I must have traveled in the region of 4,000
miles a month. I was living in Warrington, the
Company was in Hampshire and I was traveling
all over the UK. I was selling to new and existing
customers, in order to get the new range of
Contour Carpets "off the ground". Perhaps with
the benefit of hindsight, carpets, "on the ground"
may have been better!" I was barely at home

during this time, but for some reason, although the new range was selling well, there were other dark factors at work affecting the company. The 90's recession had taken such a heavy toll on the company, its cash and its markets. It looked as if the company was in serious trouble. I started soul searching. As General Sales Manager, it was down to me to achieve the sales objectives, but I could not carry the entire burden. There were other factors hovering ominously in the background. On my visits to the office, there was a general feeling and ground-swell, that all was not well! There were whispered conversations, that I was not a party to. Slowly but surely, it began to dawn on me that the company was in deep trouble and even a big order book, would not get it out of the mire.

In little over a year, my decision to go to a smaller company was proven to be an erroneous one. The original Caravelle Company had been a thriving manufacturing company, owned by a Mr. Tony Bedford, a local entrepreneur. Being close to retirement age, he had sold the company to a group of businessmen known as the Orb Group. Whatever went wrong is up for discussion, but the end result was that the company went from a thriving business into a bankrupt company within a very short time indeed.

Whereas larger companies could ride a financial storm, smaller companies were badly bitten by the desperate recession in the nineties. In September 1990, along with all the other employees, I received my redundancy letter from my boss and Managing Director, Martyn, who was also made redundant. The company had gone into a voluntary liquidation.

That was the sixteenth job of my career in less than eighteen years and I had already suffered three redundancies during that period of time. Perhaps this could be some sort of record, but not one to be especially proud of. Perhaps it all went back to my instability and inability to adapt to life in the world outside of the monastery, where everything was stable and reliable, even though in the final analysis, it had not been the correct life for me.

There was however a silver lining to my third redundancy within a few short years. I had negotiated a three month rolling contract with Contour Car Mats, otherwise known as Caravelle. Once again, this came to my rescue. It gave me a financial buffer, until I was able to find another job. It would also give me a financial nest egg, should I quickly get back into employment. I had been harboring thoughts that I would like to start my own business, to be in charge of my own destiny and my redundancy severance could go a long way towards forming a financial fund, which could get me started up in my own company.

News of the demise of Caravelle had spread throughout the industry. Within a matter of days of being made redundant, I received a phone call from the Managing Director of Stylex Auto Products, a medium sized automotive company not dis-similar in size and market share to Caravelle. The automotive industry was a very incestuous group of companies and people became well known in the industry. I had known Stylex from exhibiting at an automotive show and knew some of their staff. The MD asked me if I was interested in joining their ranks as Sales Manager. By that stage I had a good background in the automotive industry due to my time at Holt Lloyd and Caravelle. I had good contacts in the business that would be useful to their company. I was still unemployed at that time, so I readily accepted their offer of a job, as it was similar to the company and the job I held at Caravelle. Stylex was to be my 17th. Job in just 19 years. Although this was not a good statistic in terms of job stability, it had given me a broad and varied experience of business in a relatively short time.

After about nine months I was beginning to make inroads into developing the business for Stylex, when completely out of the blue, I received a mysterious phone call. It was from Tony Bedford, the original owner of Caravelle before he sold it to the Orb Group. He was still really upset that his beloved company had disappeared into oblivion within a year of him selling it. He had decided that retirement was not for him and that he was going to start up a new business from the ashes of the old Caravelle. There was still a gap in the market that had not been filled and he wanted to start a new company to take advantage of the opportunity. Tony was a true entrepreneur from the old school. Although I did not know him, I certainly knew of him. His reputation went before him. He was aware of me from my short time at Caravelle.

On the telephone he said to me: *"Stephen, may I speak to you confidentially. I could not stand to see what they have done to my company [Caravelle]. I am coming back out of retirement and I am going to start a new business. I would like you to join me, to front up the business and I have invited my previous production manager David Atkins to join me as head of manufacturing. Are you interested in joining us?"*

It came like a bolt out of the blue. Although I had settled reasonably well at Stylex, I never really felt completely at home there. When Tony outlined his plans for the new company, it sounded like an exciting project. In the new company I would be a key player along with David and Tony. The plans were terrific and although it was another start up business, Tony had many years' experience, and more importantly, he had a terrific drive and determination to succeed. I was to head up the drive for new business and David would manage the production unit, I could not turn down the opportunity, it was exciting and too good to miss.

I handed in my notice to Stylex. They were surprised to say the least. I had not been there for a year and it was all going fairly well. I could not tell them where I was going, as we would be competitors, once my new job was up and running. Even though the new company was not yet formed, I had to resign at Stylex, to become involved in setting up the new Car Mat business.

Once I had worked my notice at Stylex, I immediately made the move to the new company [still to be named]. Although I was based in Lincolnshire at Stylex, I knew that I would have to relocate to Hampshire to work with the new company. At this stage, the new company had not been formed, and we had no premises, so we held all our business meetings at Tony's home. His wife would always attend the meetings and she would act as the secretary. I was taking something of a risk in joining a company that was yet to be formed, but fortune favours the brave and it seemed a chance worth taking. At the last such meeting, all the arrangements for forming the new business were completed. Tony was to fund the business 100% and he was to give David and myself a 5% stake in the business with an additional profit share scheme for making the venture a success. All that remained was for Tony to form the company and for us to get started on developing new sales and turnover. What could possibly go wrong?

Within a couple of days of this meeting, Tony called another unscheduled meeting at his home. Nothing too unusual with that. He was always quite impulsive and unpredictable. However, this was on a Sunday evening and although I was curious to know why it was so important, I was not prepared for what he had to tell us. I thought it unusual that his wife was not at the meeting. She was normally acting as the secretary, but on this occasion she was out of sight in the kitchen. Tony seemed sheepish! That was unusual for a person as ultra-positive and decisive. He started by telling us that his wife was cooking dinner and that we were invited to join them. At that point, I could smell a rat! Was he sweetening us up for something? I was unsure, but he came straight to the point.

"Guys, I need to tell you something. I'm not sure you will like it, but, on the positive side, it's going to be a big opportunity for both of you." We didn't twig it! He was trying to butter us up in advance of the news. Without his usual calm and authority he stuttered: *"My wife has persuaded me that I should not come out of retirement to take on such a big project, and after considering it with her, I agree that it is the right thing to do. I am not going ahead with the new company. I am pulling out of it. I am going back into retirement!"*

I cast a glance at David. He didn't know what to say and neither did I. We were both rendered speechless. We had not been expecting that. After all, both of us had burnt our bridges by giving up our jobs to join him. Nobody spoke. In order to ease the uncomfortable silence, Tony continued the conversation: *"Look Guys, I'm not going ahead with the business, but if you want to do it yourself, then it's a big, big opportunity for you."*

Well, that was his view-point. The goalposts had moved completely and we had to consider whether there really was an opportunity for us to take on a new business without his finance and without his massive experience in running a company. He had been the owner of his own operation for many years and he knew all the ropes. By comparison, David and I were complete novices.

Dinner was served. The meal had been a sweetener after all. Tony was trying to let us down gently and try to sugar coat his decision, with a fillet steak and a few glasses of fine red wine. David and I just ate the meal and said very little. Tony continued to justify his decision by rabbiting on during dinner about a new opportunity for us. His wife interjected at regular intervals, to say that Tony's health would not be up-to the stresses and strains of managing a new company, after working in the industry for nigh on forty years. I did not say as much, but could not understand why they could not have reached that conclusion before they had asked us to leave our jobs and before he had taken weeks in preparing for launching the new business. He had already bought company cars for David and me and had committed to other major capital expenditure. He then offered us two options. Option one, was that we walk away and find another job, another career. I believe that he felt bad about this option, as he had clearly let us down badly. Alternatively, he suggested that we could go forward with option two. It was that David and I could start up the business on our own. He offered to give us the benefit of his considerable help and experience, in starting up a new automotive company. He made his terms quite clear. He told us that he would help to get the new company started, but that would not include any financial assistance from him and his wife.

In reality he was just looking for an exit route that would give him back the money he had already spent on the project. Tony seemed to want to have an immediate decision from us, over dinner, as to what we were going to do, but I told him that David and I needed to talk alone and decide what was in our best interests. He didn't seem happy, as he always wanted immediate decisions, but there was no way he would get one that night. At that, we made a hurried exit and went back to our hotel. It was a big decision and we needed to think hard.

Tony had spent money on business plans, finance arrangements, and rather prematurely, he had bought two company cars for David and me. He seemed to want reassurance that he would get his money back. That meant that we would have to buy them from him. I told David that we needed to sleep on it and decide the next day, when we had fresh minds and could make our own decision.

The following day, over a long working breakfast at the hotel, we decided in principle, that we would go it alone and set up the business. I had plenty of sales and marketing experience, while David had been Production Manager for several years. What we lacked was finance and experience in running a company. I asked David what money he could muster to fund the fledgling business. Surprisingly, he said that he had no money, but he could scrape together about five grand. It wasn't going to be easy to start up. Fortunately for me, I had put aside all the funds from my three redundancies for a rainy day, and it was now starting to pour down! So I put in £25k, an 80% share and became Managing Director in my own company. We paid Tony off, and true to his word, he gave us some valuable help and assistance over several weeks. I think he owed us that much! We set up the new business in a rented factory unit in

293

Basingstoke, paid Tony off for the cars and his other expenditure. The rest, we sank into buying or renting old machinery and buying stock. Fortunately, much of the machinery from the defunct company, at Caravelle Carpet Mats, was still unsold, and several of the staff from the liquidated company would come and join us in this new venture. One company had failed but another company was about to rise from the ashes, Profile Car Mats was born. This was to be the first ever business I had owned and I badly needed it to be a success.

Chapter 16

My Own Boss.

Profile Car Mats was born and in business. This was to be my Job No.18. It was a big risk with a recession in full swing, but we were either good judges or just foolhardy. Only time would tell.

We set about winning some business. It was just me at first. I had plenty of contacts from Caravelle, Holt-Lloyd and Stylex and I set about knocking on the doors of anybody who would listen. It was mainly car dealers initially, but there was a growing market for personalized car mats and we were there to fulfill that requirement. David hired several of the redundant machinists and workers from Caravelle, and we were up and running and manufacturing car mats in Basingstoke.

It was never going to be easy, but we built up a good business over a two year period and were profitable, albeit in a low key way. In fact, we developed from initially selling to car dealers and developed sales into some major automotive and DIY multiples customers like Homebase.

The main problem with rapid growth was cash-flow! We had won a number of large multiple customers. We had good sales, but large customers paid slowly, and if we were to have a major breakthrough with the large accounts, then we would have to fund large amounts of stock and wait for payment for up-to ninety days, despite our payment terms being thirty days. This put enormous pressure on our cash-flow. I went to our bank and asked for further funding, but the price of their help was far too high. Our bank was not keen to take that risk, unless I put my home up as collateral, and I was not willing to do that, as it was far too big a risk. To keep the cash flow flowing, we had to borrow funds, in the short-term, from my wife's business, but had to pay this back quite quickly. Running a profitable business is one task, but funding its growth required a further substantial cash injection and this may have been beyond our reach.

It was at this stage of our development, and while we were pondering our future options for growth, that we had an offer to buy the business which made us think very seriously about our future.

When we started the business, David lived close to where we worked. I was living in a small apartment in Old Basing, close to Basingstoke. I was on my own from Monday to Fridays and only went home to my wife at weekends, back in Warrington. Even when I was at home, the worry and the pressure of the business was never far from my mind. When an offer for the business came in, it was against this backdrop, that I had to make the decision. The be all and end all, was not the success of the company. I also wanted some quality of life and I had not been getting much of that for nearly two years since we started. On the other hand, I also had to consider not only myself, but my partner David and twenty-three company employees in the factory.

It all started when I was approached by a third party consultant, acting on behalf of his client. He called me out of blue one day and asked me if I would like to sell the business. I enquired who his client was, but he was not forthcoming, unless I told him I was willing to sell.

Why would I want to sell? We had built the business up in just two years and although life was tough and profits were small, no outside party would know that. I hedged my bets and told him that we were not keen to sell, but we would listen to any generous offers that came along.

That night, David and I had a tete a tete and I put him in the picture regarding the potential offer to sell the business. He was not at all keen on the approach, fearing that a takeover would lead to job losses or even worse. Even so, we were both keen to know who it was that wanted to buy our business and why. We were even flattered that somebody or some company would think enough of our business to want to buy it. But why?

We had earlier received an offer from an Indian businessman just a couple of months earlier. I told him to put his offer in writing, which he duly did, but it turned out to be a derisory offer and we turned it down without so much as a 2nd. thought.

When the second company wanted to make an offer, it made us wonder if we had struck gold! Why would anybody want to buy a young, albeit progressive company, when just two years earlier, Caravelle had gone into liquidation with no takers? Even so, we were keen to find out.

We were both intrigued to find out who else wanted to buy Profile Car Mats. I contacted the consultant again and told him that we would be willing to listen to the mystery buyer's offer. When we received his answer, it all started to fall into place. The mystery enquirer was none other than my former Managing Director at Caravelle.

Martyn was extremely bright, but he was likewise made redundant when Caravelle went belly-up. Martyn had formed a new alliance with a big player in the business. He approached a former supplier to Caravelle, a huge Dutch Company named Visshermatten, which would set him back up in the UK business and at the same time, would allow Visschermatten back into the UK market.

Martyn formed a new business named Visscher-Caravelle, supplying Motor Companies and major automotive retailers.

Why would Martyn want to buy little old Profile Car Mats? Profile started up business by supplying Car Dealers with tailored carpet mats, but having secured sales to several hundred, we turned our attention to the large multiple retailers, where we were having considerable success. Martyn certainly believed that by amalgamating our company into his, he would not only take a competitor out of the market, but it would give Visscher Caravelle greater market share. David was not keen on selling, but I had to consider whether we had the ability and funding to take Profile to the next level. It would have required significant funding and I did not believe that the bank would have supported us at that stage, without greater security and I was not willing to put our family home at risk for the business.

A bid for the business finally arrived, but it was nowhere near acceptable. Eventually Visscher Caravelle made an offer that was difficult to turn down and I was about to start my nineteenth job! By this stage I had decided that I could not run a business forever, whilst living 300 miles from home. Moving home to Basingstoke was not an option for me. Taking all matters into consideration, we decided to accept. The sale duly went through, but Visscher Caravelle did not want to continue running the business from its Basingstoke factory. Their plan was to close it down and amalgamate it into his much larger business in Milton Keynes. The factory in Basingstoke closed and although the staff were offered jobs in Milton Keynes, it was not a viable option for them. The main condition of the purchase, was that I went to work for Visscher Caravelle as Sales Director and David as Production Manager. This was for a minimum contract of one year, to secure the good-will of the customer base, that I had brought to the company and that Visscher Caravelle had purchased. I had it in mind, that I would rent a flat for a year and then return home and start a small business in my home town. I had already spent far too much time traveling up and down motorways and staying in hotels and I wanted to put down my roots once more and experience my family life. That was my master plan, but I was unsure if it would ever happen, given my track record to date.

As things worked out, it did not quite happen that way. Martyn and I worked well together despite various ups and downs, and I became totally embroiled in the business at Visscher Caravelle.

Instead of renting a flat for my one year contract with the company, I decided to buy a really pleasant apartment in the lovely rural town of

Stony Stratford. It was very comfortable and that helped me to settle down. Time just seemed to fly by. A year came and went, and I was still there. There had been no discussion about me leaving and I did not feel inclined to do so, despite missing my family life. My wife would visit me at Stony Stratford at weekends, on the occasions when I did not travel home. In fact, home became something of a rarity and all I seemed to live for was the business. I had fully integrated my Profile customers into Visscher Caravelle and secured their business, but then I just became immersed in the young and thriving company. In the end, I remained there for three years. This was the longest period I had ever remained in any one job. I may well have stayed even longer, but I was becoming tired of forever living out of a suitcase and not having a real home life. I wanted a change of lifestyle, and not just another change of job. I had certainly had plenty of those over the years.

It was at a time when there was a lot of pressure in the job, that I had a big fall out with my M.D. It was all about achieving objectives via my sales team and I felt we were being treated unfairly. Martyn could be a fiery character and I could be stubborn when backed into a corner and attacked.

One night, I was alone in my apartment. I was feeling depressed and being alone was not a good way to deal with it. I remember polishing off a bottle of red wine and this was not me. I had always been a happy drinker. I rarely had alcohol to drown my sorrows. I preferred a drink when I was happy or to celebrate something.

That night was to be the tipping point. In a flash of inspiration, I just concluded that I did not need this enormous pressure anymore and that there was more to life than corporate business and all that it entailed. I told my wife that I regretted selling my business and that I wanted to be my own boss again. If there was to be huge pressure in my work, then I wanted it to be my own stress, and not the pressure coming on me from a boss of a big company. I had often played number 2, playing the supporting role and coped with it, but I had also experienced being No.1, the top dog, and I wanted to feel that experience once again.

The very next day, I told Martyn that I was going to resign my position. Martyn could sometimes be a difficult boss, dominant, unreasonable and not easy to work for. Yet on other occasions, he was easy to get along with, reasonable and when not at work, he was extremely sociable and practically a friend. When I gave him my resignation letter, he seemed extremely disappointed and practically begged me not to go. He said he liked having me as his No.2, despite often treating me as his whipping boy. I had heard this line before, in a previous company

Surprisingly, we arrived at a solution that partly met my requirements. Martyn asked me to stay with the company, managing the major accounts, but no longer as head of salesforce. In addition, he said that I could be self-employed, as a consultant and that I could base myself at home and just visit Milton Keynes Head Office, say, once a week. Martyn always seemed to get what he wanted, albeit in an alternative way and it seemed a decent solution to a tricky problem. I would be self-employed, still my own boss and yet I would be doing a similar job to what I had been doing while employed. How could I refuse? It sounded like a brilliant solution from Martyn or was it?

The following week, I gave up the relative security of a good salary package, for the less secure and less well-paid role of self-employed Sales Consultant. I was to name this business, Platinum Consultancy, and this was to be my twentieth job!

The new role meant that I remained as Head of Sales for the major accounts, worked from home, and was to all intents and purposes, self-employed, yet still accountable and responsible to Martyn. I invoiced the company every month for the agreed consultancy fee and commission for achieving the agreed sales targets. At first, it all worked extremely well. I was my own boss, I was based back at home and just got on with it, without having to report daily to Martyn and take part in meetings after meetings, which had become the bane of my life!

The new arrangement seemed to work well for a period of time, but after a while, our agreement seemed to be forgotten and it just seemed that it was returning to the previous arrangement when I was an employee. The time arrived when our business was not as it had been agreed. Little by little, Martyn seemed to forget that I was a self-employed consultant and began including me in all sorts of meetings and company events. He began to phone every day, several times a day, and wanted this report and that. Over the period of a year, I came to the sad conclusion that I had effectively become an employee again, in all but name, and that is how Martyn viewed me. The changes to my job and status were all there on paper, but, I was doing everything I used to do as an employee, without any of the salary, pension and security benefits, that I had enjoyed before. It seemed to me that, reluctantly I was going to make yet another career and lifestyle change. I told Martyn that the current role was not working for me, but that I had another potential solution that may suit both him and me. Neither of us seemed to want to let go and call it quits, so between us we came up with yet another compromise plan.

I was going to start up a new specialist business back home in Warrington named "Sterling Auto

Products", not in competition with Visscher Caravelle, but working with them and buying most of my stock and materials from the company. In addition, to supplement my business and assist my cash flow, I would continue to sell to, and service, many of the Visscher Caravelle's major customers. It seemed that we were destined to work together forever, in one way or another. My new role was a duel one: Platinum Consultancy plus Sterling Auto Products. It was yet another compromise and it was my 21st.Job since 1972.

I busied myself finding premises, and I purchased a small 800 square foot production unit in Latchford, Warrington. I purchased all the necessary machinery and stock and started up the business. It was great to be working from very close to home again and I still had the relative security of an agreed consultancy fee from Visscher, for working an agreed two days a week. I also worked three days a week for Sterling Auto Products. It sounded like the perfect solution. For the first time in years, I could travel just five miles from home to work and come home nearly every night. I was in seventh heaven, at least for a while.

I loved the new business. I was doing work that I was largely familiar with and I had years of experience in the car mat business. Importantly, I was my own boss once more. I was manufacturing specialist high quality carpet mats for premium cars and specialist vehicles. We quickly developed a core business and a customer base of regular car clubs and dealers. In addition, I still had to balance this with selling on behalf of Visscher for two days every week. As companies, we were still as intertwined as ever. I bought all my carpet and stock from them and sold the products to a market that we were not competing in. It was a win, win situation and my relationship with Martyn became a strong one which we both seemed happy with.

The core business was top range tailored mats for Jaguars and Mercedes although there was a specialist element too. We would produce tailored mats for vintage and sports car clubs. Perhaps the most unusual contract was fitting out a range of carpet mats for a group of funeral hearses! That was a spooky job! Another specialist job was fitting out new 75-ton trucks for ERF, the haulage company with fitted carpet mats in their cabs.

I considered myself fortunate, that I had employed a young man named David who was extremely bright. While I was devoting my time to my responsibilities with Visscher, he practically ran the factory unit single handed and he was a very important right hand man. I had hoped he would have stayed and together we could have built Sterling into a substantial specialist business with him being an integral part, perhaps even a partner. Although the business was growing, it was slow progress and I really needed to put more of my time and effort into developing new customers, yet all the time I was put under increasing pressure to spend more time on my major account work for Visscher Caravelle. Once more, it had become difficult to balance the demands of the two businesses and I could see yet another conflict with Martyn, on the horizon in the near future.

With hindsight, I had relied on David too much. We should have spent more time working together. I had it in my mind that I would give David more responsibility and a much increased remuneration package. I wanted him to have a share in the business, which would free me up to continue my role with Visscher. This would have funded the growth of the business and enabled me to fund David's share in the business. Unfortunately, before I did so, David told me he was leaving. It was a great shame, but his mind had already been made up. He told me that he wanted to go back into further education. He had his mind set on another career path in computer technology and he needed to study for it.

Sterling Auto products had been working well for about twelve months, but as always, something happened to upset the apple cart. I was trying extremely hard to balance the responsibility of developing Sterling Auto Products with my responsibilities to Visscher Caravelle. I tried hard to be fair in allocating the correct amount of time to both projects. At first, both parties seemed happy, but eventually I became so busy, that managing the two businesses became untenable, as the demands from both were pulling me in opposite directions. Characteristically, Martyn reverted to type and became even more demanding. He was expecting much more than the two day's work that we had agreed to. He always seemed to want more of me and despite my "part time" tag, he still treated me as an integral and full time member of his staff. Something had to give.

I believed that I would be unable to replace David because he had done just about everything in the unit, from production to administration and I relied on him for all of our I.T. which was not my strong point. I interviewed several potential replacements, but none seemed to fit the bill. It came to a stage where almost 70% of the income was coming from Visscher and just 30% from Sterling Auto Products. I could have coped with that, but the joint workload was pulling me apart.

I had a huge decision to make. Sterling versus Visscher. One of the two had to go. Despite my efforts, dividing my time between both was proving just too difficult. After extensive soul searching and with great reluctance, I decided that I had to sever my ties with my own business, Sterling Auto Products. It was a wrench, because

I enjoyed running my own business, but in the end I had to do what was right for me. The tipping point, was when Martyn offered me a large salary package to go back there as Head of Sales. It was just too good a deal to turn down. He practically owned me anyway, so I decided to return to the corporate lifestyle and all the responsibility that the job entailed. It would mean long hours and long days, and traveling extensively all over the U.K yet again. At least I would be working from my home base in Cheshire and not Milton Keynes.

Sadly, I decided to close down Sterling Auto Products and I sold the machinery and stock back to Visscher. All the customer base I had worked so hard to build, would be serviced by Visscher Caravelle. It felt as if I was selling Profile Car Mats all over again. I had turned a full circle. My final act was to rent out the unit, which gave me an income, all in all it turned out to be for the best.

It was onto job No.22, back to Visscher Caravelle. I was back in the fast lane. I had not stayed in the slow lane for very long and it seemed that I was always drawn back to the hurly burly of corporate life and there was no chance of me taking it easy. As with everything in my working life, jobs had been a-plenty, but longevity was not a feature of my career. Some may say that it showed a lack of staying power, and stability. I take the view that practically every time I changed job, I had made some progress or earned a promotion of some kind, perhaps an increase in remuneration.

It was good to be back in the mainstream business. I had enjoyed my time running my own company Sterling Auto Products, yet it was difficult and even lonely on occasions and I would miss the cut and thrust of being part of a large team and the camaraderie that went with it. I had missed the challenges and the satisfaction of achieving sales objectives and the "buzz" that made it worthwhile.

I was to spend almost another two years with Visscher Caravelle, with all the ups and downs that the position entailed. It was never easy, but I was well rewarded for my efforts and I accepted the long hours, the stress and the huge mileage it entailed, in being the Company Sales Manager.

Everything was fine for a while, but I began to suffer a number of issues, health wise. I was being troubled by arthritis in my knee and hip, making it painful to drive long distances. I also developed an irregular heart beat and worst of all, the stress and anxiety attacks that went hand in hand with them.

One day, after leaving home at 5am to get to a client meeting for 9am in Milton Keynes, I was sat in the meeting, listening to somebody giving a presentation, when I realized that I was not really listening at all. I was day dreaming. Martyn asked my opinion on what had just been said and I had no idea what they were talking about. I just blustered my way through an answer, but it did not even sound convincing to me, let alone my colleagues and the clients. In truth, at that moment I was feeling tired out, stressed and anxious and not really party to what was going on around me. During the rest of the meeting and in a quiet moment at my desk later on, I seriously asked myself what I was doing there? Around the table, at the meeting, had been a group of mainly twenty and thirty somethings! They were young energetic and full of enthusiasm. I looked at myself. I was nearing 60 years of age and had been doing this routine for almost twenty five years, much of it entailing long hours of driving all over the UK. I realized that my enthusiasm was on the wane and I was starting to feel out of place in the lineup. On the drive home that evening, I knew that I would not be home until about 9pm, which had meant a sixteen hour day. As I drove through the inevitable traffic delays, I thought about the family life I was missing, and that the long hours and driving were taking their toll on my body and my mind.

On arriving home, my wife Anne, had a hot meal ready and waiting for me as always. I refused it. It was just too late, and I was too tired to eat it. I asked her for a hot chocolate, had a bath and told her I had to go to bed, as I had yet another early start the next day and a long drive to Scotland.

"Is it worth it any more Steve? "Anne said: "Why don't you pack it in? We will manage, and at least we will have some sort of life" she said to me. That night, I lay in bed and I began to come round to her way of thinking. Things needed to change once more. I had to get my health back on track again and I would never be able to do that by working at the pace that was demanded at Visscher Caravelle. I really had no idea what I would do next, if anything at all, but at last, I did know that I was going to bring the curtain down on working full time in the corporate business.

I arranged a time to have a talk with Martyn. I told him that this time, I really wanted to finish and that this final time, it would be permanent and there would be no going back.

Despite our many ups and downs, Martyn did not want me to leave and in some ways, neither did I, yet on this occasion I knew it was the right decision to make. We had worked together at Caravelle, and had both been made redundant. We both set up our own companies and Martyn bought mine, and bought me, as I went to work for him again. Since that time, we had worked together in various guises, but all good things come to an end and this time there would be no going back. With some misgivings and reluctance, I resigned, yet we have always kept in touch and remained as friends.

Chapter 17

Winding it down.

Before I resigned for the second time at Visscher Caravelle, I had no clear idea of what I was going to do afterwards. Certainly, I knew that I had to continue working. I was not far off being sixty and although I knew that I could draw down my occupational pension then, it would not be sufficient to keep me in the standard that I had had been used to, while I was working full time. I had to continue until I was at least sixty-five years of age, so there had to be a plan "B," to enable me to resign from my full-time employment.

One of the biggest features of my work over the past twenty years, had been that I had always driven extensively as part of my employment. In just about every job, I had traveled about 50,000 miles a year in pursuit of my work's objectives. Therefore, one of the skills that I was competent at, was driving, even though the excess traveling, was one of the reasons I had left Visscher Caravelle. It was hardly surprising then, that driving came to mind when I was looking out for another career path, albeit a part-time or temporary position.

I knew that I needed an occupation, not just one

which would give me an income, but I also wanted it to be comparatively easy, without the level of stress or anxiety that I had been accustomed to, and where I could work the hours to suit my chosen lifestyle. It was quite a big "Ask" then!

Over the years, there had been many occasions when I had required a taxi or private hire vehicle. On several of these occasions, I had been quietly critical of the standard of service and quality of vehicle, that was offered to business men. There did not appear to be many good quality Private Hire Companies which specialized in providing premium service to business people. Too many of the taxi companies had poor vehicles and the drivers themselves left something to be desired in terms of their service level and customer relations.

I decided that I was going to start a private hire taxi service, aimed exclusively at business people and at the high end of the market. I planned to use the brand of my consultancy name at Visscher-Caravelle and called the new business "Platinum Executive Travel." My latest job, No.23 was launched. Nobody that I knew, thought that the new job was a good idea. After my frequent changes of career and direction, nothing would surprise them, but many of my friends and family raised an eyebrow, when I told them what I was planning to do. After all, I had been in the top level of business management and had owned my own company. Others thought it was something of a comedown for me. What they may not have understood was that a "comedown" was precisely what I had in mind. I wanted to work, but without the same high level of commitment and stress that went with it. At that stage of my life, all I wanted was a job that required less thinking and more action. I wanted to be able to just fall out of bed and do the job, without doing hours of preparation.

14. Platinum Executive Travel - Peugeot 607

I decided to buy a really good quality motor car, at least as good a quality as my budget would allow. I saw a beautiful large vehicle, a Peugeot 607. It was a huge beast of a saloon car, with a three litre engine, automatic transmission and with cruise control. The interior was plush and comfortable, just as my potential customers would be expecting. I bought it there and then, even before I had applied for a license to become a private hire driver. The main limiting factor, was that the market was extremely competitive and customers would only pay a small premium to travel in a top quality private hire vehicle. Otherwise, I would have gone for a top of the range Mercedes Benz. I felt that there could be a market for it, but was unsure if customers would pay for the privilege.

If I had known beforehand what was entailed in gaining a license, I may not have bothered. There was the dreaded "knowledge" to be learned. It required knowing every single street, road and place of interest in the local area of operation. Memory had never been my strong point and remembering the names of roads and places did not come easy. In any case, the "knowledge" was rapidly becoming something of a white elephant! Why was it necessary for a driver to learn every back road in each area, when that wonderful new Satellite Navigation system, would do it all for them? It seemed pointless, yet the council, still in the dark ages, insisted that the "Knowledge" was learned in the same old fashioned way.

Unsurprisingly, I failed my first knowledge test. My memory got the better of me and I could not recall off the top of my head, the route from A to B and naming every road and side street along the way. I could have driven it without a problem, yet I could not remember the names of the roads!

It meant that my lovely new car had to sit in the garage and I could not use it until I passed my knowledge test. I was not used to failing examinations. Since I first failed my eleven plus as a young boy, I had not been used to failing and it did not go down well with me. I had passed my 25 metre swimming test, my driving test 1st time, all seven GCE O Levels and so to fail a silly knowledge test was a major aggravation. I re-applied straight away to re-sit the test and spent night after night studying the A-Z road maps and memorizing the road names and page layouts. Fortunately, it worked and I re-sat my Knowledge Test four weeks later and passed with ease, at the second time of asking. It was a huge relief.

My new business developed surprisingly quickly with the help of others in the trade. People would ask me how my taxi business was coming along. I was not trying to be clever or snobbish, but I would correct them and inform them that I was not a taxi driver! I told them that I was a private hire owner, specializing in executive travel. The truth was, that I felt more at home dealing with business people, as I had been doing that during my entire working career. I had a quality vehicle and I would always dress as smartly as they were, in a suit and tie. I targeted business people and wanted to drive them to and   from Airports, Rail Stations,

Theatres, Restaurants and the Races. It didn't concern me that it may be viewed as being subservient to business people, because a couple of years earlier, I had been in their position. I had been there, done that and worn their business T-shirt. I was very much enjoying being in their company and mixing with them, but without the level of pressure associated with their jobs anymore. I offered a business type, private hire service, which I know they wanted and appreciated. In the mornings I would always have a copy of the Times or the Telegraph in the car for them to read. Some would ask me why I was doing that job and simply, I would reply that I enjoyed it and that unlike them, I could go home and forget about the business, at the end of the day's work.

It wasn't all mundane trips to railway stations, airports and the like. There were some memorable trips that were often enjoyable and even interesting, as well as being profitable. Most journeys were worth just a few pounds, but occasionally a job would come up that had the potential to be both enjoyable as well as profitable.

Perhaps one of my most memorable and surprising jobs was when I was booked by a firm of Solicitors from Manchester's commercial quarter. Initially, I was only told that we were to go to a place close to the O2 in London's Docklands area. I was told that it would be a long return journey and to quote my fayre based on me collecting them at 11am in

Manchester and returning them in the early hours of the following day!! It was a good fayre, and I quoted them £350 for the return trip. They did not seem unduly phased by the price, so despite the unsociable hours, I was happy to accept the job.

It was the strangest of days. It started out so demurely. I collected three of my passengers from Manchester, all solicitors and dressed typically as one would imagine; male, dark suits, standard tie and black shoes. The first few hours of the journey were what I expected. They all had mobile phones glued to their ears and they were engrossed in conducting their business. There was plenty of conversation among them, as they were discussing serious cases of business which were all highly confidential. Clearly, I could hear exactly what was being said and much of it was extremely interesting, as it involved criminal matters. It was as though I was not there. I was sat close by them, yet they were oblivious to my presence. The subject matter being discussed was extremely personal and yet they were trusting me and my professional confidentiality. I felt good that I was offering a business service for professional people. Perhaps it was because I had been a similar type of professional, for much of my career and that I understood what it was that they wanted from me; i.e. a business to business private hire company, offering complete confidentiality. Coincidentally, I felt like just a priest in a confessional. Of course,

I very nearly was. I would hear all, see all, but say nothing to anybody else. There was a strict bond of confidentiality. Nothing had been said about it, but my absolute silence was clearly understood.

As we reached Central London I was asked to make an un-scheduled stop off at a London Soho restaurant, where we were to collect their fourth member of the team. I waited patiently for well over an hour on a parking meter, [at an additional charge!], and at around 4pm, the clients all spilled out from the restaurant looking and sounding decidedly worse for wear. The fourth solicitor was a young lady, but she was not dressed for business at all. She was all glammed up for a night on the town. The male solicitors had also made a change of attire. They were then dressed, to my amazement, for a rock concert, torn jeans, and all of them sporting loud t-shirts emblazoned with the image of the Hard Rock band, Led Zeppelin. Unbeknown to me, the band were playing at the O2 Arena, that day, on 10th. December 2007. The band were the surviving members of the Rock Legends, reunited for their first full-length concert in nearly thirty years. These not so young, middle aged solicitors, were massive fans of hard rock icon Led Zeppelin and had been so, since their youth, around thirty years earlier. "Hard Rock" was definitely not my scene. I was strictly a "Rock and Roll" fan, from a different era and as the saying goes. "Vive la Difference!

Suddenly, the entire journey took on a totally different persona. From being a quiet and formal business journey, the whole event had changed to a loud, swinging group of fans, off to a rock concert. As soon as we departed Soho, the leader of the group changed identity completely. Instead of being just a driver, I was now his best buddy and he became chatty and ultra-friendly. On the journey south, he had barely uttered so much as a word to me, but now he was chatting away about Led Zeppelin and about the amazing reunion concert they were going to see. They were clearly excited and at lunch they had plainly oiled their vocal chords with plenty of alcohol. He handed me a CD containing Zeppelin's greatest hits and asked me to play it, which I did. I played the CD, but not too loudly. I should have known better. You can't play Hard Rock music quietly! I switched it up to top volume. I had a brilliant Panasonic music system in the car with great speakers and the car rocked! Suddenly, as their greatest hits blared out, the rock concert groupies, who an hour earlier had been sedate solicitors, turned into head-banging, party going revelers. The car shook and vibrated to the music. The revelers were singing along at the top of their voices and violently throwing their heads back and to, in rhythm with the music. I thought to myself that they had better hold something back for the concert or they would be a spent force by the time we arrived at the O2 Arena.

We arrived there at 7pm. and I was still in a daze. I was in a type of shocked admiration at the complete transformation of my previously sedate passengers, into gregarious groupies. I arranged to meet them at an agreed pick up point at 12 midnight and off they trooped to see their heroes of yesteryear, reunited. I completely understood it. I was just as much an Elvis Presley fanatic as they were Led Zeppelin fans. For me, Elvis had been dead for thirty years and it was still as if he were here in person and still performing live concerts.

I had five hours to kill. I was tired after my six-hour journey to the O2, particularly with the head-banging music, still ringing in my tinnitus affected ears. Already I was dreading the return journey and another five or six hours with that lot in my car! Which group would turn up? Would it be the Solicitors I collected in Manchester or the hard rock groupies I had dropped off at the O2?

I was starving. Unlike my passengers, I had not eaten since 9am that morning, so I walked into the O2 complex. Outside of the actual music arena, the complex had turned into a myriad of eateries and entertainment. It was 7th.December and it was far too cold to stay in the car. I found myself in a pizzeria and ate alone, satisfying my hunger pangs. After that, I had a walk around the outside of the O2 and it was still only 8.30pm. What was I going to do until midnight? I had an idea. There

was a multiplex Cinema and there was a choice of films. Well, it wasn't far off Christmas and I chose a shmaltzy Christmas Rom Com, for some light entertainment. Frankly, I could have chosen anything, because I was so tired that I just knew I would fall asleep, but at least it was lovely and warm in the cinema. I watched the film intently for all of ten minutes and then drifted off into a cozy oblivion, woken up suddenly from my slumbers by the movement of people leaving their seats at the end of the film. So, I missed the cinema, but glancing up at the clock I noticed it was gone 11pm and after a double shot of strong coffee at Costa to keep me awake, I returned to my cold car and awaited the return of my "lively" passengers.
It must have been around 12.30am when the drunken "gang of four" rolled up at the car. What a site they were! Glassy eyed, reeking of alcohol and all on such a "high" that I thought they would never come down, this side of Christmas! The three males crawled into the back of the car. The female got another taxi back into London to her home. I genuinely hoped that the guys would slink quietly into their seats and drop off to sleep. Not a chance! No sooner had I set off on the long road north, then they gave me another Led Zeppelin CD and asked me to play it loudly. Reluctantly I slid it into the CD player. I thought that they would have had their fill of Zeppelin by then, but apparently not. They were on one almighty high and they wanted to listen to more of it all the way home.

Thank goodness, that tiredness and alcohol got the better of them by the time we reached Birmingham. After I was sure that they had all slumped off into unconsciousness, I quietly turned off the music. My ears were still ringing from the blaring music and my tinnitus was worse than it had been in years. I glanced into the rear-view mirror and the three solicitors were slumped together, sleeping like new born babies. It put a brand new perspective on my idea of these professional gentlemen. I had a secret giggle to myself, at the images flitting through my mind. By the time I had dropped off the last of the three solicitors at their homes, it was 4.25am and I finally arrived back at my own home at 5am, £350 better off, plus a well-earned tip of £50. It had been quite an experience, but not one that I would care to repeat, at least in the immediate future.

There were other memorable trips, but not too many that I care to remember. On one occasion, I broke my own rules and took on a job that was nothing to do with professional people. Close to home there was a Music Festival which was famous throughout the UK. It was the renowned "Creamfields" festival and it took place less than a mile from my home. I could have "filled my boots" with driving jobs and made good money from them, but I told myself that I did not want that kind of work. Even many of the standard taxi drivers shied away from Creamfields because of its bad reputation in the trade, for drink and drugs! I had a phone call from one of my regular business clients who told me that her nephew and two friends were attending the festival. I was right to have reservations, but I accepted the job as a favour to her, after convincing myself that it would be alright. I was even more assured when I was asked to collect him and his friends from a nearby motel at 11am the day after the end of the festival.

There were no warning signs when I collected the young people at the hotel, except that all three boys were extremely quiet after I asked them how they had enjoyed the festival. I glanced into my rear-view mirror, shortly after moving from the hotel and one of them seemed very pale. Then, without any warning whatsoever, he vomited in a projectile manner, the contents going all over the rear of the car, covering the lovely velvet seats with vomit. It stank, throughout the car. I stopped on the roadside straight away and told them that I would drop them back at the hotel and that there was a compulsory charge of £50 for passengers who vomit in the car, after becoming intoxicated. Reluctantly, they paid up, after I threatened to tell the lad's aunt or call the police. I had to cancel my other appointments that day while I cleaned up the car and fumigated it. The smell lingered in the car for the rest of that day. It was not a pleasant experience and from that time onwards, I refused to take any passengers, business or not, if I suspected that they had been drinking to excess.

Perhaps the most frequent question that taxi and private hire drivers are asked is: *"Have you ever driven any famous people?"* I guess this is because celebrities and well known people frequently use private hire transport. The answer is: Only once, and my passenger would be known to people only in the North of England. I was asked to collect D.J. and Radio presenter, Miss Becky Want from Radio Manchester. She was a lovely lady, not at all pretentious and she talked incessantly about her young son, clearly the love of her life. I drove her from her Cheshire home to the Lowry Hotel in Manchester to a dinner date function. I listen all the time now, to her daytime radio magazine show.

The other frequent question that taxi drivers are asked is: *"what is your worst ever journey?"* Well, mine is not a difficult one to recall, as it is lodged in my mind and will be for a very long time.

I was booked at 9am to take a couple of business people from an office complex in Warrington to Manchester Airport. They had to be at the airport by 10am for their flight. This should have been a routine job and would normally take about thirty minutes to the airport and about the same time back to base. As a private hire driver, I always kept a watchful eye on the weather forecast and traffic conditions, as these are the two most frequent events that can affect a journey and make it late.

On this particular morning, the weather forecast was very precise. It was for extremely high 60mph damaging winds, of up to gale force. I was wary about this and had considered not accepting the job. With hindsight, I wish I had listened to them.

I collected my passengers and set off on the M6 towards the M56. No chance! I could see there was a lengthy queue and my local radio station warned me that the Thelwall Viaduct, the main bridge on the M6 was closed. Several high-sided vehicles had been blown over and were blocking the carriageway. All the local roads were becoming grid-locked. I eventually managed to exit the M6 before the closed bridge. I knew of a small toll bridge called the Warburton Bridge in Lymm, that would enable me to cross the Manchester Ship Canal and then I could take the back roads to the airport. It had already turned 11am and the passengers were in danger of missing their flight. That is, until we heard on the radio that Manchester Airport had also been closed, due to the high winds affecting take-off and landing. We were then in no man's land as the Warburton Bridge had a three mile queue waiting to cross it. We decided that we would take the "A" roads and side roads into Manchester. The passengers had given up on their flight and now wanted to be taken into Manchester City centre, to a hotel. We crawled all the way to Manchester at about 10mph due to the grid-locked traffic and to avoid falling trees, walls and slates which were being blown into the road. Eventually, we arrived in Manchester at their hotel at 2.30pm. They were alright in their comfortable hotel. I was paid just £18 for a five and a half hour journey which normally takes half an hour. The fayre was based on the mileage driven and not the time taken. I did all I could for them and I didn't even get a tip!

Worse was to come. After creeping slowly out of Manchester at no more than 5mph towards the M56, I eventually reached the Motorway at 4pm. Within about two miles of driving at a snail's pace the motorway came to a complete halt. After sitting in the queue for forty-five minutes, the radio station alerted us to the fact that the Motorway had been completely closed, about two miles ahead of us and the Police were unable to say when it would be re-opened. I switched the engine off and waited for the traffic to move. It was November and by 5pm it was dark and it was very cold. I had not even had a warm drink since 8am and had not eaten anything at all, except for a two finger "kit-kat," that I gratefully found in my glove compartment. Nature also called. I was desperate for a No.1 and managed to relieve myself in bushes at the side of the M56 Motorway, before returning to my cold dark car. I could not run the engine to create heat, due to the exhaust fumes and using up the diesel fuel. I did manage to call my wife on my mobile to let her know I was at least safe. I sat there for a further two and a half hours until the traffic began to move again, after the police had re-opened the motorway. Once that had happened, I was just twenty minutes from a very welcome and warming home, some food, drink and relaxation. It was by then, 7.30pm and I had been in my car all day since 9am that morning. I had been driving for ten and a half hours, and all for the princely sum of £18 less my fuel costs. All in all, it had been a day to be forgotten.

To add injury to insult, my wife came to me with a cup of hot chocolate and said: *"It's worse than that, we have lost several ridging tiles and a number of slates off the roof due to the high winds"*. That was to cost me another £200, so it had not been a profitable day. I should have listened to my own gut feelings and the weather forecasts that morning and not gone out to work!
It had never been my intention to do the private hire job for very many years. I was doing it as a stop gap job until I was ready to retire. However, there are times in life when decisions can be taken out of your own hands and this was the case in my private hire career. I was enjoying it, despite the unsociable hours and relatively poor reward for the time I put into it. But I was not expecting it to finish as suddenly as did.

I had lived for years with a condition called Atrial Fibrillation, and although it was not a pleasant condition, I coped with it and it did not interfere too much with either my life or my work. Therefore it came as a bolt out of the blue when I had to attend a regular independent medical examination, required for all private hire drivers. I told them without any concern, that I had the condition called A.F. I was not expecting a negative reaction to this admission. Imagine it then, when The G.P. consultant informed me that he was suspending my private hire driving license immediately, and until further notice. I was absolutely flabbergasted. The doctor informed me that atrial fibrillation could cause a much higher incidence of stroke and heart attack and that my private hire license was suspended until my condition was cured or brought under control.

So, that was that! My license was taken away and I was suspended from driving the general public. It meant that I was unable to drive my private hire vehicle until my A.F. condition was sorted out to their satisfaction. It gave me time to take stock of my life. I had to tell all my regulars that I had been suspended on health grounds and unable to work again until further notice. My wife though was delighted, not that I had been suspended, but because she did not like the fact that I had been working more and more unsociable hours. I had been getting up as early as 3.30am some days, to meet early flights to or from far flung destinations like Dubai. Likewise, as my business grew I had been working Saturdays and Sundays, early and late, and it was not going down well with "she who must be obeyed!" She wanted me to finish the job.

I had recently turned 60 years of age, and I had taken my occupational pension, but I still needed to work and could not do without the income. This was the first time in my working life that I had been unemployed and it was strange to wake up of a morning and not go to work. I felt like a spare part. I "signed on" as unemployed, but I was never paid any unemployment benefit. It was an alien action for me to take and against my principles. I believed in earning my own money and not being supported by the state unless it was necessary.

After about twelve weeks of kicking my heels at home, I had another hospital medical, and to my huge relief I was deemed fit for work again. My Atrial Fibrillation condition had been rectified by an operation which was called a "Cardioversion". This involved using a drug which medically stopped my heart, while I was put to sleep, and then it re-started it. It was the medical equivalent of "jump-starting" a car!

When I woke up, my heart was back in a regular rhythm and I was fine again, fit and healthy, well at least for a period of time. Quite soon, I was feeling a lot more like my old self. It was such a relief. I did not feel even close to being a pensioner. I was feeling as fit as a fiddle once more and looking forward to working again and being able to carry out physical activities, that the atrial fibrillation had put a temporary halt to.

I considered starting up the business again, but somehow, I did not feel quite the same about it anymore. I was yearning to lead a normal life again, having a real family life and not having to work at strange and unsociable hours of the day and night. I did not have to do anything, because the business had already ceased trading, but I had made the decision in my mind, that I was not going to go back to it. My wife fully supported me, in fact cajoled me into this course of action.

I wrote to all my regular customers and told them that I would not be re-starting the private hire business. I thanked them for their loyal support and for their business and referred them to other colleagues in the trade that I felt I could recommend, should they need private hire travel. I felt confident that the other private hire companies I had recommended, would offer the same standard and quality of service, that I had always tried to give to my customers. It was hard to let the business go, but the time was right, once again, for me to change direction, but what, if anything was to follow next?

Chapter 18

Glitz and Glamour

So, job No.23 had ended. Would there be a job No. 24? Yes, was the resounding reply! It was never in any doubt, because I was still searching for something, but I was not sure exactly what the "something," was. My life had never felt entirely fulfilled, since those traumatic young days in the monastery, to any of the crazy, disastrous, even high-powered jobs I had held over the years. There was no way I could finish my career without gaining true fulfillment from something, but what would that something be?

At the time, I was not seriously considering anything in particular. I was rather hoping that whatever came next, would hit me like a slap to the face! After 23 jobs, I felt that I had still not fully reached my potential. I was still searching for that something different. I felt un-fulfilled.

I had recently spoken to a colleague in the Private Hire business. He was involved in the glitzy end of the trade. He was in the stretch limousine business. This was a private hire company that dealt with the entertainment side of the taxi business. It was all about group days out, nights on the town, weddings, hen and stag nights, and teenage promenades. It was the fun section of the business, at least for the customers, but it could also be enjoyable for the chauffer, at least on occasions, and a sociable way to make a living.

We were speaking together one day, when I let it slip that I had decided to finish my private hire business. I told him that I had been given the all-clear, health-wise and that my private hire license, to drive the general public, had been reinstated. I could see that it had suddenly sparked his interest.

"As it happens, Steve I am looking for a part time Limousine driver, hours to suit, if you are interested?"

Well that would be something different! I had never even been in a stretch limousine, let alone driven one. I don't know why, but driving a stretch limousine for a job, had a certain appeal. It seemed such a fun and sociable way to earn some money. I loved anything glitzy, with a touch of showbiz. Initially, he offered me a job covering for him, when he was not available or when he needed time off. He had a beautiful vehicle. It was a full length sixteen seater Stretch Limousine, in a brilliant white finish, with full leather seating and with all the glamourous trappings and features you would expect from such a lovely vehicle. Driving it would certainly be an eye-catching event as Limo's always seem to attract people's attention.

I had only recently been granted back my private hire license, so I was very tempted to make good use of it once more. It didn't take me long to make a decision. I was really excited about it. I had been out of work for around twelve weeks due to my health suspension and I was really itching to be doing something useful again. I was aware that some of the work would entail anti-social hours, but not all of it, and anyway, it sounded fun, and it was only part time cover, when all said and done.

It was up, up and away with job No.24, and this job was to be something entirely different. I knew that it was not going to be full-time, and maybe not even permanent, but I was really looking forward to it, for as long as it lasted. I thought of it as a job without real pressure and the money would be very useful. I thought it could be a job I could enjoy, but without all the normal pressures of work.

15. White Stretch Limousine.

335

My first job as a limousine driver turned out to be a really tricky one. I had spent only about fifteen minutes learning to drive the Limo and it was a tense start! I had to collect a group of ten women for a pre-wedding party. OK, it was a Hen Party by any other name. I had to pick-up the group of party revelers from the other side of town. I was to collect them from an old council estate and my first problem was getting to the house to collect the ladies. The roads in and around the council estate were exceptionally tight and narrow and there were parked cars on either side of the road. This was causing genuine problems to a vehicle of this length. The Limo was 11 to 12 metres long and it was exceptionally difficult in maneuvering the tight roads. It had a poor turning circle.

All my life I had a genuine hate of being late, even by one minute and despite allowing myself thirty minutes leeway, it was looking as if I may be late for my first job, due to the difficult driving conditions, on the estate where I was to pick-up.

I was squeezing past parked vehicles with only inches to spare on either side. The driving was very nervous. I did not want any crunches or scrapes on my first night out, but I really needed to get there on-time and I was not used to driving a limousine of this length, especially one with such length and a poor turning circle.

After painstakingly negotiating the next corner, there they were, standing outside of the house, champagne glasses in hand, and chattering excitedly with each other. This group of party ladies were dolled up to the nines, and ready for serious action. I had made it in time, but only just and my nerves were already shredded. I tried not to let it show and I smiled and welcomed them one by one, on board my luxury limousine. I was still not very confident with women, especially in groups, although I was more at ease on a one to one basis. I came across as shy and nervous. Once seated, I served them with the "champagne" that came with the group deal. It was called "Charlemagne," a budget sparkling Perry that would never pass for champagne, but it went down well, even though it was only 4 per cent proof. It didn't seem to matter, as most of the ladies seemed well oiled already and were just up for a good night out. The journey to Blackpool was surprisingly serene. Perhaps it was to be the calm before the storm. I wasn't quite sure what to expect from them. Maybe they were saving themselves for later on. I dropped them off at their venue in Blackpool, after agreeing to collect them at a pre-determined rendezvous at midnight, for the return journey, back home to Warrington.

The next part, was the most difficult section of the evening. I had four hours to kill, until I collected the ladies to take them home. I did not have another job in between, so it would be a waste of money and fuel to go back to my base. I did what everyone would do in Blackpool. I went for a long walk along the promenade, bought myself the traditional fish and chips and then went back to the Limo for a well-deserved sleep in the driver's seat, until it was time for the pick up at midnight.

I awoke from my slumber at 11.30pm and readied myself for the return leg of the journey. I had never seen such a transformation in a group of ladies, within just a few short hours. On the journey to the coast, they had been reasonably subdued, polite and friendly. When they arrived back at the Limo in dribs and drabs, they had been transformed into a band of disheveled, loud and foulmouthed wailing banshees! I was taken aback. I had to avert my eyes from the ladies, due to the various wardrobe malfunctions, or just brazen flirting. I just smiled, kept my eyes on the road and concentrated on my professional job of driving them back home safely. I made sure that each and every one of them was escorted, unsteadily on their killer heels, to their front door. I doubt that some would be able to find the hole for the front door key, due to their over-intoxication, so I took it onto myself to ensure that they arrived back home in a safe, if rather drunken condition and I did not leave them until they were safely inside.

Back home and safely tucked up in bed by 2am, I

lay there contemplating my first trip and wondered if I had made a huge mistake in taking on this job. I feared that this could be the first of many such experiences. Not only had I been their driver, but I ended up practically being their nurse and carer. I felt responsible for their safety and well-being, but I had not bargained for that part of the job.

Some of my Stretch Limousine jobs were rather interesting and quite enjoyable, considering it was work, but it was generally a rather sociable way to earn a living and the job had a certain status to it. I did not wear a chauffer's peaked cap, yet I always dressed in a formal dark suit, shirt and tie. It gave me an air of quiet authority and respect, that was sometimes required when being their driver, as some customers needed control and care.

The main types of venue for the Limousine, were race courses, theatres, seaside destinations and such like. It was also gratifying to see people enjoying themselves. Most of the time, alcohol was an integral part in the journey, and usually the outward journey was much more pleasant than the return leg, where drunkenness was the norm. After all, vomit in the limousine was most unpleasant and anti-social, yet it happened to me on several journeys. Sometimes there was aggression and foul language, as a result of too much drink. Customers could become awkward and difficult and it made it an unpleasant journey on the way home. On reflection, I was there to drive the limousine, not to act as peace-maker, and take care of passengers that were unable to look after themselves. Many of the revelers were rendered incapacitated by drink. I had not bargained for that, and I was unsure that it was worth all the effort, late hours and the trouble.

I could cope with most of the irritations, although cleaning up vomit was a major turn-off and I detested it. I was also finding out that many of the limousine runs were evening jobs with a very late finish, of around 2am or 3am, with all the nasty experiences that the job sometimes entailed. I was getting to the stage, where I would dread the next job, because of all the negatives and I was concluding that it was not all glitz and glamour after all, much of it was really hard work, unsociable and often very anti-social.

My next Limousine job turned out to be the straw that broke the camel's back. Although I enjoyed driving the limo, too many of the journeys were proving arduous and stressful. I was booked to drive a group of twelve children to a "Promenade," at a local hotel in Frodsham, Cheshire. I collected my passengers, one by one, from houses on a local council estate. Again, the roads were narrow and full of parked cars, creating really difficult driving conditions. The limo was twelve metres long and did not negotiate tight bends very well at all.

Squeezing past parked vehicles without damaging my pride and joy, turned out to be a nerve racking experience. Eventually, I had picked up all of my twelve passengers. They were a mixed group of kids aged between eleven and thirteen. Not an easy age group to deal with, but they were excitable and really talkative, as this was their first experience in a stretch limousine for most of them. I took them on a mystery drive before taking them to their promenade destination at the hotel. One of the girls in particular, kept coming up-to the sliding glass partition separating the driver's cab from the main section of the limousine. She was about thirteen years old going on eighteen! She told me her name was Bethany. She was really inquisitive and very advanced for her years. She wanted to know all sort of things about the vehicle. That was no problem, I answered her questions, although I really wanted to concentrate on my driving. After all, I had a group of children to look after. She was very friendly and outgoing, and she stayed at the screen, even though I asked her to sit down. She wanted to know my name, how long I had been driving, was I married and what was my wife's name? I just put this down to the exuberance of youth and her excitement on her special day out.

Late afternoon, I dropped off the twelve excited youngsters at the hotel for their Promenade. It involved a dance, music, party food and general fun and games. They were to have about five hours at the venue. I was due to collect them at 9pm which was not too late, as it was a Friday, so no school the next day. Before leaving them, I told the group that I would be outside the front door of the venue at 9 O'clock and that they must not be late.

As was my normal custom, I was ready and waiting to collect the children by 9pm. I knew that their parents would worry if they were late home. The kids arrived in dribs and drabs, two or three at a time and by 9.10pm, I had ten of the twelve children safely back in the Limousine. I waited for another five minutes, but the remaining two did not appear. I asked the others who was missing and I was told it was Bethany and Lucy.

Shortly afterwards, Lucy came running up-to the Limousine. She seemed rather stressed, somewhat agitated, but she came across as a sensible and likeable young girl and she told me that she had tried to get Bethany to come out of the hotel, but that she would not come. I started to get worried! I thought to myself:

"I am not a parent, and not a school teacher. In fact, I am not actually in charge of this group of young children. I am merely paid to drive them safely from A to B and back again. They should have an adult who is responsible for this group!"

I felt sure that my responsibility should not go

beyond that. I had a dilemma and I was unsure quite how I should deal with it.

I asked Lucy to go back into the hotel and tell Bethany that she must come back to the limousine immediately. Minutes later, Lucy raced back once more and told me that Bethany was going to stay. She was with friends and she wanted to make her own way home sometime later.

I was horrified. I started to wonder exactly what my duty and responsibility entailed. I did not want to overstep the mark, yet she was in my care, after a fashion and I had to do exactly the right thing.

After weighing up all the odds, I came to the conclusion that I had to take decisive action. Again, I asked Lucy to be my messenger. I did not want to leave the others alone in the Limousine, yet I did not want to get into direct confrontation with a young girl, who was just my passenger and nothing more. At least, that's how I viewed it.

I asked Lucy to go back into the hotel, and to tell Bethany that we would not be leaving without her and that if necessary, I would contact her parents or the police and tell them what was happening.

Thank goodness! That seemed to work! Lucy came running straight back to the Limousine, with Bethany, clearly in a huge sulk, and dragging her

343

heels, a good ten yards behind her. She slammed the door to the Limousine and sat back into her seat, in an awful mood and glowering at me. Lucy told me she had been drinking and it certainly looked that way. There was no telling what she may have done, in the mood she was in, so I kept a respectful distance and just ignored her.

On the way home, I felt that I had been put into an intolerable position. I honestly felt that I was just a hired driver, tasked with transporting a group of children that I did not know, to a party. I should not be accountable for any of their actions, only my own. I felt that the group of children should have been accompanied by an adult who knew them and was responsible for their behavior and safety. It was with huge relief that I returned all twelve kids home to the safety of their parents. I heard no more from anybody, but I never wanted to be put into a similar situation to that again.

The next day, I spoke with Mike, the owner of the stretch-limousine and told him about the episode the previous night. He seemed to think that it was all part and parcel of the job, but I disagreed. My mind was already made up. That was to be my last job as a Stretch Limousine driver. It was with some reluctance, but with even more relief, that I told him I did not want to do the job any longer. He was disappointed to lose me as a driver, as it had all been going so well, but I could not cope with more episodes like the one I had just experienced the previous night. So there it was. Job number 24, was another job been and gone.

That night as I lay in my bed pondering yet another short-lived job of work, I concluded that while it had not lasted overly long, that it had certainly been "quite an experience." I chuckled to myself at some of the antics that I had experienced while driving the Limousine, but I was more than relieved that it was finally finished and I looked forward to doing something more normal and mainstream. It had been quite an experience.

Over the next few weeks, I was still not working and I was finding it hard to occupy myself fully at home. I was still feeling unfulfilled and in need of something! After almost forty years of work, I realized that I did not have enough to do in order to gainfully fill my time. It dawned on me that I did not have any hobbies, interests or male friends. All our friends were couples or friends to my wife and me. But I did not have a mate, a close friend who I could confide in, or do things with. I was not a golfer, did not play squash or go walking. In fact, I did not do much of anything at all, other than work and family life. I realized that I had to do something about it. I was coming around to the idea of taking up badminton, cricket or learning to dance. I needed a job or an interest, just something to help me to get to know other people, make some friends and have a varied social life.

The fact was, I still needed to work because the small private pension I had taken at sixty, did not fill the void that my salary had left, when I finished my full business career. Even so, I slowly came round to thinking that maybe I should retire, whether I could really afford to or not. I was quietly warming to the idea of putting my feet up, doing the gardening and watching daytime T.V, when by chance, my mind was made up for me. My daughter Julia and son in law Chris came to visit one day. They had recently set up their new Solicitors business in personal injury litigation. It was going pretty well, but they needed more hands, yet they could not afford to take on another member of staff at that stage of their development.

It was Julia who asked me. This was a clever move on her part! She knew, like all daughters do, how to get around her Dad and to get him to do just about anything, with a disarming smile and a coy look, glanced in my direction:

"Dad"! She said sheepishly, yet cunningly.
"Well, you know you said you were at a loose end".

"Well, I don't actually remember putting it quite like that, Julia" I retorted.

346

"Well anyway", she continued, not wanting to lose her momentum. *"Would you like to help us out in the business? You are an experienced businessman and you did say that you don't have enough to do at the moment. Would you like to come and work in the family Solicitor business?"*

When your only daughter looks at you in that disarming and manipulative manner, what else could I possibly do? If I had been seriously contemplating retirement, then my mind had just been made up for me! I had little choice in the matter! I would not be putting my feet up with the slippers and pipe, for a while to come.

Instead of being a job like some of the unfortunate ones that I had recently undertaken, they were offering me a respected position, part time, and a job that I could do from home. It was for my family too. How could I possibly say "No"? I was to act as the first real point of contact for potential clients, who thought they may have a personal injury claim. I would vet the claim and if it met the required criteria, I would then pass it onto the solicitors to handle. It freed up the time for them to do their legal work, and I would act as the main point of contact for the new clients. This was to be my twenty fifth occupation. It had taken a total 25 jobs over a period of 45 years for me to achieve my longest job ever. I started in the family business in 2008 and called time on it, towards the end of 2017 after nine years, bringing more than a thousand-new client claims to the business.

As with many of my other jobs, there were interesting and humorous stories that could be told, but client confidentiality prohibits this, so they will remain locked up in my memory box "ad infinitum"!

Since around 1972, I have worked in some twenty-five different jobs. That equates to just under one job every two years. It may be something of a record! Certainly, in the earlier years it did indicate a lot of uncertainty and insecurity. It involved a lot of chopping and changing. It was not an employment record to be particularly proud of. However, as a general trend, I had shown progression in terms of status and financial gain, as I went up and down the employment ladder. One thing for certain, is that I gained a valuable and broad experience of life, as I moved from one type of work to another. I have held a host of business positions, interspersed sporadically with jobs such as Nursing, Child Care, Security, Taxi Services and even as a Stretch Limousine driver. The fact that I continue to work, albeit, not full time, indicates that I am not a person for sitting down and putting my feet up. I need a challenge all of the time and need to be kept interested. Perhaps I will never fully retire.

348

I think perhaps it was due to my lack of friends and hobbies, that I was desperately searching around for something to occupy my time and give me a real purpose in life again. Since I had given up my full time work, I had been doing a variety of part-time tasks, but I still had time to spare and the desire to keep myself gainfully occupied. What else was around the corner, or on the horizon?

Chapter 19

A job with no pay

It was while I was on holiday in my motorhome in 2010, that I was speaking to a friend of mine, Keith Daniel, over a drink or two. As frequently happens, the subject eventually turned to politics. Once that topic had been done to death, or we had fallen out about it, the conversation moved onto religion and the meaning of life. At some point, the same question was always asked: "Do you actually believe in God?" Very few people have no view on it, and people rarely do not have an opinion on it at all. I have always held the view that a man would be foolish not to even consider the possibility that there may be a God. The fact is that no-one knows for certain that there is an almighty being that created this universe, as there is no positive proof one way or another. It is all a matter of belief, and one day every one of us will either know the answer for certain, or we will know nothing at all because, we will be dead.

Whilst the four of us were putting forward our various "drink fueled" opinions on such matters, the conversation drifted around to my own unusual background and upbringing. I find that people are fascinated to hear of my life spent in a Monastery.

It appears to belong to a long bygone era, another moment in time, so unusual was the life of a Monastic, that I had lived as, from an early age.

Keith showed a particular level of interest in my upbringing, asking me a variety of questions about my life in the Monastery. He did not however, express any opinions one way or the other about it. However, what he did say starting me thinking. He said: *"Steve, you should write a book!* "His comments were the catalyst for me deciding to write my first book: "The Nearly Man" which was published in 2014. The Nearly Man tells my true story, from being a young eleven-year-old boy, who is told that God has chosen him to become a Catholic Missionary and Priest; the choice is not his to make. He joins the Redemptorist Order and spends the next 11 years being schooled in the way he is expected to live for the rest of his life. He must leave his family to lead a secluded monastic life, making no close friendships and taking vows of poverty, chastity and obedience.

When doubts arise in his mind he strives to overcome them, studying all the harder, but eventually he realizes that he is not happy in the only life he knows. When he spends time in hospital and falls in love, his thoughts crystallize. Only then is he able to make his final decision about the type of life he wants to live. The autobiographical work brings his true story to life and its moving narrative comes to a truly dramatic and emotional conclusion.

Most of the people who have read the first book, "The Nearly Man," commented that the book had finished far too early, leaving them up in the air. They wanted to know what happened afterwards, and where my life went to after that. This was how this present book came into being. It tells of my early struggles to come to terms with life after the monastery. In particular, it focuses on how I found it difficult to form personal relationships, finding the right career, after a mammoth tally of 25 jobs in a 45 year working career. Some of the jobs were huge mistakes, totally unsuitable, but with the benefit of hindsight, it is easy to understand why they were entered into, in the first place.

I had never seriously considered that my autobiography, "The Nearly Man" would be anything other than what it is; a one-off book of my early life. As interesting as it seemed, I believed that after leaving Hawkstone in 1970, that it would be final, and an end of the story.

It came as a genuine surprise to me, that most of the readers, family, friends and acquaintances, that had read the book, told me that although they had enjoyed reading my story, that they were disappointed that it finished where it did. Of course, I was just 22 years old when my monastic journey came to its conclusion. The age of 22 is an unusually young age to finish any autobiography, yet I believed that the story people would want to read about, had finished, and I did not believe that there was more to be told that was worthy of documenting. Perhaps the story could have continued further, but where would it finish? As I began to explore the possibilities, it dawned on me that there was indeed much of the story that could, and maybe should, have been told about my return to the monastery. Although the return was merely for a visit, it would in fact complete the tale and bring closure to it. The difficulty was that, to explain how I adapted to life outside of the cloister, it was necessary to explain what happened afterwards, including the various jobs and career paths I had chosen. Thus, "from Monk to Elvis", was born. Whilst my life and career had taken a topsy-turvy path, it concluded with me feeling somewhat unfulfilled and still wanting to do something more, something different that would also bring closure to an unusual and varied lifetime of work.

In the twilight of my 25-job career, still feeling unsatisfied after such varied experiences of life, there was a constant desire and a drive to do, or be, something different and perhaps unusual.

That desire goes right back to that time on 16th.August 1977. I was on my way to a meeting at work, when I was suddenly shocked to hear on the car radio that Elvis Presley, the King of Rock and Roll had died. I had to pull my car over to the roadside to take it all in. I was in deep shock. The surprising thing was that, at that moment in time, although I liked Elvis, I was not what one would call a big fan. However, something that day struck a chord. I had already bought a new karaoke machine, and I started playing his music and singing along to it. Prior to that, I had enjoyed singing songs from a more demure era, from Sinatra and Nat King Cole, that style of music.

Since that fateful day, I became a closet Elvis Presley fan. I would listen to him and sing his songs, in the privacy of my own home, but nothing more. Life was too demanding and far too busy, to spend any more time on it. It was not until I seriously began thinking of my retirement, that I started to sing and perform the music of Elvis Presley. It seemed a strange decision, to start singing in public, at a time when many performers are considering retiring from it.

I could never really have claimed to be a singer. I was in a choir at the Erdington Monastery in the 1960's and I had a passable and pleasant voice, as part of a choir. Even so, it was not a particularly good voice. I was never selected to be a solo singer. During my monastery years, I did of course sing regularly, but this was monastic singing or chanting, in the choir. It did help me to sing well, to sing in tune and breathe in all the right places.

Throughout the years, I would sing occasionally, at parties and the like, but I recall that with the advent of karaoke machines, that I learned to sing properly. Even so, this was a closet event. I saved my singing exclusively for myself, in the privacy of my own home. Occasionally, we would have parties at home and I would sing Sinatra and middle of the road songs. However, little by little, after Elvis died on 16th.August 1977, I began to put words to his music and sing his songs at home. When I was alone, I would start to put more into the songs. I would begin to move like Elvis, to use his mannerisms and facial expressions. Finally, I would try to sing in a similar manner to Elvis. It was far from being even close to the "King" himself, and I could never dream of reaching some of the notes and power that he put into his songs. It was only when I decided to try and look like Elvis too, that a better picture slowly started to emerge. I bought an Elvis suit from an online fancy dress store. It was amazing what a difference it made. When I was alone in the house, I would dress in the Elvis suit and sing along to his music. There was no way that I would do this in front of other people. I was far too self-conscious. I did not think that I was in anyway near good enough to imitate the King of Rock and Roll. In any case, Elvis was only 42 when he died, and arguably still

356

in his prime. I was well into my late fifties by this stage and I thought I could be something of a laughing stock if I sang in public.

Even so, we would have parties at home, at times like Christmas. We would invite friends to our home and after a suitable amount of drink, to provide plenty of Dutch courage, I would reluctantly put on an Elvis performance for family and friends, as part of a party evening.

I recall that my first "public" appearance was for some friends, Denis and Barbara. They had seen me doing a bit of Elvis and they were holding a Christmas Party at their home. They had a huge cellar, large enough to hold around 60 guests. Dennis was an out and out showman and he would often sing, even though he didn't have a great voice, so it gave me the confidence to do the same. He asked me to do an Elvis routine at his party. It was nerve-wracking. Both my wife and I had been feeling ill, due to flu, on the day of the party. But as the saying goes in showbiz, "The Show must go on". I gave the best performance I could, despite having a rather husky voice and it went down a storm, mainly due to the drink-fueled enthusiasm of the audience. In those days, I was still sporting a moustache, as I had worn one ever since I was about 23 years old. When I looked back at the first photograph of me as "Elvis," and sporting a Groucho-styled moustache, I decided that the moustache just had to go. It simply wasn't Elvis!

16. Steve's Early Elvis Tribute with moustache

I decided very early on in my "Elvis" career, that I would not be doing my Presley Shows to earn money for myself. I frequently went to see professional tribute artists doing their performances. They ranged from average to absolutely fantastic, but they certainly earned their money, even the not so good impersonators. I reasoned, that if I did not charge anything for doing my show, just performing it for pleasure, then the viewing audience had no grounds for complaint, even if it was poor! It was free entertainment, so they had nothing to lose.

I convinced myself that as, arguably the oldest "Elvis" in town, I was not really good enough to make money from my shows. In addition, I did not think that my show or my voice, were good enough at that time, to charge money for my performances. That certainly showed a lack of confidence on my part. I decided to set my stall out. I would do Elvis performances in public, but just for the fun of it and for pure entertainment.

It was at that time that several members of my family and friends were suffering from Cancer. I decided that, here we were, generally healthy, happy and enjoying ourselves and that it would be a decent thing to do, if we held a collection in favour of Cancer Research at any future shows.

As I became better and more "professional" at doing the Elvis shows, I felt more confident that I was offering value for no money, a good and enjoyable night's entertainment. All we asked for in return, was a donation, at the end of the night towards my favourite charity. It worked very well. The audience would enjoy a free evening's entertainment and contributed generously to Cancer Research.

The more shows I did, the better and more

confident I became. My voice was becoming stronger, sounding a bit more like the "King" and the whole show began to take on the appearance of the professional shows I had regularly watched.

I used to visit the genuine tribute artists, not only because I loved being totally engrossed in everything Elvis, but because I could also learn a lot from them, how to sing, how to perform and how to put across a really professional show. I would take notes at their shows and remember how different artists would do various things. At one show featuring a top Elvis Tribute Artist, I watched the local entertainer from Cheshire performing his version of the "King" under the banner of "Pure Presley". He was a fantastic guy called Paul Larcombe. He used to be a top night club singer, and he could also play the ukulele and perform as George Formby, yet his portrayal of Elvis Presley was sublime. He was as close to the "King" in both appearance and sound and as good as any other Elvis tribute artist, I had ever seen.

I chatted to him after the show and told him how much I had enjoyed it. I plucked up the courage to tell him that I also did an Elvis tribute. I went to great pains to let him know that I was hardly a competitor to him. I was not a professional like he was, and that I only did shows locally, on a small scale and just for fun or to raise money for Cancer Research. He was more than helpful. He clearly did not see me as competition! He gave me many tips and advice over a couple of years and I would regularly go to see his performances. He even gave me some of his backing track music, to make mine sound better than the karaoke backing tracks I had been using up until then.

At first, I would do some of my shows with my great mate Eddie. We had been buddies since 1975 and had kept in touch as friends over the years. We played football together for an awful team, the infamous "Griffin Growlers". It was a pub team to beat all others, except where it mattered, on the pitch. We had terrific times over the years, mainly going on foreign football tours with the "Growlers". We toured to Malta, Spain, Belgium, and Holland among others. I recall that too much alcohol and local "fire water" were the main problems. We were usually too hung over to perform well on the day of the match. Well, that was one of the problems. We were fairly old for an amateur football team, ranging from late twenties to well into the forties. We would sometimes come up against young Spanish teams aged between 18 and 20 years of age. They frequently ran us off our feet, whilst many of us were still sporting hangovers from the previous nights and days. Eddie was a flying left winger in those days, always fit and lithe, no matter how much drink he had the night before. Some forty years on, he is still the same weight and build. Eddie would play his Ukulele in the Spanish Pubs or wherever else we would be on tour and he was the life and soul of the party. We rarely, if ever won any games, but who cared? a great time was had by us all.

Eddie loved his music and he really enjoyed performing. He went down an entirely different route to me. He started off by playing the Ukulele, mainly the George Formby music. It was not just the old folks that loved "When I'm cleaning windows". It was fun and quirky, and Eddie sounded and often looked just like the late great singer and actor, George Formby himself.

Eddie would often visit our home, sometimes over Christmas and we would party on my Karaoke. I would sing Sinatra or Dean Martin and Eddie played and sang Formby with his trusty Ukulele. He would burst into song and play in pubs and clubs, on the coach, and just about anywhere. He gained the nickname from me as: "The Great Edwardo", referring to his singing and playing in Spanish pubs and clubs on the "Griffin Growlers" football tours. In my early Elvis shows, Eddie would also strut his stuff. It added variety to the performance. By this time, he was doing less Ukulele and Formby and was performing more Swing music, largely the music of the 1950's and 40's including a lot of Frank Sinatra music. He would always bring his own equipment, but sometimes we would share it and Eddie would act as my "Roady" and sound man, looking after my running order, acting as M.C and D.J. This continued for several years. We would do a few shows a year, but we were still very much amateurs, yet enjoyed doing music for just fun.

One memorable show, was to celebrate one of my wife's "significant" birthdays? We hired a double width, party canal boat and had about 60 guests on board, as we cruised the length of canal from Preston Brook to Stockton Heath near Warrington. It was hardly on a footing with a Pacific Cruise, yet it was just as good! We hired a professional singer guitarist who really set the scene. The boat was rocking from side to side. Eddie did his usual slot and acted as DJ and sound man. I did a Buddy Holly routine followed by an Elvis set. The passengers were well and truly in the zone. The lashings of champagne and other alcoholic beverages were getting everybody up on their feet to the strains of Elvis's "Wonder of You". The canal boat on the way back to Preston Brook was practically bouncing and lurching from side to side, to the movement of the revelers on board. It was amazing to see the onlookers on the canal side watching in wide eyed amazement at this group of mature passengers throwing away all their inhibitions and rocking and rolling on board. The boat however was perfectly safe. It would have been hard to drown in less than three feet of water!

17. Bridgewater Canal Boat Cruise

18. Canal boat cruise party – Roger's 60th. 2005

Such was the success of the Elvis Canal Boat booze cruise, that my friend Roger, [Dodger to his mates!] who had been a guest on that day, requested that we did the same thing for his 60th. birthday, later that same year. It was a case of "Groundhog Day", just like the hit film. We organized the same boat, the same entertainer and Eddie and I did our music routines on board. It was largely a different group of passengers, but the result was exactly the same. After a quiet and calm start to the cruise, the canal boat suddenly came alive. It was an exact repeat of the 1st cruise the year before, as the motley band of boozy senior citizens, rocked and rolled to the strains of the sixties on Roger's Bridgewater canal cruise.

About this time, my Elvis show was becoming slicker and looking more professional. My friend Denis who hosted our inaugural show in his cellar a couple of years earlier, was about to celebrate his 40th.birthday. Denis would never do anything by halves. He was an out and out showman. If he organized an event, it was an event to remember with no expense spared. He hired a major hotel in Stretton, at The Park Royal Hotel, and hosted a 40th birthday party to remember. He had a Las Vegas themed evening. Of course, who was one of Las Vegas's most famous sons? The one and only Elvis Presley! The night kicked off with a gambling casino, entertaining the tuxedo clad list of guests. After their money had been squandered,

"Elvis entered the building", moving among the guests on his way to the stage in Las Vegas style.

This was a first! I had never done a show of this size before. Up-to then, it was just for small groups and venues of up-to 50 people. The Park Royal Hotel was throbbing to the sound of Vegas, with around 300 dinner-suited guests. The expectation was high. There was a lot to live up-to. I had to walk for a nerve-wracking 350 yards from my hotel room to the "Vegas Casino". My nerves were shredded. I had never done a show of this magnitude before. Even though I was sporting my new Elvis Vegas suit, which gave me extra confidence, I was a bag of nerves. I needn't have worried. Nobody seemed to notice that I was a beginner, an amateur, and as the music blared out to "Viva Las Vegas" the whole room was vibrating and pounding to the sound of the guests singing along at the top of their voices. They were certainly in Las Vegas mode. The Elvis music, the gaming tables and the fantastic atmosphere, made it a night to remember for Denis and Barbara and his 300 guests on his fortieth birthday celebration.

The Vegas show was the real start of my public performing. I knew that I still needed to improve the performance aspect of the show and so I invested in new music equipment and more Elvis attire. I bought two new Elvis jumpsuits, a blue one-piece and another white suit called "The

Fringe". Both were imitations of Elvis's favourite suits. On one occasion I had been watching another tribute artist from Yorkshire at a golf club in Lymm. I was chatting to him in the interval. He knew that I was a rookie performer, and he told me he had a couple of suits for sale. I jumped at it. One was worth around £500 when new, but he was letting it go for £100. Co-incidentally, we were about the same height and build and it turned out to be a good acquisition for my Elvis wardrobe.

Park Royal Hotel Stretton.
Denis's 60th with Elvis Gina + Blonde Hula Girl.

This had been the breakthrough for me. I felt that I was a now a genuine Elvis tribute artist, even though, unlike the professionals, I did not do my shows for money. One of the main differences was that the professionals earned their living from the shows, whilst I did them either for the fun of it, or to benefit Cancer Research. The benefit of earning money was that the "pros" could afford to dress just like Elvis and have all the top equipment. I could not compete with that, but I dug deep to buy myself an Elvis Jumpsuit that was not out of place. I paid £550 for the Elvis "Golden Eagle" jumpsuit, arguably Elvis's favorite outfit. It was tailored to fit me perfectly and what a difference it made. Suddenly, I looked and felt like an Elvis tribute. Fans were in awe of it and were wowed, as I strutted out onto the stage, the rhinestones shimmering and glittering under the bright stage lights. I knew that the only thing to do was go the whole hog. I bought a tailored Elvis hairpiece, followed by the glittering rhinestone belts. The transformation was amazing. I felt like Elvis, when I was fully dressed for a show. It gave me the confidence to go out and act just like Presley. The knock on effect was that it improved my performance, my singing and the way I would move and act on stage. It was as if I had morphed into Elvis. Looking at the audience, they too were in the mode. When the music was blaring, some were acting as if the man in the white suit was Elvis himself. They loved him so much that they wanted to believe that it is Elvis re-incarnated, if only for a couple of hours. There is no harm in that kind of fantasy imagination. It takes the audience and the performer out of their normal hum-drum routines, and just for a while, they too can be transported back to Las Vegas in the early 1970's. The next show would be my first show featuring my new Elvis jumpsuit and the new musical equipment. It gave me a big lift in confidence and I felt that my performances improved as a result.

For several years we had owned a Motorhome, some know it as an R.V, a [recreational vehicle]. It is most certainly that. We have traveled the UK and many parts of Europe. It is a traveling home on four wheels. Often we would attend Motorhome Meets. The Rallies are meetings of Motor-homers from clubs, such as Motorhome Facts, and Motorhome Fun. At such an event, we would gather at the chosen venue. Many of the Rallies organize entertainment. I was asked to perform my Elvis show at Hatton World, an entertainment venue near Stratford on Avon. There were about sixty Motorhomes attending which meant about 120 people. The entertainment was due to be held in a Marquis outside. Although it was August Bank Holiday, it was an awful day and it rained hard, right up-to the late afternoon under heavily laden clouds. I could not see how the show could go on. I was partly relieved, but mainly disappointed. Then at about 7pm, the skies suddenly cleared and it was decided that the show would go ahead. It was cold and damp, the audience were sat or standing in coats and blankets, but as they say in showbiz; "The Show must go on!" It went on, under the bright stage lights in a marquis, although the audience were sat outside. It turned out to be a fantastic night and the show was a glitzy highlight, despite the awful weather, which the audience did not worry about.

A personal highlight was that my grand-daughter, Amber who lives in Stratford on Avon, came to see me. She was nearly 6 years old, maybe one of my youngest ever Elvis fans, but despite the late show time, she really wanted to see her Grandad Steve performing his Elvis show for the first time. Being a "Grandad Elvis" didn't do a lot for my image with the girls, but Amber was really happy.

Before the show, Amber came to the Motorhome [Elvis's changing room.] She was most amused to see her Grandad having stage make-up put on and dressing up as the King of Rock and Roll. She was amazed and excited at the transformation.

We had arranged, that during a particular song in the repertoire, that Amber would walk out from the audience and put a Hawaiian Garland around Elvis's neck. It's what Elvis always did in his Vegas shows. At the agreed time, Amber [only six!], walked up-to the stage and tried to put the garland around my neck. The problem was, the bright stage lights blinded me, as it was pitch black outside. I could not see her in the lights, all 3 foot 2 inches of her, and I was stood nearly 6 feet tall.

She jumped to try and reach me, but failed and then she raced back to her Dad in floods of tears. Fortunately, at the interval break, I was told about the aborted garland and we arranged that Amber would try it again at a specific song in the 2nd set. That moment duly arrived. Amber sidled up to me, I knelt down in front of her and she gave me a hug. Then she placed the garland around my neck and ran happily back to her Dad. At last! One happy little girl and a new Elvis fan for the future? well maybe!

From that time onwards, I would often perform at various local community centres and clubs, sometimes to raise funds for the centre, but always for Cancer Research. Performances ranged from Pwglass near Ruthin in North Wales, to Corfe Castle in Dorset. There was also a fund-raising show for by brother, Arthur. He is the parish priest at St. Mary's, Catholic Church in Littleborough. We were raising money for the church funds, by doing an Elvis Christmas show in the Parish hall. The regular churchgoers were inquisitive to see Father Arthur's brother performing as Elvis and there was a sell-out crowd. Unusually, I was told, while I was changing, that there were a lot of quite rowdy young children in the audience and that they were running up and down on the stage and being quite excitable. It was not normal to have children at my shows because of the late time of the show, but they had come with their parents after going to church and then onto the show. I was concerned for their safety because my radio mic had failed and I had to rely on my wired microphone for the show. I was worried about the children tripping on the microphone wire if they came too close, as I mingled with the audience.

As I walked on to the stage to the strains of "That's All Right Mama", I quickly spotted that the children seemed fascinated by the white Elvis suit, the flashing neon lights and that they had all sat down together at the foot of the stage. They were gazing up at the stage in open-mouthed amazement and hanging on my every word and movement. At the most, they were around 9 to 11-year old's. It seemed as if they had never seen Elvis before, neither had they heard of him. I decided to include them in the show and get them involved, so that they would enjoy it and not become restless. In between songs, I put the mic in front of one of the children and asked: *"Have you ever heard of Elvis Presley"? "No!" came back the honest reply! "Are you enjoying it?"* I retorted; *"Yes, Elvis!"* she said; I think perhaps that we may have been nurturing a young group of a dozen or so of Elvis's youngest fans for the future. Time alone will tell.

During the show I performed a number called; "G.I.Blues". It was a song from Elvis's army days. As part of the song, I marched up and down the

372

hall, acting like I was a G.I. soldier. I would also salute in U.S army style. As soon as I did that, the whole group of children got up and followed me up and down the hall, mimicking me with every step and movement. It was hilarious and the audience including their mums and dads were delighted at this new bunch of young Elvis fans.

20. Elvis & Father Arthur Littleborough

Another memorable occasion was when we traveled in the Motorhome to the west coast of Spain, close to Benidorm. It was a Motorhome Facts rally at Denia. We arrived a couple of days later than most of the group and as we pulled onto the site there was a post besides one of the pitches saying: "Reserved for Elvis". I was curious to know how this came about, as I did not think that anybody at the rally knew me. It turned out that several of the ralliers had been to the Elvis show at Hatton World a couple of years earlier.

It was there in Spain, that I met my new "Roady" to be, Alan Lord. He too was a motor-homer from Bury, the home to the famous Bury Market in the land of the Black Pudding! He was on the rally, and we met after playing a Boules match in Denia. After chatting together a few times, it became clear that we had quite a lot in common. We were both big fans of Elvis, as well as being very keen on Roy Orbison and Buddy Holly. Oh! and of course, we were both owners of Motor homes.

Alan was something of a frustrated closet singer. The problem was, he could not sing. That was not my evaluation. It was his! He openly admitted that he would have loved to have been a singer, but he could not hold a tune or string two notes together. On the credit side, he was brilliant at anything technical, computers, music and anything electrical. It goes back to his time when he worked as the owner of a television rental shop. Thus his Motorhome Facts handle of "Teleman"

It was Alan that offered to help me with my music shows. As a big Elvis fan, he loved the music and the whole Elvis scene. He asked me if he could be my "Roady". Until then, Eddie had generally helped me with the music, when I was performing. It was difficult though! Eddie was not quite as mobile, and he had his own George Formby and Swing Music shows to perform as a busker.

It was at this stage that Alan made a suggestion that I move away from using mini-disks as my backing tracks. They were the older technology and it was easier and more flexible to use backing music on a laptop or a similar hi-tech device. This was something that Eddie did not feel very comfortable with and he preferred to use his mini disks and traditional equipment, whenever he did his shows and when he went busking, as he frequently did.

In recent years, many of the shows we performed were for the largest motorhome group in the UK named "Motorhome Fun". The clue was in the name! The group was for motor-homers who wanted to have "Fun", and most of the rallies, which were all over the UK, featured a full programme of in-house entertainment from the members. It included a Ukulele Band and the "in-house" rock and roll band which kept the Motorhome troops entertained.

I did my Elvis and Buddy Holly Shows in 2013 at The Cotton Arms in Wrenbury. Corfe Castle in Dorset was the venue for shows in both 2013 and

2014. In addition I did shows to collect for Cancer Research at the working men's club in Bank Quay Warrington, The British Legion Club in Runcorn and The Tunnel Top at Dutton in Cheshire.

It was a win, win situation all round. I loved performing the shows with my team, which was made up of Anne, my manager - often known as Colonel Parker, the legendary manager of Elvis Presley. She prefers to be known as "Priscilla", Elvis's wife. There was Alan, my Roady, better known as "Lord Alan", [he owns a square foot of land in the Scottish Highlands!], and then to complete the team is Lady Margaret, who acts as a general helper and "goeffer!" It is a team effort, and I could not do my Elvis shows without my team's valuable contribution.

Chapter 20

Matador V Bull

This occasion was a rare "home" performance. I was to perform an Elvis and Buddy Holly show. I had agreed to donate the takings to the Village Hall funds, if there was also a collection for our favoured charity, Cancer Research.

This was on the occasion when I had been ill, due to a sudden attack of atrial fibrillation just before the show. It very nearly did not go ahead, and I was advised not to perform, because of the potential for a heart attack or stroke. I felt ill, and far from my best, but how could I let down over 100 punters who had come to support the function. The show just had to go on. Adrenalin is a powerful weapon. In the wild it alerts animals to imminent danger and heightens their alertness, to deal with any threat. Inside me, that night, just when I was feeling ill and at a low ebb, it galvanized me to such an extent, that for two hours, my body was able to overcome the illness and ignore its symptoms. For two hours only, this was a pure case of mind over matter.

The Villagers were well and truly up for it! They had supported the show in large numbers so that it was a sell-out. As it was a local venue and just a couple of minutes' walk from my home, there were plenty of family, friends and neighbors in the 100 plus audience. There was a raucous feel to the show. It seemed that half of the people had been drinking before they arrived! One in particular seemed to be particularly well oiled and had seemingly left all her inhibitions back at home.

It was terrific that the audience were taking part. It indicated that they were enjoying it. This was something that I encouraged and built into the show. Many were on the dance floor especially for the faster rock 'n roll numbers. They all knew the lyrics of the songs and were heartily singing along and dancing. I never liked being up on a stage and far away from the audience, as I like to mingle with them and build them into the act. It's what Elvis used to do in the seventies. The stage area was unusually on the same level as the dance area and so it was not difficult for the audience to be dancing alongside Elvis. That was fine by me, but there is usually one that takes it a little bit too far.

On one occasion while I was performing a show at The Cotton Arms in Wrenbury, Cheshire, I was singing an Elvis love song called "Love Me!" During this song I would mingle in the audience and select a lady to put a beautiful silk scarf around her neck. It always went down well, often with the ladies clamoring to be selected for a free silk scarf. One lady was particularly well in the mode. She

sidled up-to me and danced provocatively
alongside me. As she faced me, I was about to
place a red silk scarf around her neck, and
comment humorously that it would match her red
eyes! I was unsure, but she did seem to have had a
"few", despite her protestations to the contrary.
Instead of the traditional kiss, she took the scarf
which was still around my neck and pulled me
tightly to her, planting a kiss somewhere on my
face. I was still trying to sing, but we were locked
together, and I was unable to either sing or move.
The music continued playing all on its own, to the
great amusement of the audience, if not to my
watching wife!!

It was really all good clean fun and just goes to
show how people can get so involved, that they
almost believe that the man in the big white
jumpsuit was Elvis Presley himself.

Returning to the show at Preston Brook, one lady,
a very pleasant and mature lady, acted completely
out of character. I was told somewhat later, that
uncharacteristically, she had been drinking brandy
before coming to the show and had then continued
to drink wine. She was well and truly without
inhibition by the time she hit the dance floor! The
lady was on a mission and seemed intent on
confronting Elvis. In her muddled mind, at that
moment, she seemed to believe that the man in the
jumpsuit was in fact Elvis Presley! She wanted to

grab hold of him and do something, but I was not sure what. I did not wait around to find out. I had people to entertain, I moved swiftly around the dance floor, moving among the audience, but she seemed intent on following me and "getting at me". Her friend could see what was about to happen and danced between me and the lady, my tormentor! As I sang and danced, I would move and swerve around the floor to avoid her approach. It was good natured banter, but I knew I needed to continue moving. I was quicker and more sober than she was and fortunately, she could not get at me. I too was completely in the Zone. Elvis and I had morphed into one and the same person. My tormentor was facing me down the dance floor, she at one end and I at the other. The other dancers had drifted away from the dance floor to watch the warriors and had left the confrontation to the two of us. The audience were in roars of approval, believing that the confrontation was all a part of the show. I was the Matador; she was the Bull [and a raging Bull at that]. I started to sing the famous Elvis "blues" song: "Trouble". She stood twenty feet away from me staring down her drink fueled and red bloodshot eyes. The music started up and the lyrics began with: *"if you're looking for Trouble, you came to the right place" If you're looking trouble, look right in my face!"* And she did! I sang the song, as if my life depended on it. Every word was aimed at my tormentor and not only to my audience who were embroiled in the

380

confrontation and hanging on every word, to see how it unfolded. The raging bull strode down the dance-floor, her stilettoes loudly clicking to the music, her arms pointing to the sky and her eyes transfixed onto mine. I continued singing to her, unperturbed. I was gazing at her with a fixed stare, to the strident lyrics of the song. As she moved closer to me, her fingers flicking, her stilettoes clicking, my left arm shot out in her direction. My first and second fingers were pointing outwards and towards the flared nostrils of the Raging Bull. She drew up to a sudden and grinding halt, my fingers in her face as my final lyrics belted out;

"So, don't you mess around with me, yeah"?

21. Steve sidesteps the Raging Bull!

The audience absolutely loved it. They were embroiled in a real life musical confrontation. It was no longer a duel. It had become, unwittingly, a part of the act and yet, it was for real. Never had my Elvis show become such a real life impromptu event. The audience was an integral part of it. For two hours, they believed that I was Elvis Presley. In their minds, their escapism, they wanted to believe it for a short while. How else can it be explained, that at the end of the show, people were queuing up to have photos taken with "Elvis", a sixty-five-year-old grandad with a heart problem. Only a year or so before, I had been suffering from a heart condition called Atrial Fibrillation. It did not affect me all the time, but it could be triggered by several factors; overwork, stress or partaking in over energetic activities. When I was in a state of A.F. I would feel extremely tired, washed out, and my heart would race in a crazy and irregular rhythm. At times such as this, there was a vastly increased chance that I could suffer a heart attack or stroke.

It was serious enough, that about two years before, my private hire driving license had been suspended indefinitely, until I had a medical procedure that had temporarily rectified it.

I had been given an operation to try and mend the condition. It was a Cardioversion. It involved a general anesthetic, after which my heart was electronically stopped, using chemical medication and then re-started by shocking my heart back into rhythm. It worked! My heart was restored to its normal rhythm straight away and lasted for almost two years, before gradually starting to fail again. Over the previous months I had been suffering further bouts of this debilitating Atrial Fibrillation.

On the day of the Preston Brook show, and just two hours before taking to the stage, my heart had gone into a crazy and fast beating arrhythmia. The stress of putting the show together, coupled with humping around the heavy musical equipment had caused my heart to fly off into a fast and irregular rhythm. What a terrible time to become ill!

I should never have taken to the stage that night! Without being over dramatic, in that condition, I could quite easily have suffered a heart attack or a stroke! Was that going to stop me performing? Not on your life. If I was going to die, I would be far happier dying, performing as my favourite singer Elvis Presley and dressed in my Elvis jumpsuit, rather than some twenty years later, in some insignificant care home and forgotten by everyone but my close family. So, as they say in the land of the theatre:

"The Show must go on!" And go on it did: My audience was in the zone, queuing up at the back of the hall, to have their photos taken with Steve,

383

alias, the one and only Elvis Presley. Oh yes! And as the saying goes: for "One Night Only", in the eyes of my audience; I was **"Elvis"**

22. Steve with Elvis Fans – Preston Brook

Chapter 21

Return to the Monastery.

I wrote my autobiography when I was 65 years of age. The story finished when I was just 22 years. With the benefit of hindsight, and after listening to readers of "The Nearly Man", I had to agree with the majority, who believed that my book finished somewhat too early. I thought that I had told the essential story, but now I believe that there was a continuing story still to be told.

In any case, at the greatly more mature age of 69 years, I can now take a more expansive view of those happenings, all those years ago, during the decades from the fifties to the nineteen seventies.

I trust that my second autobiography now answers all those questions raised in the reader's minds, that arose from the rather premature finish to "The Nearly Man". The previous chapters have certainly delved deeply into the transition from the monastic life to civilian life, in previous decades.

It covered the interesting diversity of jobs and careers that I had taken on. Many of them were totally unsuitable for me and my abilities, although they were undertaken by a desire to adhere closely to the values and strengths that I had developed during my early life in the monastery. It left me with a lack of satisfaction at my achievements and a desire to do something more than I had done. It covers the public side to my life, and some of my private life remains precisely that; private. Thus, there have been many omissions. I have already laid bare my life and my soul, much more than I had ever intended to. Yet it had to be so, to inform readers of the complete story, honestly and in its entirety.

23. Hawkstone Hall, Shrewsbury.

24 Hawkstone Hall Mansion – Full view.

When I departed the Hawkstone monastery in 1970, to go back to civilian life, I did not return there again for well over forty years. There were many occasions when I thought about my life there. Yet there had been happy times, as well as unhappy times, during my periods at the three Redemptorist Monasteries. The time I had spent there, especially in the final year, was just too painful to re-live. I left eventually, because the life of a monastic was just not right for me. I was unable to commit to a life of celibacy and the loneliness that the celibate life had entailed.

Even so, I had many regrets about leaving. Over the ten years, I had spent many happy and contented periods. My time there meant a lot to me. Initially I felt as if I was a failure, a deserter, but now, I do not believe that to be the case. That is not to say that I regret the life I have had since then. I have returned to all three Redemptorist Monasteries over the past few years. It has helped me to put my story to bed. It helped me to come to terms with the decisions I had made and to put all my life's experiences of the monastery into genuine perspective.

Perhaps my return to the Juvenate at Erdington was the easiest of the three. I was young at the time and it was like many other boarding schools, except that it was very different. The difference was that we were training to enter the monastery. I had many good times during my six years there, and experienced terrific camaraderie with many of the boys. Yet in the end, I felt that I had carried the entire burden of all the boys that had left. By my final year, in the 6th form, many of my friends had already left the Juvenate, to return to their families. Of the sixty or so boys who started with me at the beginning of 1960, there were less than twenty when I came to transfer to Perth in 1966 and only four remained from my 6th form class. The weight of expectation on me was immense. In truth, I had serious doubts, during the 6th form, about my desire to carry on to the Monastery at Perth. It is now a fact that I carried on and went to Perth, but on many occasions, I asked myself what was my motivation for doing so. Was it because I was called by God to be a Monk and wanted to go to Perth? Was it that I was expected to do so by others? Was it that I did not want to disappoint all those people who were willing me to do so? With hindsight I now believe it to be the latter.

[25. Erdington Abbey]

When I returned to Erdington in 2013, I was disappointed, but not surprised by what I found. The Juvenate section of the Monastery was now a girl's public school, but no longer directly associated with the Monastery. The Church was still the same, which was a relief and it is still a thriving part of the community. It brought back to me many memories, both good and not so good. As would be expected after almost 50 years, there were many changes. The grounds had been sold off for houses. The farm and football field that had been an integral part and parcel of my life there, had both gone, to be replaced by housing.

The cemetery in the monastery grounds brought back the most vivid of memories. We tend to remember our teachers and colleagues as being much younger, but the teachers were now all departed and our colleagues are now the same age as we are, if indeed they are still alive. The happiest moment of my return visit, was to learn that one of the students of my class of 1960 was still there, and he is presently the rector and parish priest of the Redemptorist Parish. His name is Father Gabriel Maguire. The name gives it away. He is of course an Irishman.

I could not wait to go to the presbytery to see him again. Excitedly, I knocked on the door. I had been with him as a boy at Erdington Abbey and again during my time at Hawkstone, where we were both Monk's together, but even that was over forty years ago. I did not know what to expect. Would he recognize me? Would he even remember me?

The front door opened. I am not sure why, but I expected Gabriel to answer the door and I was disappointed, when it was a lady that came to greet me. I asked for Gabriel, but he was out. She told me she would ask him to call me. I drove away, but by the time I received a call on my mobile, I was too far away to return. When I answered the phone, it was him! I recognized his voice straight away. *"Gabby"* I blurted out with a huge smile on my face! Gabby was his nickname at the Juvenate and even at Hawkstone. *" Nero! Be-Gorragh, sure it's yourself!"* It was a statement not a question. It seemed as if we had last spoken only the day before, and not over forty years ago. "Nero" had been my nickname at Erdington, short of course for "Nearey". It was great to hear his dulcet tones after all those years, and to hear how his life had moved on and changed for him, since those heady days, way back in the early 1960's.

Unfortunately for the Redemptorist monasteries, the general picture has been one of severe decline, as fewer and fewer men join the religious orders. It is a reflection of the general demise of religion in the western world and like all the others, the monastery at Erdington has changed almost beyond recognition. It made me wonder what I would be thinking about life in the monastery now, should I have stayed on as a Redemptorist Monk. I feel that I would be greatly unhappy at how the Redemptorist Order had demised, and that I would not have stayed the course over all these years. With some regret, I realize that I have taken the right decision about the direction of my life.

I also went back to Perth as described earlier in these pages. The expression goes *"that you should never go back!"* as you will almost certainly be disappointed. On my return in 2013, I was not so much disappointed, as upset at how the life had since changed. The Monastery building at Perth had barely altered at all. In fact, from the outside, it looked as imposing and historic as it ever did way back in 1966. On the inside, it was a different story. The people and the atmosphere seemed entirely changed. Certainly, it was less austere, not so dour, and naturally it was much more up to-date. That was entirely good. Way back in 1966 the monastery was still stuck in the dark ages and by my previous admission, it had to update itself to survive, let alone to thrive. When there were people around, it had a much more vibrant spirit to it. There were monks, but monks of today, not yesteryear and they were trying to be relevant to the needs of the modern world today.

For me, I could see the differences and yet the monastery at Perth felt as if it was still haunted by the ghosts of 1966 and bygone years. The monk's cemetery reminded me of those men who had given their lives to the cause and had since moved on. The attic cell which I had called my home for a year, had barely been touched since those days. They were not in use anymore, just a ghostly reminder of times past. I experienced an unusual feeling of regimentation, discipline, austerity and silence and it sent a shiver down my spine. In addition, I could feel the claustrophobia that I had experienced back then and which still remains with me today, as an uncomfortable reminder.

In one way, I loved returning to Perth. It had been life-changing and an important part of my life. I had developed a love and a hate for it, at the same time. I wished I could have returned to see it thriving and vibrant, but it was not to be. It was a shell of the calm and austere monastery that I had experienced and I had pangs of regret that it had changed to such an extent. On leaving again, I was still feeling the austerity and the loneliness that I had endured during my time there. It had a lasting effect on me, after life there some 45 years ago.

I have returned to Hawkstone on about four occasions over recent years. Until then, I had deliberately not done so since 1970. At that time, I was in a deep and dark depression about my future. I was afraid that I could experience all those bad feelings once more, even after, so many years since I had departed the monastery.

My first return there in 2013 was a completely different experience to what I had expected. There, I felt more at home. Indeed it had been my home. I had lived at Hawkstone Hall for almost four years. I felt privileged to have resided in one of Shropshire's finest stately homes, which in my time was a seminary and monastery, owned by the Redemptorists, to train priests and care for the local community. Despite its purpose as a home for the Redemptorists, it has retained nearly all the original features of centuries gone by. As a religious monastery, it did not have the sumptuous glamour that a private owner would have lovingly bestowed upon it, but it was still a wonderful property, and an iconic place to live. The Roman Catholic Redemptorists bought it for the princely sum of £10,000 in 1926, as a seminary to train priests. From the 1970s, Hawkstone Hall was turned into a pastoral centre. Visitors would come from right across the world to attend a variety of religious courses, conferences and Christian Renewal, in the Hall and it's grand surroundings.

The present rector of the house, Father Maurice O'Mahony, said the hall was being sold as part of "restructuring plans" by the Redemptorists. He wrote: *"I think many religious congregations, especially in Europe, are experiencing a downturn in the numbers of people coming in to the ministry so that's had a knock on effect.* Hawksone Hall is a grade-one listed mansion house in Shropshire and has been put up for sale for £5m. Whoever is the next owner, will be buying a jewel in the heart of the Shropshire countryside, along with 88 acres of prime farming land and beautiful landscapes.

I had happy times within it's confines, as well as sad. The camaraderie was special, even if close personal relationships were not encouraged. I loved the mansion, the beautiful countryside and the peace and tranquility. This became a lifeline for me when I was battling with my conscience. I had to decide if I would continue in the monastic life or whether I would be leaving it forever. I had suffered depression, illness and a serious operation in hospital. It was while I was in the hospital that I met a nurse, Margaret, and fell in love with her. I temporarily went back home to convalesce, only to find out that my biggest battle was yet to come. I could not decide if I would return to the monastery and only did so under duress and due to my own feelings of guilt. On my return to Hawkstone Hall, my overall feeling was of great unhappiness, even to the point of feeling suicidal, on one of my lonely visits to the 120-foot monument. It was this episode, that was to be the catalyst for my eventual decision to leave the monastery and finally return to civil life.

Only now, some 45 years on from those troubled days, do I feel comfortable in returning to that same place. I now do so with a fondness for the people, the Monastery and the organization that did so much to welcome me and to include me in their community. I was one of their brothers and I will always have a special place in my heart for the

Redemptorists, the institution and my former colleagues. It had been my home, and each time I return there, I am made welcome, like a returning son. The heartache I suffered, has long since disappeared, and I now have only pleasing memories left in my mind, with no sign of bitterness or regrets.

At the time of finalizing this manuscript, the Redemptorists at Hawkstone have closed the large wooden front doors, for the final time, awaiting a buyer. This act brings down the curtain for one final time, as the memoirs of my life as a Redemptorist Monk, draws to a fitting conclusion.

The Monastery and Hawkstone will always hold a place dear to my heart as I remember that I was

"The Nearly Man, who was going to change:

"from Monk to Elvis."

Chapter 22

From Monk to Elvis

When I was a Monk, way back between 1966 and 1971, I dressed in the single long garb of the monastery. I wore a full length black habit. Even then, I was a type of performer, a preacher of the gospel. I reached out to my congregation, my audience. I projected an image so very different to the real person inside that robe. As any actor or performer will verify, once they don the garb and take to the stage, another person emerges, and that person takes on a completely different persona to that, by which he or she, is usually recognized.

Elvis Presley was indeed a very spiritual man, religious in many ways and despite his many flaws and failings as a human being, he was always a god-fearing man. Despite his outward appearance, and theatrical lifestyle; the women, the drink and the drug problems, deep down, Elvis was a loving and caring country boy, with a deeply spiritual interior. By contrast, when Elvis took to the stage, and buoyed by his raucous audience, a new, vibrant, exciting persona emerged. He was brash, flamboyant and showed a confidence, that belied the person normally seen outside of his trademark white jumpsuit.

When I was a young man, I was a person in a monastic habit, a robe of religion. It portrayed me as a quiet and contemplative man, deep thinking, respectful and quietly shy, yet, when asked to perform my monastic missionary duties, my persona somehow changed out of all recognition. Instead, the habit portrayed me as a man of God, a preacher and a leader of men. This was an image though, that did not come naturally to me.

In later years, I tried to mimic Elvis. I wanted to show the world that the quiet "Nearly Man" had something inside of him, that was bursting to emerge. He could not possibly do so as plain and simple Steve Nearey, the quiet man. No, the truth was that, he had to hide behind another persona. It could have been anybody, but not himself. Once he donned his big white suit, the Elvis trademark, the large collar, and the flared pants, it was as if he had grown in stature overnight. Then he added the big hair, the make-up and the glasses. These were all items that he could hide behind. The massive rhinestone incrusted belt, made him stand out in a crowd and the outfit was then complete. The transformation was final. Instead of a quiet 65-year-old man, emerged what appeared to be a six-foot man mountain, like you have never seen. The large white boots added to the appearance and the rest was pure theatre. The music started up, the lights thrust him into the spotlight and it was as if he had burst into life, not his own life, but the life

398

of another. The voice was not of course, Elvis. How can anybody compare? Yet many try and some come extremely close. For the Nearly Man, he was there to entertain, to raise funds for charity, and any audience would forgive his imperfections in trying to portray Elvis, "For One Night Only," as the saying goes. The audience sees only Elvis. They only want to see the "King" and they will imagine that it is Elvis Presley that is stood in front of them. For a while, an hour perhaps, they can forget that the King of Rock & Roll had died in 1977 and that the person in front of them is the same man. The voice may be different, almost certainly weaker than the King, who had an expansive voice, a vocal range of gigantic proportions, and a sound that was so very different. Yet this was just Steve Nearey, not even a professional performer, just an amateur singer, trying to entertain and raise funds for charity. Until recently, he only entertained family and friends in a fairly low key manner, before going public.

Instead of an elderly gentleman standing in front of the audience, there was now a Tiger, a man so possessed and full of confidence, that he could even overcome his own physical limitations. He was performing in the manner of a thirty something, gyrating across the stage. "For One Night Only", he would forget the pain of the arthritis in his knees and hips, as he moved quickly across the dance-floor to the lyrics of "Blue Suede

Shoes". His wife would wince as he went down on one knee to the sounds of "Suspicious Minds", fearing that he may never get up again, yet he always did. Yet, in times of stress, the mind is far greater than the matter, and up he would get, endeavoring not to wince as he did so. He would feel the pain the following day and he would deal with it then! But for tonight, he was Elvis Presley, The King of Rock and Roll. He was young, daring and vibrant. His audience, for one moment in time, believes him to be Elvis Presley and the roar goes out; "Elvis, Elvis Elvis"! It rings out and resonates across the auditorium. He walks onto the stage as his iconic entrance music strikes up the "2001 Space Odyssey", followed by the iconic introduction song of: "That's All Right Mama"

It helped that most of his audience were in the same age bracket. The large majority of Elvis fans come from that same era, and yet such is the image, the persona of Elvis Presley, that today's youngsters will try to emulate him too, and this is borne out by the large numbers of young men, and a few women, who are Elvis Impersonators, or tribute artists, as they prefer to be known. Even the audiences, although largely mature, are liberally sprinkled with teenagers and twenty somethings, who by rights should not be interested in this 1970's icon. Yet such is the pulling power of the man who changed the world of music in the 1950's, that his legacy, with the help of Elvis

400

Presley Enterprises, continues to live on and thrive in the modern era and into the youth of today. There is no other performer, either in Rock 'N Roll, or any other music genre, that is more popular now, than he was before his untimely death, over forty years ago. Dying at the age of 42 means, that Elvis will never become old, even though, had he lived now, he would be 83 years of age. Elvis will never grow old, and if anything, he is developing a fan base of young people who can feed on the music and his amazing life story. His impersonators are becoming even younger, and teenagers and twenty-somethings are now donning the white one-piece jumpsuits to the tones of Blue Suede Shoes. Who knows how long this phenomenon can continue?

26. Elvis & his Hula Girls – Grange, Latchford.

401

Chapter 23

The Final Reckoning

Throughout my unusual and varied life, I have felt that I have never quite fulfilled my true potential. True, I had very humble beginnings and a really slow start to my young life. I was slow to grow up, slow to start doing well in my education and slow in making an impact in everything I attempted.

I had spent eleven long and hard years, with the Redemptorist Monks in Erdington, Perth and finally Hawkstone, whilst training to become a Priest. I fell at the final hurdle, feeling that I was unable to go on and make the final big decision. It was not that I was unable to do the job. Hard as it was, I had more or less mastered the requirements of being a Monk, but I was unable to commit my life to being a celibate Priest, unable to marry and have any special relationships. Life would have been far too lonely and in my final analysis, I was unable to commit to a life of celibacy and solitude. For me it was a case of so near and yet so far.

Back in the big wide world, my early years were a complete disaster, as I selected a series of totally unsuitable jobs in double quick time. Although matters later became significantly better on the employment front, for a long time, I was forever No.2, always playing the support role, but never quite achieving the number one job. Eventually, I did get the number one position, in my own business, but with hindsight, I ended up with the unenviable record of having had twenty five jobs in forty five years. It was not a great record, although there were several highlights during those years. Even so, it worked out that each job over my working lifetime, lasted for an average of under two years!

Looking back over my working life, following my Monastic period from 1960 to 1971, it seemed to me that I had never quite found my niche in life, that I had not quite done what I wanted to do, or achieved my goals in life. I still have a strong feeling of un-fulfilment, of nearly achieving something in my life, but never quite. The description of me as "The Nearly Man" is the one that readily springs to mind and seems a true measure of me as a person.

Of all my 25 extremely varied jobs, the nearest I ever came to being fulfilled, was the one job that was not really a job at all. It was a job that did not pay me any income. I did receive money, but it was not for me. The funds were raised by entertaining people and it was donated to the very worthy cause of Cancer Research.

Although I had been a massive fan of Elvis since 1977 and had regularly performed his music, it had only ever been for my own entertainment and not usually for the general public. It was when I was coming to the end of my full-time working career in 2010, that I was persuaded by my wife to do a full Elvis tribute show. I guess I could have done this some 30 years earlier, but I was too busy then with work and family, and anyway, I would not have had the confidence at that time, to perform in public. "Better late than never," springs to mind.

Although I considered that I had a reasonable singing voice, I never believed that it would be good enough to warrant singing for money. That said, with the correct vocal training, then who knows how good my voice may have become? It is too late to know now. What I do know, is that I have heard men singing Elvis Tribute Shows for money, and their voices have not been as good as my own. At least that gave me the confidence to sing as Elvis in public. The one definite decision I made, was that I would not sing Elvis for my own monetary gain. When I performed, I would ask not for payment, but for donations to a very worthy charity, Cancer Research U.K.

And so it has been, since 2010 to the present day. I now perform several times each year, not just to entertain people, but to raise money for the charity.

Of all the 25 jobs throughout my varied and checkered career, none of that work has given me the satisfaction that singing like Elvis Presley does. I don't regret that I was unable to perform it for a living, but I feel at my most fulfilled, when I put on that big white suit and I morph into the big man himself – Mr. Elvis Presley, the King of Rock and Roll.

I was **"The Nearly Man"**, who after training for eleven years, became a Redemptorist Monk, and nearly, but not quite, a Catholic Missionary Priest.

I then spent over 40 years in employment and business. I have been a Nurse, Social Worker, Encyclopedia Salesman, and a Milkman and undertook all manner of weird and unusual jobs, some good and others totally unsuitable. Of these 25 jobs, I would want to be remembered for just the one. When I am in the zone, when I am dressed as Elvis Presley, in my mind I take on his persona. My lifetime's journey to date has been:

"from Monk to Elvis"

The End

27. Steve - Elvis at Warrington Sports Club YOLO Fundraiser.

28. Steve – From Monk to Elvis.

407

408

Printed in Poland
by Amazon Fulfillment
Poland Sp. z o.o., Wrocław